OF GERMANY

MEMOIRS OF THE CROWN PRINCE OF GERMANY

CROWN PRINCE WILHELM

The Naval & Military Press Ltd

Published by
The Naval & Military Press Ltd
Unit 10, Ridgewood Industrial Park,
Uckfield, East Sussex,
TN22 5QE England
Tel: +44 (0) 1825 749494
Fax: +44 (0) 1825 765701
www.naval-military-press.com
© The Naval & Military Press Ltd 2005

In reprinting in facsimile from the original, any imperfections are inevitably reproduced and the quality may fall short of modern type and cartographic standards.

CONTENTS

	PAGE
IMPULSUS SCRIBENDI	11

CHAPTER I

CHILDHOOD DAYS	13
1. Boys will be Boys	13
2. My Father's Nature	25
3. Princes, Sovereigns and Sayings	31

CHAPTER II

SOLDIER, SPORTSMAN AND STUDENT	38
1. The Value of Prussian Drill	39
2. Queen Victoria	44
3. Student Life	45
4. In Command of the Foot-Guards	50

CHAPTER III

MATRIMONIAL AND POST-MATRIMONIAL	57
1. Freely Chosen, Freely Given	58
2. Recollections of Russia	62
3. Statecraft Studies in Germany and England . .	66
4. The Row in the Reichstag	85
5. How the Kaiser Worked	91
6. Our pre-War Policy	94
7. Travel Impressions	102

CHAPTER IV

STRESS AND STORM	108
1. The Cloud on the Horizon	112
2. The Cloud Bursts	119

CONTENTS

STRESS AND STORM, *continued—*   PAGE
  3. Our Military and Civil Leaders 132
  4. My Memorials 137
  5. Hindenburg and Ludendorff 154

CHAPTER V

PROGRESS OF THE WAR 163
  1. Battle of the Marne 164
  2. Verdun 173
  3. Princes and Politicians at the Front . . . 183

CHAPTER VI

THE GREAT COLLAPSE 195
  1. Foreseeing the End 195
  2. Mistaken Proceedings 198
  3. Wilson and Foch 218
  4. The Wrong Man 224

CHAPTER VII

SCENES AT SPA 229
  1. Schulenburg : Gröner 233
  2. The Value of Ideas 242
  3. The Forged Abdication 247
  4. The Council of Officers 250
  5. The Kaiser's Ejection 261

CHAPTER VIII

EXILED TO HOLLAND 267
  1. Waiting for Berlin 268
  2. Accepting the Inevitable 273
  3. What was Done in My Absence 275
  4. Farewell to My Troops 280
  5. The Decisive Step 281
  6. Wieringen 287
  7. My Message 294

LIST OF ILLUSTRATIONS

The latest portrait of the Crown Prince . . *Frontispiece*

	FACING PAGE
The Kaiser (as Prince Wilhelm) with his eldest son . .	16

THE CROWN PRINCE—
    As a sportsman 40
    As an artist 40

CÄCILIENHOF—The Crown Prince's Elizabethan House, Potsdam 64

The Crown Prince's residence at Oels 64

The Crown Prince with his wife and family . . . 96

A remarkable Royal group 96

THE CROWN PRINCE IN INDIA—
    An antelope hunt 104
    With his first elephant 104

German Head-quarters: the Crown Prince with General von Hindenburg 168

The Kaiser and Prince Henry of Prussia visit the Crown Prince at his Head-quarters in France 168

AT VERDUN—The Kaiser with the Crown Prince . . 176

Three Kings visit the Crown Prince's Head-quarters in France 192

THE CROWN PRINCE—
    In pre-war days 200
    At work at Head-quarters 200

	FACING PAGE
In the trenches at La Fère ; receiving a report from General von Gontar, 25th March, 1918	224
The Crown Prince in the midst of a convoy of wounded, St. Quentin, 1918	224

WIERINGEN—

The Crown Princess visits the Exile	272
The Crown Prince with a native	276
At work with farrier Luijt, making horseshoes . .	280
The Crown Prince, Crown Princess and family, with the Mayor and Mayoress	288
POTSDAM, 1914—" Sanssouci " (The New Palace) . .	292
WIERINGEN, 1922—" The Parsonage " (the present home of the Exile)	292

IMPULSUS SCRIBENDI

March, 1919.

IT is evening. I have been wandering once more along the deserted and silent ways between the windswept and sodden meadows, through greyness and shadow.

No human sound or sign. Only this sea wind driving at me and thrusting its fingers through my clothing. A March wind! Spring is near at hand. I have been here four months.

In the vast expanse above me sparkle the eternal stars, the same that look down upon Germany. From the horizon of the Zuyder Zee, the lighthouses of Den Oever and of Texel fling their beams into the deepening night.

On my return I find my companion waiting anxiously at the little wicket-gate of the garden. Had I been gone such a long time?

I am now sitting in this small room of the Parsonage. The paraffin lamp is lighted; it smokes and smells a little; and the fire in the grate burns rather low and cheerless.

Not a sound disturbs the silence, save this ceaseless moaning of the wind across the lonesome and slumbering island.

Four months!

In this seemingly endless time—which I have spent in one unbroken waiting-for-something, listening-for-something—the thought has recurred again and again to me: " Perhaps if you were to write it out of your heart ? " This idea has seized me again to-day; it was my one companion as I trudged the silent roads this evening.

I will try it. I will write the pages that shall recall and arrange the past, shall bring me out of this turmoil into calmness and serenity. I will retouch the half-faded remembrances, will give account to myself of my own doings, wishes and omissions, will fix the truth concerning many important events whose outlines are seen at present by the world in a distorted and falsified picture. I will depict all events honestly and impartially, just as I see them. I will not conceal my own errors, nor inveigh against the mistakes of others. I will compel myself to objectivity and self-possession even where recollection's turgid wave of pain, anger and bitterness breaks over me and threatens to sweep me along with it in its recoil. With the distant days of my youth I will begin my reminiscences.

* * * * *

CHAPTER I

Childhood Days

WHEN I look back upon my childhood, there rises before me as it were a submerged world of radiance and sunshine. We all loved our home in Potsdam and Berlin just as every child does who is cherished and cared for by loving hands. So, too, the joys of our earliest childhood were, for sure, the same as the joys of every happy and alert German lad. Whether a boy's sword is of wood or of metal, whether his rocking-horse is covered with calfskin or modestly painted —this, at bottom, is all one to the child's heart; it is the symbol of diminutive manliness—the sword or the horse itself—that makes the boy happy. We played the same boyish tricks as every other German boy— except, perhaps, that we spoiled better carpets and more expensive furniture. Whenever and with whomsoever I have talked of those childhood years, I have found full confirmation of the truth that—be he child of king or child of peasant, son of the better-class or son of the workman—every lad's fancy has a stage of development in which it seeks the same bold adventures and makes the same wonderful discoveries, undertakes expeditions into roomy and mysterious lofts or dark cellars; there are happenings with rapidly opened hydrants which refuse to close again when the water gushes out, and secret snowball attacks upon highly respectable and punctiliously correct State officials who, forgetting all at once their reverend dignity, turn as red as turkey-cocks and shout: " Damned young rascals."

As far back as I can remember, the centre of our existence has been our dearly-beloved mother. She has radiated a love which has warmed and comforted us. Whatever joy or sorrow moved us, she always had understanding and sympathy for it. All that was best in our childhood, nay, all the best that home and family can give, we owe to her. And what she was to us in our early youth, that she has remained throughout our adolescence and our manhood. The kindest and best woman is she for whom living means helping, succouring and spending herself in the interests of others; and such a woman is our mother.

Being the eldest son, I have always stood particularly close to our beloved mother. I have carried to her all my requests, wishes and troubles, whether big or little; and she, too, has shared honestly with me the hopes and fears of her heart, the fulfilments and the disappointments which she has experienced. In many a difficulty that has arisen in the course of years between my father and myself, she has mediated with a calming, smoothing and adjusting hand. Not a heart's thought of any moment, but I have dared to lay it before her; and this loving and trustful intercourse continued throughout the grievous days of the war; nor has the relationship been destroyed by all the trying circumstances which now separate me from her. I am particularly happy to know that, in these painful times, she is still, in misfortune, permitted to be the trusty helpmate of my sorely-tried father as she was once in prosperity, and I give thanks to heaven that it should be so. She has been his best friend, self-sacrificing, earnest, pure, great in her goodness, perfect in her fidelity. As her son I say it with ardent pride, she is the very pattern of a German wife whose best characteristics are seen in the fulfilment of her duties as wife and mother, and, in her, they display themselves only the purer and clearer now that the pomp of Imperial circumstance has vanished and she stands forth in her simple humanness.

The relations between us children and our father were totally different. He was always friendly and, in his way, loving towards us; but, by the nature of things, he had none too much time to devote to us. As a consequence, in reviewing our early childhood, I can discover scarcely a scene in which he joins in our childish games with unconstrained mirth or happy abandon. If I try now to explain it to myself, it seems to me as though he was unable so to divest himself of the dignity and superiority of the mature adult man as to enable him to be properly young with us little fellows. Hence, in his presence, we always retained a certain embarrassment, and the occasional laxity of tone and expression adopted in moments of good-humour with the manifest purpose of gaining our confidence rather tended to abash us. It may have been, too, that we felt him so often to be absent from us in his thoughts when present with us in the body. That rendered him almost impersonal, absent-minded and often alien to our young hearts.

My sister is the only one of us who succeeded in her childhood in winning a warm corner in his heart. Moreover, all sorts of otherwise unaccustomed restraints were experienced at his hands. When, for instance, we entered his study—a thing which never exactly pleased him—we had to hold our hands behind us lest we might knock something off one of the tables. In addition to all this, there were the reverence and the military subordination taught us towards our father from our infancy; and this engendered in us a certain shyness and misgiving. This sense of constraint was felt both by myself and by my brother Fritz, though certainly neither of us could ever have been characterized as bashful. I myself have only got free from the feeling slowly and with progressive development.

In recalling my father's study, I am reminded of an incident of my childhood, which has imprinted itself indelibly upon my memory because it involved my first and unintentional visit to Prince Bismarck. It was early in the morning. My brother Eitel Friedrich and I were about to go to Bellevue for our lessons, and I was strolling carelessly about in the lower rooms of the palace. Accidentally, I stumbled into a small room in which the old Prince sat poring over the papers on his writing-desk. To my dismay, he at once turned his eyes full upon me. My previous experience of such matters led me to believe that I should be promptly and pitilessly expelled. Indeed, I had already started a precipitate retreat, when the old Prince called me back. He laid down his pen, gripped my shoulder with his giant palm and looked straight into my face with his penetrating eyes. Then he nodded his head several times and said: " Little Prince, I like the look of you, keep your fresh naturalness." He gave me a kiss and I dashed out of the room. I was so proud of the occurrence that I treated my brothers for several days as totally inferior beings. It was incredible! I had blundered into a study and had not been thrown out—not even reprimanded. And it was withal the study of the old Prince.

The nature of our later education tended to estrange us from our father more and more. We were soon entrusted entirely to tutors and governors, and it was from them that we heard whether His Majesty was satisfied with us or the reverse. Here, in the family

THE KAISER (AS PRINCE WILHELM) WITH HIS ELDEST SON, 1887.

and in our own early youth, we already began to experience the "system of the third," the unfortunate method whereby, to the exclusion of any direct exchange of views, decisions were made and issued by means of third persons, who were also the sole mouthpieces by which the position of the interested party could be stated to the judge. This principle, so attractive to a man of such a many-sided character and so immersed in affairs as unquestionably the Kaiser has always been, took deeper and wider root with the advance of years, and in cases in which place-seeking, ingratiating and irremovable courtiers or politicians have gained possession of posts that gave them the position of go-between, has caused the suppression of disagreeable reports and the doubtless often quite unconscious distortion of news with its consequent mischief. The "department" (Kabinet), especially the Department of Civil Administration, was fundamentally nothing but a "personal board"; the head of the department (*chef de cabinet*) was the mouthpiece and intermediary of any and every voice that made itself heard in this sphere of activity; he also carried back the Imperial decisions. The idea of such a position presupposes unqualified and almost superhuman impartiality and justice—doubly so, when the ruler (as in this case the inner circle was well aware) is susceptible to influence and is shaken by bitter experiences. Then the responsibility of these posts becomes as great as the power they confer, if their occupant goes beyond the clearly-drawn line indicated above.

Then, and still more when they tacitly combine their influences so as to strengthen their position, they and their helpers at court become distorters of the views upon which the ruler must base his final and important decisions. It is they who are really responsible for the wrong decisions that were issued in the name of the ruler and which possibly sealed his fate and that of his people.

But who would think now of discussing the sins committed against the German people by the heads of many years' standing of the Civil Department and the Marine Department in the duologues of their daily reports? Closely and firmly they held the Kaiser entangled in their conceptions of every weighty question. If, after all, a mesh was rent, either through his own observation or by the bold intervention of some outsider, their daily function gave them the next morning an opportunity of repairing the damage and of removing the impression left by the interloper. I am aware that none of these men ever wittingly exercised a noxious influence. Every one considers his own nostrum the only one and the right one to effect a political cure.

Turning from those who were the pillars of this principle back to the principle itself, I know too that a *chef de cabinet* who would have influenced and moulded the decisions of the Kaiser in quite another way might have proved a blessing to the Fatherland and to us all, if that *chef* had been a firm, strong and steadfast personality. But unfortunately destiny placed among the Kaiser's advisers no men of such a stamp with the single exception of the clever and resolute Geheimrat von Berg, whose appointment to the responsible post of Chief of the Civil Department took place in the year 1918— consequently too late to be of any effective service. In general, the notions of the rest were characterized by dull half-heartedness. Wherever they had to suggest men for the execution of new tasks, the men whom they proposed and recommended were only too often mediocre. Anyone who was willing to go his own road with a resolute tread was carefully avoided. Hence, instead of a determined course, there was eternal tacking—instead of any steadfast and clear-sighted grasp of the consequences of such a policy, there was masking of the imminent dangers and a deaf ear for the louder and louder warnings of anxiety and alarm, until at last the cup of fate which they had helped to fill flowed over.

It was in the obscurity of their departments that these "advisers of the crown" laboured, and it is into the darkness of oblivion that their names will disappear. But the taint of their doings will cleave to His Majesty's memory where no more guilt attaches to him than just this: not to have displayed a better knowledge of character in the choice of his entourage, and not to have been more resolute in dealing with his advisers, when the wisest heads and the stoutest hearts among all classes in Germany were but just good enough for such responsible positions.

It was a fundamental mistake that only the Imperial Chancellor made his report in private. All other ministers were accompanied by the chiefs of their respective departments; for the reports of the Military and Naval Ministers, indeed, Adjutant-General von Plessen was also present. In this way the Departments acquired a certain preponderance over the minister or the man who was responsible.

But this theme has led me far astray. I must return to the recollections of my youth. I stopped at the system of the third party. In regard to us boys, the result was that when we acquired military rank, the Kaiser's intercourse with us was generally conducted through the head of the Military Department or through General von Plessen; and, indeed, in quite harmless matters of a purely personal nature, we occasionally received formal military notices (Kabinetts-Orders). Amicable and friendly discussion between father and son scarcely ever took place. It was clear that the Kaiser avoided any personal controversy in which decisions might be necessary; here, again, the third party was interposed. For trivialities, which, under other conditions, a few paternal words might have settled, intermediaries and outsiders were employed and thus made acquainted with the affair; in my own case, since nature has not blessed me with a taste for such punctilious formalities, the tension was often increased. It is quite possible that these gentlemen, who were penetrated with the very profound importance of their missions, were not always received by me with a seriousness corresponding to their own self-esteem and that they rewarded me by taking the first opportunity to express to His Majesty their views on my immaturity and lack of courtesy and dignity. Most certainly these intermediaries are in no small degree answerable for misunderstandings, and for the fact that small conflicts were occasionally intensified or caused all kinds of prejudices and imputations. Sometimes I received the impression that these little intrigues assumed the character of mischief-making. Everything I said or did was busily reported to His Majesty; and I was then young and careless, and I certainly uttered many a thoughtless word and took many a thoughtless step.

In such circumstances it was for me almost an emancipation to be ordered before the Kaiser in regimentals and to receive from him in private a thorough dressing down on account of some incident connected with a special escapade. It was then that we understood one another best. Moreover, one might often, in such colloquies, give rein to one's tongue. An absolutely innocent example comes to my mind. I had always been an enthusiastic devotee of sport in all its forms: hunting, racing, polo, etc. But even here there were restrictions, considerations and prohibitions. One felt just like a poacher. Thus I was not to take part in races or in drag-hunting on account of the dangers involved. But it was for that very reason that I liked this sport. Now I had just ridden my first public race in the Berlin-Potsdam Riding Club, and was hoping that there would be no sequel in the shape of a row, when next morning the Kaiser ordered me to appear before him at the New Palace in regimentals. There was thunder in the air.

" You've been racing."

" Zu befehl."

" You know that it is forbidden."

" Zu befehl."

" Why did you do it, then ? "

" Because I am passionately fond of it, and because I think it a good thing for the Crown Prince to show his comrades that he does not fear danger and thereby set them a good example."

A moment's consideration, and then suddenly His Majesty looks up at me and asks:

" Well, anyway, did you win ? "

" Unfortunately Graf Koenigsmarck beat me by a short head."

The Kaiser thumped the table irritably : " That's very annoying. Now be off with you." This time my father had understood me and had appreciated the sportsman in me.

The older I grew, the oftener did it happen that serious men of the most varied classes applied to me to lay before the Kaiser matters in which they took a special interest or to call the attention of His Majesty to certain grievances or abuses. I took such matters up only when I was able to inquire into them thoroughly and to convince myself of the justification for any interference. Even then their number was considerable.

In most cases the subjects were disagreeable; and they concerned affairs which my father would probably never otherwise have heard of and which he nevertheless ought, in my opinion, to be made acquainted with.

The most difficult matter that I had to take to him was unquestionably the one I was forced to deal with in the year 1907. It was then that I had to open his eyes to the affair of Prince Philip Eulenburg. Undoubtedly it was the duty of the responsible authorities to have called the Kaiser's attention long before to this scandal which was becoming known to an ever-widening circle. But they failed to lay the matter before him; and since they left him in total ignorance of it, I was obliged to intervene. Never shall I forget the pained and horrified face of my father, who stared at me in dismay, when, in the garden of the Marble Palace, I told him of the delinquencies of his near friends. The moral purity of the Kaiser was such that he could hardly conceive the possibility of such aberrations. In this case he thanked me unreservedly for my interference.

In contrast with the Eulenburg affair, most of the questions which, on my own initiative or at the suggestion of others, I had to bring before His Majesty were questions of home or foreign politics, or they concerned leading personages, nay, rather persons who were irresolute and flaccid, but who stuck tight to posts which ought to have been occupied by clear-sighted and steadfast men. In such cases the Kaiser generally listened to me quietly, and frequently he took action; more often, however, he was talked round again by some one else after I had left. It was inevitable that, in the long run, my reports and suggestions should affect him disagreeably. As he travelled very much, I saw comparatively little of him. In consequence, our meetings were mostly encumbered with a whole series of communications and questions by which he felt himself bothered. I myself was fully conscious of the pressure of these circumstances, but saw no means of altering them. In any case, I considered it my duty to keep the Kaiser frankly informed of all that, in my view, he ought to know but would otherwise remain ignorant of.

Notwithstanding all this tension, and although my father was annoyed by certain idiosyncrasies of mine —above all by my disinclination to adopt the traditional princely manner—he was, in his own way, fond of me, and in the secret recesses of his heart proud of me too.

Naturally, much was whispered, gossiped and written in public about these personal relations of ours. If I had been a person to take all this sort of thing seriously, I might soon have appeared very important in my own eyes. Repeatedly there was talk of marked discord, of sharp reprimands on my father's part, of open or covert censure. In all this, as I have shown and as I would in no wise cloak or disguise, there was sometimes a grain of truth—a grain about whose significance a mighty cackle arose among the old women of both sexes. To reiterate, there were early and manifold differences of opinion, and many of them led to some amount of dispute. In so far as these conflicts were concerned with personal affairs and not with political questions, they were, at bottom, scarcely more lasting or more serious than those which so often occur everywhere between father and son, between representatives of one generation and another, between the conceptions of to-day and those of to-morrow; the difference lay in the enormous resonance of court life which echoed so disproportionately such simple events. Thus, these rumours do not really touch the heart of the matter. The frequently recurring fact that father and son differ fundamentally in character, temperament and nature, appears to me, so far as I know the Kaiser and know myself, applicable to us. It is, indeed, regularly observable in the history of our House.

It is possible, too, that there has come between us the great epochal change from traditional conceptions to a broader view of life—a change which seems to have inserted itself between people of the Kaiser's years and my contemporaries, and by which I have benefited while he has viewed it with hostility. At any rate, many of his notions, opinions and actions appeared to me strange and even incomprehensible; they struck me so at an early period of my life, and the more so the older I grew. The first group of the questions towards which, even as a lad, I felt a certain inner opposition, concerned court ceremony as it was then practised. It was painful to me to see people losing their freedom through stereotyped and often thoroughly musty regulations. Each became, in a way, the actor of a part; nay, under the influence of these surroundings, men who were otherwise clever lost their own opinion and yielded here nothing more than the average. Hence, wherever possible, I myself later on avoided everything courtly, pompous or decorative; and, as far as was feasible, I suppressed all formalities in my own circle. For my recreative hours I desired, not endless *réunions* and ceremonious gala performances, but unrestrained intercourse with people of all kinds, sociability in a small circle, theatres, concerts, hunting and sport.

Intercourse with persons of my own age always had a greater attraction for me than association with people much older than myself, though I never designedly avoided the latter. Furthermore, my natural inclinations leading me perhaps more into actualities than was possible to my father and giving me the chance to talk with and listen to a greater number of unprejudiced persons of all professions, I frequently felt impelled by the convictions thus gained to warn and to contradict. But I have ever recognized in the Kaiser my father, my Imperial overlord, to whom it was my duty as well as my heart's wish to show every respect and every honour.

* * * * *

I have been perusing the pages which I penned recently as reminiscences of my childhood and of my attitude towards my parents. The perusal suggests to me that my jottings are not quite just to my father's character, that they speak only of petty weakness, that, if I am to give a complete sketch of his personality, I must dwell upon him more in detail. When I try to distinguish his deepest characteristic, a word forces itself upon my attention which I am almost shy of applying to any man of our own day, a word which seems hollow and trite because, like some small coin, it is flung about so continually and thoughtlessly; it is the word *edel* (noble). The Kaiser is noble in the best sense of the word; he is full of the most upright desire for goodness and piety, and the purity of his intellectual cosmos is without a blemish and without a stain. Candour that makes no reservations, that is perhaps too unbounded in its nature, ready confidence and belief in the like trustworthiness and frankness on the part of others, are the fundamental features of his character. Talleyrand is said to have uttered somewhere the maxim: " La parole a été donnée à l'homme pour déguiser sa pensée." With my father it has often seemed to me as though speech had been bestowed upon him that he might open to his hearer every nook and bypath of his rich and sparkling inner world. He has always allowed his thoughts and convictions to gush forth instantaneously and immediately—without prelude and without prologue, an incautious and noble spendthrift of an ever-fertile intellect which draws its sustenance from comprehensive knowledge and a fancy whose only fault is its exuberance. Moreover, he is by nature and by ethico-religious training free from all guile; he would regard secrecy, dissimulation or insincerity as despicable and far beneath his dignity. The idea that the Kaiser could ever have wished to gain his ends by false pretences or to pursue them by tortuous routes is for me quite unimaginable. It may be that, with all this unreserved and unrestrained self-expression, the passion for complete frankness implanted in every virtuous being found, in the Kaiser, its strongest support in his evident over-estimation of his momentary personal influence. In a personal exchange of ideas he believed himself to be sure of immediate victory and to need the expedients of trickery or dodgery just as little as he did wordy diplomatic skirmishing. I have a thousand times observed the effects of his personality to be indeed very great, and have seen men of otherwise thoroughly independent nature fall an easy prey to his frequently fascinating, though perhaps only transitory, influence.

Nevertheless, such successes, experienced from youth onwards, and, still more, the consequent expressions of admiration and the flattery of complaisant friends and courtiers in the end clouded his judgment concerning the expediency of thus sacrificing every final reserve, as well as obscuring his insight into the fact that the individual—even though he be an emperor and a never so energetic personality—is of little ultimate weight in comparison with the vast world-shifting currents of time.

To this lack of perspective in estimating his personal relations and his personal influence may be partly attributed his remaining so long unconscious of the full significance of the approaching danger. Many a false estimate was formed by him in this regard, and his confiding trust was not seldom lulled into security by clever opponents.

So it happened that, even when the enormous pressure of economic and political forces was uncontrollably driving the world towards the catastrophe of war, he believed himself able to bring the wheels of fate to a standstill by means of his influence in London and Petrograd. The capacity to estimate men and things correctly—that is, impartially and objectively and without any personal exaggeration—is of the greatest moment to rulers and statesmen. It has not been liberally bestowed upon the Kaiser, and my impression is that responsible individuals and the heads of the various " cabinets " have not, by any means, always intervened with the energy necessary to correct erroneous conceptions of this description.

In the depths of his nature my father is a thoroughly kind-hearted man striving to make people happy and to create joyousness around him. But this trait is often concealed by his desire not to appear tender but royal and exalted above the small emotions of sentiment. He is thoroughly idealistic in thought and feeling and full of confidence towards every collaborator who enters fresh into his environment. Present and future he has always seen and gauged in the mirror of his own most individual mental cosmos, which became more and more unreal as the secret and the open struggle for our national existence grew more and more difficult and oppressive both within the realm and without, or as one fragment after another of this cosmos of ideas was harshly snatched away and crushed by the hand of destiny.

In the chivalrous ethics of the Kaiser his conception of loyalty is of great moment. He demands it without reserve, and there is scarcely any dereliction which he feels more keenly than actions or omissions that he regards as breaches of trust. I quote one example: he has never, from the bottom of his heart, pardoned Prince Bülow for not giving him that support which he might have expected in the November incidents of 1908. As a matter of fact, unless I am mistaken, those severe conflicts, with their stormy Reichstag sittings and their innumerable Press attacks, meant for him far more than an affront to his Imperial position or dignity. It was only to outsiders that they appeared to have this effect. Possibly I was able at that time to see deeper into the heart of my Imperial father than anyone, save my dear mother; and I am firmly convinced that, from experiences which were for him barely conceivable and scarcely tolerable, his self-confidence received a blow from which it has never recovered. His joyous readiness of decision and intrepid energy of will, till then undaunted, were suddenly broken; and I believe that the germ was then planted of the lack of decision and vacillation noticeable in the last ten years of his life and especially during the war. From that moment onward, the Kaiser allowed affairs to glide more and more into the hands of the responsible advisers in the various Government departments, eliminating himself and his own views either partially or even entirely. A secret and never-expressed anxiety concerning possible fresh conflicts and responsibilities which he might have to confront had come over him. Where strong hands were needed, complaisant and officious persons pushed themselves forward, and, making use of the opportunity to usurp functions that should never have come within their scope, they dragged into the sphere of their own small-mindedness matters which, so long as the then current constitutional ideas remained valid, ought never to have been withdrawn from the range of the unhampered Imperial will. Still I will not be too hard upon these advisers; I do not wish to be unjust to them; it may be that, in the anguish of those dark days, His Majesty was sometimes even grateful to them for so busily troubling their heads— it may be that they believed themselves to be acting for the best, while in reality creating only evil.

The Kaiser, too, in those years of self-repression and of weakness, just as in his days of unbroken self-confidence, desired to do his best, and he regarded as the best the peace of the realm. Nothing should destroy that; with every means at his command he would secure that to the empire. The terrible tragedy of his life and of his life's work lay in the fact that everything he undertook to this end turned to the reverse and became a countercheck to his aims, so that finally a situation arose in which we were faced by enemy upon enemy.

April, 1919.

Weeks have passed since I last occupied myself with these pages. Tidings have come to hand which are enough almost to break one's heart—which show our poor country to be torn by internal dissension and to be conducting a desperate struggle with a pack of heartless and greedy " victors." In the face of these monstrous events and problems, I have felt as though the individual had no right whatever to review and determine the petty incidents of his own life and destiny. Thus spring has had to come before I could revert once more to my task—spring with its sunny green pastures in which droll little lambs are skipping beside the dirty winter-woolled ewes, and across which blow the clear sea-breezes in ceaseless restlessness.

In this radiance and in the revived colour everywhere visible, all things look better, and people too have more genial faces.

When I think of these first months here in the island! With the best will to make the best of it, there was not much to be done. Distrust and reserve in every one—among the fisherfolk and among the peasants, and among the tradespeople in Oosterland, in Hippolytushoef and in Den Oever. A shy edging to one side when you came by: "De kroonprins"—and that was as much as to say: "That Boche—the murderer of Verdun, the libertine." What the Entente with the help of their mendacious Press and their agents had hammered into the minds of these good people had got thoroughly fixed. Nor was there any possibility of an explanation with them concerning this nonsense. Moreover, my quarters can scarcely be heated, since these little iron stoves will not burn, and our famous single lamp smokes and can only burn when petroleum is to be had. Therefore, as soon as it is dark, one crawls into bed and lies there sleepless to torture oneself with the same matters over and over again, and gets half mad with worrying over the question: "How did it all happen?"—"Where lies the blame?"—"How might one have done better?"

Now, all has grown less hard and is more tolerable. To-day, the people of the island know that none of all the slanders that have been circulated about me are justified. Their distrust has vanished; their simple, unsophisticated nature now meets me frankly. Every one greets me in a friendly manner, and most people shake hands. I also receive occasional invita-

CHILDHOOD DAYS

tions and then sit in these clean little rooms to sip a cup of cocoa and make trial of my acquirements in the Dutch language.

One person in particular has done much to enlighten people and to smooth my path, namely, Burgomaster Peereboom. At the outset, he was the only one who thrust aside all prejudice, and sought to see and to help the human individual—he and his family. And to him and to his warm-hearted and active wife I am indebted for many a little improvement in my modest household at the Parsonage as well as for many a wise hint that taught me to understand my new environment. One or two Germans also tendered me immediate help; among them the experienced Count Bassenheim of Amsterdam, who knows Holland as well as he does his beautiful Bavaria; then the clever and ever-faithful Baron Huenefeld, formerly vice-consul at Maastricht, whose care for me has been most touching; further, there are several German business men of Amsterdam, faithful, self-sacrificing men to whom I owe a lifelong debt of gratitude. And so there only remains unchanged the anxiety as touching my old home, my country, the longing for her and for those to whom I belong.

But not of that now. I will talk here of that other life which to me, in the seclusion of this island, often appears so distant as to be separated from the present by a whole train of years.

* * * * *

Born heir-apparent to a throne, I was brought up in the particular notions valid by tradition for a Prussian prince. No one in the family had ever cherished a doubt as to the suitability and excellence of these principles, for in their youth all its male members had traversed exactly the same path.

While fully recognizing the undeniable value of the old Prussian traditions, I believe, nevertheless, that the narrow, sharply-defined and hedged-in education of Prussian princes (in which the rigid etiquette of the court combines with the anxious care of the parental home to provide directions for mentor, tutor and adviser) is calculated to produce a definite and not very original product adapted to ceremonial duties, rather than a modern man capable of taking his unswerving course in the life of his times. If I had submitted tamely to the system, it would in time have led me into a position in which I should have been ignorant of the world, sequestered and secluded. The worst of such a position appears to me to be, not the Chinese Wall itself, but the ultimate incapacity to see the wall, so that the immured imagines himself free while in reality his mental range is closely circumscribed.

At an early age, and certainly at the outset as a mere consequence of my natural disposition, though later with growing consciousness and maturer judgment, I opposed the efforts to level out the independent features in me with the object of creating a "normal Prussian Prince." Two directly diverging views were at work here. On the one hand was the traditional notion stressed so emphatically throughout His Majesty's reign, the notion of the augustness (*erhabenheit*, exaltedness) of the ruler, the notion—figuratively expressed in the word itself—that the Prince, King, Kaiser must stand elevated high above the level of the governed classes; on the other hand was my own conception that he must become acquainted with life as it is and as it has to be lived by people of every station. It remains to be said that the endeavour to be true to my conviction in thought and act caused me many a struggle and many an unpleasantness.

CHILDHOOD DAYS

The upbringing and the daily life of us children in the Imperial parental home was simple. We certainly were not indulged—least of all by our military governors.

My first military governor—I was then a lad of seven years—was the subsequent General von Falkenhayn. I remember him with reverence and gratitude. He did not pamper me; permitted no excuses; and even in those childhood years he impressed upon me that, for a man, the words " danger " and " fear " should not exist. In the best sense, he passed on to me the undaunted freshness of his faithful soldierliness. There was in me from infancy a passion for horses and riding. General von Falkenhayn arranged our rides in the beautiful environs of Potsdam in such a way that we had obstacles to surmount. Hedges, fences, walls, ditches and steep gravel-pits had to be briskly taken. He used to say on such occasions: " Fling your heart across first; the rest will follow." That saying I have taken with me through life; again and again, and in recent circumstances when the drab hours of my destiny and my loneliness here in this island have threatened to stifle me, the General has stood before my mind's eye and has helped me over my difficulties with his brave soldierly philosophy.

Even when a lad I had to prove myself as patrol and scout, and I was also instructed in reading maps. Gymnastics, drill and swimming were ardently practised as physical training.

An event that made a deep impression upon my young mind recurs to me. I was permitted to present myself to Prince Bismarck in due form and not in the unofficial way in which I had done so when, as a youngster, I suddenly surprised him in his den. From my father I received instructions to don my uniform and meet him at Friedrichsruh; I was going to the eightieth birthday of the ex-Chancellor (Alt-Reichskanzler).

To don uniform was, even in that early period, the acme of delight to my boyish heart; and to this was to be added a visit to the man whom, then as now, a healthy instinct taught me to regard as a sort of legendary hero. In the night before this journey, I did not sleep a wink.

Bismarck was suffering severely from gout, and leaned upon a stick to welcome us in the castle. At lunch he displayed an astounding liveliness and vigour; but, as a consequence of the excitement naturally experienced in this first " official " appearance of mine, this general impression is all that I have preserved in my recollection. Moreover, it must be confessed that I was rendered somewhat anxious during the meal by the Prince's big boarhound, who suddenly laid his cold nose on my knee under the table, and growled very unmistakably whenever, unobserved, I tried to free myself from his attentions.

After lunch, His Majesty mounted horse and, on a piece of ploughland close to the castle, awaited Bismarck at the head of the Halberstadt Cuirassiers, whose chief the aged prince had been appointed. I had the honour of accompanying the old gentleman in his carriage. In a truly paternal manner, he pointed out to me all the beauties of the Friedrichsruh park. My father delivered a very fine speech and presented the prince with a sumptuously-wrought sword of honour. The prince replied with a few pregnant words.

Then we returned to the castle. I noticed that the prince was very weary and fatigued; the prolonged standing had doubtless put too great a strain upon him. His breathing was quick and heavy; and finally he tried to open the tight collar of his uniform, but failed. Almost startled by my own boldness, I bent over him and undid it; then he pressed my hand and nodded gratefully.

We left the same afternoon. On this beautiful day, which I would not, for all that is dear to me, have blotted out of my memory, I had seen for the last time the greatest German of his century.

Our first scientific education we received from our private tutor. I cannot approve of this method, for the pupil misses the stimulating rivalry of comrades. When I entered the Cadet School at Plön as a lad of fourteen, in April, 1896, large gaps manifested themselves in my knowledge, which necessitated a good deal of extra work.

In my Plön days the future General von Lyncker acted as governor to me and to my brother Eitel Friedrich. He was a typical high-minded Prussian officer of the old school. His unswervingly serious nature made it rather difficult for him to enter into the ideas of us immature little creatures or to discover the proper methods of managing us. And we were real children at that time. For him there existed only orders, school, work and duty, and again orders and duty. When I grew a bit older, we often got to loggerheads. As a youth, I certainly was not a pattern being for the show-window of a boys' boarding-school; but that there was so much to complain of as General von Lyncker managed to discover, day in day out, I really cannot believe. Moreover, although quite unintentionally on his part, his somewhat hard and unyielding manner hurt me. But it was this very General von Lyncker whom the Kaiser afterwards employed as go-between when disagreeable conflicts arose. Although I readily and gratefully acknowledge, that in this task imposed upon him, General von Lyncker never adopted the rôle of time-serving tale-bearer or consciously increased the friction—anything of the kind would have been totally irreconcilable with his sincere and lofty character—still, I cannot help saying that the importation of his frequently brusque manner rather tended to widen the breach than to diminish it.

As Plön cadets, we were very fond of Frau von Lyncker. At that time a special School of Princes was formed at Plön for my brother Fritz and me. Each of us had three fellow-pupils. In harmony with the totally false educational principle which this displayed, any association with the other cadets was looked at askance. Nevertheless, from the very first day onwards, we continually leaped over the barriers and seized every opportunity of cultivating comradeship and friendly relations with the other lads of the corps. The football, the rowing matches and the snowball fights are still pleasant recollections for me. Many of my then "corps" companions, drawn from the most varied classes, have become good friends of mine with whom I have remained bound by close ties ever since. During the war, I often quite unexpectedly ran up against one or other of my old Plön comrades in distant France; and then, amid all the grim harshness of the time, the long-lost, care-free days of youth rose before our memories like a sweet smile.

In acquiescence with my special wish, I was permitted to apprentice myself to a master turner. Among the Hohenzollerns it is customary for every prince to learn a trade. In general, of course, such princely apprenticeships must not be regarded too seriously, though the tradition is a valuable symbol and "un beau geste." Now, while I will not assert that I could make my way in the world with my turner's craft, I can say with truth that I have practised it with pleasure again and again, and that master and apprentice took the matter quite seriously. My good master kept me hard at it, and I was an ardent and willing pupil, and felt thoroughly happy in the atmosphere of the turner's workshop and in his simple, cleanly household.

CHILDHOOD DAYS

In these last few weeks of spring on my island I have often recalled my apprenticeship at the lathe, as just for exercise I have been working in Jan Luijt's smithy, hammering sparks from the iron while his son plies the bellows.

Our associations at Plön took us into the families of the masters, and we had also friendly relations with the grammar-school boys. Furthermore, I had a few " friends " among the farmers of the neighbourhood ; I ploughed many a piece of their land, and I still remember how proud I was when my furrow turned out neat and straight.

In the year 1887, that is, long before my Plön days, an event happened which I must recall here, as it made a strong and vivid impression on my young imagination. It was my first sea-trip. The aged Queen Victoria was to celebrate the jubilee of her reign. My parents went to England to take part in the festivity and took me with them. It was at a great garden fête in St. James's Park that I first saw the Queen—sitting in a bath-chair in front of a sumptuously decorated tent. She was very friendly to me, kissed me and kept on fondling me with her aged and slightly trembling hands. Unfortunately, I have no recollection whatever of the words she spoke ; I only know that my boyish fancy was far more occupied with the two giant Indians on guard before the tent than with the weary little old lady herself.

The huge multitude in St. James's Park, and the intermingling of representatives of almost every race, made a deep impression upon me. And if my youthfulness rendered me unable to appreciate the symbolism of the British world-power embodied in the picture, it nevertheless absorbed with awe the astounding copiousness of what it saw and for ever preserved me from underrating the significance of the British Empire.

CHAPTER II

SOLDIER, SPORTSMAN AND STUDENT

IF I regard the turn of the century as the close of my childhood and youth, I would consider the years which followed as my apprenticeship.

After I had passed my matriculation examination, and following upon the declaration of my majority on May 6, 1900, my father placed me in the *Leib-Kompanie* of the First Foot-Guards, in which regiment, according to tradition, every Prussian Prince must first serve. This was a good thing; since that regiment has always been conspicuous for its excellence, and the young princes receive in it a thoroughly strict training. I was afterwards appointed lieutenant and section leader in the 2nd Company, which my father had commanded when a young prince; accordingly, I said to myself: "You are taking here the first steps on the road which is to lead you, through years of learning, to the great tasks of life."

I was inspired by the strongest faith in my life and my future—filled with a sacred determination to be honest and conscientious. The moment when, in the venerable old Schlosskapelle in Berlin, I took the military oath on the colours of the *Leib-Kompanie* before my Imperial father and Supreme War Lord, still stands out clearly before me in all its thrilling solemnity.

The barracks of the First Foot-Guards, the regiment house and the Casino of the Officers' Corps, were now my new home; the rigid and plentiful round of military tasks were my new school. My company commander, Count Rantzau, was a typical old, experienced and conscientious Prussian officer of the line. He himself was always punctual to the minute; he never spared himself, and he devoted himself wholly to his profession; but he also required the utmost from his officers and his men. Accuracy in every detail and severity towards slackness were combined with an unerring sense of justice and a warm heart which followed with human sympathy the progress of every one. His company revered him. Now, that excellent man rests in French soil before Rheims.

Stern but just, a man and a superior of the best type, honoured and respected by me and by all was likewise my first commander, Colonel von Plettenberg. With the same feelings, I recall also my old battalion commander, Major von Plüskow; a giant even among the tall officers of the regiment, he was famous as a drill-master and, despite his strictness, much liked as an ever-kind superior.

What I learned in the Foot-Guards formed the foundation of my entire military career. The value of faithfulness in little things, the much-decried fatigue-uniform, the iron discipline and the abused, because misunderstood, Prussian drill became clear to me in their full significance as a means of concentrating the great variety of heads and forces into a single unit of the greatest strength. The army trained on these principles gained the great and imperishable victories of the year 1914. Unfortunately, in the long course of the war, this admirable Prussian method was thrust more and more into the background, greatly to the detriment of the army and its value.

On the whole, my lieutenancy was an incomparably pleasant time. I was young and healthy, carried out my duties with passionate devotion and saw life in sunshine before me. A circle of friends of like age with myself enabled me to enjoy the blessings of that comradeship which is the most important root whence a Prussian corps of officers draws its strength. To-day, alas, the green turf of France and Russia covers the mortal remains of most of the brave and trusty men who were then young and joyous and faithful; it is lonesome around me.

In those distant days of my lieutenancy and for years afterwards three dear friends stood particularly near to me; they were Count Finckenstein, von Wedel and von Mitzlaff—all of them at that time lieutenants. They shared with me joy and sorrow till fate separated us for ever. Finckenstein and von Wedel fell in the ranks of our fine old regiment—my dear Wedel at Colonfey and brave Finckenstein at the head of his company at Bapaume. Mitzlaff was, for a time, orderly officer in my staff; subsequently he took over a squadron in the East and then returned to the west front as battalion leader. A mournful shroud hangs over the memory of my last sight of this trusty comrade. It was in the summer of 1918, just before the last great Rheims attack. On a visit to the staff of my brave Seventh Reserve Division, I learned by accident that my friend Mitzlaff was with his battalion in the neighbourhood. I at once drove over to him and found him in a little half-demolished farmhouse. Seated on a broken camp-bed, and sharing some cigarettes and a bottle of bad claret which he had managed to rake up somewhere in honour of my visit, we chatted for a long time about the events of our youth and exchanged many an anxious word concerning the future. Both of us knew how matters stood and how over-fatigued the troops were. Mitzlaff himself, however, was of good cheer. Then we held each other's hand for a good

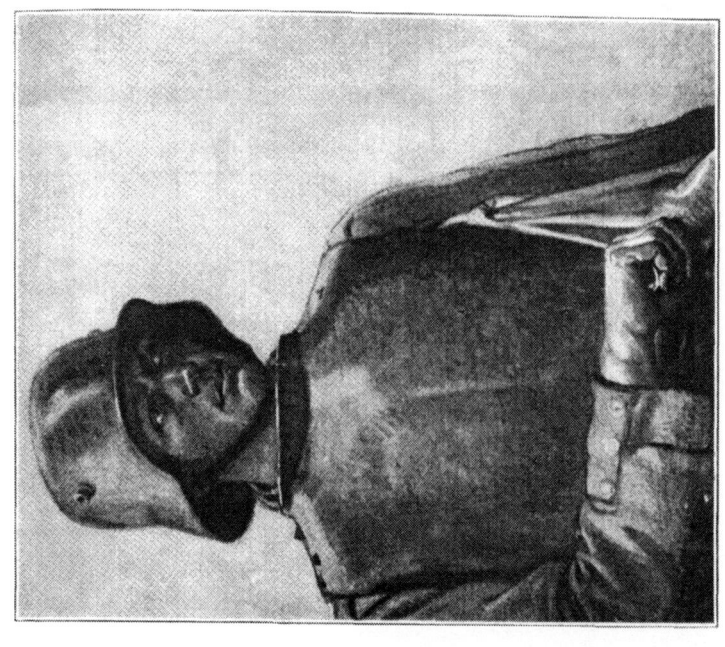

As an Artist.

A Sketch by the Crown Prince on the Western Front, 1918.

As a Sportsman.

Wins First Prize in a Jumping Competition at Schwerin.

while and parted. I drove back to my staff quarters; while he moved up into the front position with his men. Three weeks later I stood beside his simple soldier's grave; a few days after I had bidden him farewell the brave fellow had fallen at the head of his men in storming the enemy's position. He was the last of my three faithful friends.

I remained with the First Foot-Guards one year. During that time the evening order-slip beside my bed determined the hours of the following day. But, in that winter, there was not much sleep for me; for my position demanded my presence at court festivities and innumerable private gatherings. Often I did not get to bed till two o'clock, and by seven I was in the barracks, where my duties kept me busy till noon and again from two till five. Frequently, too, after-dinner attendance at the cleaning of rifles, saddlery and so on fell to my lot. This task I was particularly fond of. My grenadiers sat in the lamplight cleaning and polishing their kit. This provided a natural opportunity to approach them quite closely and humanly and to converse with them about their little personal joys, sorrows and wishes. They talked of their homes or of their civilian occupations with brightened eyes, the fine German folk-songs and soldiers' ballads filling up the intervals in the conversation. To have shared in such an evening would perhaps have opened the eyes of the clever people who babble so much about the tyranny and harsh treatment of the militarism of that time.

During my lieutenancy, as also afterwards, I devoted as much of my leisure time as possible to sport. This I did, not merely because of my natural inclination for sport, but also because I considered its practice to be of particular significance for the future head of a State; and that is, after all, what I was.

The community of sport is calculated, more than anything else, to remove internal and external barriers between people of like aims ; for it is exactly in sport that the actually and manifestly best performance is decisive. Who accomplishes it—whether *junker*, business-man or factory-hand ; Christian, Jew or Moslem —is a matter of indifference. Therefore I have repeatedly attended bicycle races, football matches, route marches and other sporting events ; and, on suitable occasions, I have promoted them by the presentation of prizes. This, again, is one of the things by which I have given offence : a properly brought up heir-apparent should, forsooth, maintain an exalted position and hold himself aloof from such noisy affairs. Very well, then, I have purposely not been this ideal of a stereotyped heir-apparent ; instead, by visiting sporting events, I have gained an insight into the life and bustle, and into the exigencies and desires of many classes of people with whom otherwise, by reason of my upbringing and general circumstances, I should never have come into contact.

In those days, however, I was, above all, heart and soul a soldier ; and it is no exaggeration to say that in the evening I looked forward with pleasure to my next day's duties. The training and the association with the rank and file, the strict old-Prussian discipline, the healthy physical exercise in wind and weather, the pride taken in the ancient regimental uniform—all this made me love the service.

As with all things else, so too with the soldier's calling, one must apply oneself to the task in hand with one's whole being and with real love and devotion if success is to be obtained. This is the spirit that must animate both the officer and his troops.

Short energetic spells of work with the utmost exercise of all one's capacity, smartness and discipline, cleanliness and punctuality, punishment for every negligence or passive resistance, but a warm heart for the meanest or the most stupid recruit, gaiety in the barracks, as much furlough as possible, exceptional distinctions for exceptional performances—in a word, sunshine during military service, formed the fundamental principle which guided me.

May, 1919.

Two bitter-sweet days have been mine in this month of May. On the sixth I celebrated the thirty-seventh anniversary of my birth. Loving letters from my family and numberless indications of remembrance from all parts of my German homeland proved to me here in my seclusion that there are still people who feel that they belong to me and cannot be alienated from me by a never so wildly raging campaign of slander. From the island and from the Dutch mainland, many touching indications of love and sympathy have also reached me—little, well-meant presents for the improvement of my modest household, flowers in such plenty that the small narrow rooms of the parsonage cannot contain them.

And then, after all the unspeakably severe and lonely experience of the past half-year, I was able, with the consent of the Dutch Government, to leave the island towards the end of the month and to celebrate a day with my mother on the estate of good Baron Wrangel. " Celebrate " ! I don't know whether the word befits the hours in which, arm in arm and no one near, we walked up and down in the rose-dappled garden, and, as so often in the better days gone by, I was able unreservedly to pour out, to my heart's content, all that burdened it. To my mother, to that ever sympathetic and comprehending woman, so clear-sighted and wide-visioned in her simple modesty, I could always come in past years when my thoughts and my heart needed the kindly and soothing hand of a mother to smooth out their tangles and creases. It was so when I was a child, it was so when I wore my lieutenant's uniform, it was so when later in life I had duties to fulfil in responsible positions; and that it has remained so to this day has been proved by those few short hours in which, after the first shock of reunion, we recovered our inward equanimity. Scarcely ever before had I felt so deeply the measure with which her nature and her blood had determined my own.

During the initial period of my service in the First Foot-Guards, a sorrowful event at the beginning of the year 1901 took me once more to London, namely, the death of my great-grandmother, the aged Queen Victoria of England.

Since the affair in St. James's Park, in which my boyish imagination had been too completely captivated by the exotic figures around her for me to gain anything but a purely superficial idea of the Queen, I had seen her twice. Each time the features of her character impressed themselves more deeply upon me; my eyes had been opened to the activities of this remarkable woman, who maintained to the end her resolute nature and strength of will.

Now, in the winter of 1901, I was to do her the last reverence.

The Queen had died at her beautiful Osborne in the Isle of Wight. There the coffin had been placed in a small room fitted up as a chapel. Over it was spread the English ensign, and six of the tallest officers of the Grenadier Guards kept watch beside it. In their splendid uniforms, their bearskin-covered heads bowed in sorrow, their folded hands resting upon their sword-hilts, they guarded, immovable as bronze knights, the last sleep of their dead sovereign.

The transport of the dead Queen to London took place on board the *Victoria and Albert*. During the entire passage, which lasted fully three hours, we steamed between a double row of ships of the entire British navy, whose guns fired once more their salutes to the Queen.

The funeral procession through the streets of London was most impressive.

A moving incident occurred at Windsor on the way from Frogmore Lodge to the Mausoleum. It was a bitter winter day; and the train that brought the mortal remains of the Queen was several hours behind time. Just as the procession was about to start, the six artillery horses of the hearse began to jib; one of the wheelers kicked over the pole; the coffin began to sway, and threatened to slip from its platform. Prompt and brief orders were at once given by the then Prince Louis of Battenberg, who was in command of the naval division drawn up at the spot. The horses were unharnessed, and, almost before one could realize what had happened, three hundred British seamen had their ropes fixed to the hearse; with calm tread and almost noiselessly, the dead Queen's sailors drew their sovereign to her last resting-place.

In the spring of 1901, the period of my lieutenancy came to an end. I was now to study, and, like my father before me, I matriculated at Bonn University.

The four semesters spent at the old *alma mater* were for me two delightful and fruitful years, replete with serious study and happy student's life and filled with all the enchantment of Rhenish charm and merriment.

In accordance with tradition I became a member of the Borussia (Prussian) Corps. Nevertheless, I was not simply and solely a " Bonner Prussian "; on the contrary and rather in despite of the strict forms of the corps, I had many friends in other corps of the "Bonner S. C."

My sport-loving heart led me to share with great delight in the fencing-practice which formed the preparatory training for duelling. Fain would I have taken active part in the latter; but, as an officer, I was only permitted to use the unmuffled weapon in serious affairs of honour. Comprehensible as this youthful impulse still appears to me and though I by no means wish to underrate the value of the " scharfen mensur " for the training of eye, hand and nerve, I believe, nevertheless, that our German studentry exaggerated its value. As in the question of weapons, so too in regard to drinking-bouts, I consider that the " Trinkkomment " (the drinking code)—for which I never had any great liking and to which, as a student, I submitted unwillingly—needs to be purged of many formulæ that have developed into abuses. This, moreover, is called for by the pressure of present circumstances. Genuine and practical love for the German fatherland, in its distress and humiliation, means work, and work and work again; it means this especially for our youth, who, in the self-training of their own personalities, are preparing values for the national entity on which may depend the fate of the coming generation.

The hours of my delightful Bonn days that were not occupied in study or in corps life I employed in intercourse with people of all classes in the Rhineland. I accepted gratefully the hospitality of professors, merchants and manufacturers, in whose families I was welcomed with genuine Rhenish cordiality. Having hitherto come into touch mainly with people of the military class, these new associations provided me with copious fresh and vivid impressions as a valuable additional gain to the intellectual stimulus of the university studies proper. To these studies I devoted myself with ardour, and I often think with gratitude of the prominent men who acted as my counsellors and mentors, such men as : Zitelmann, Litzmann, Gothein, Betzold, Schumacher, Clemen and Anschütz. With special indebtedness I recall the brilliant lectures of Zorn, the famous professor of constitutional law ; and a strong bond of confidence and friendship still unites me with that great teacher.

Out of my intercourse at Bonn with intellectual leaders in the fields of science, technology, industry and politics, there arose in me the desire henceforth to occupy myself more than ever before with the problems of our home and foreign policy, and especially with matters of sociology.

Like the lieutenant's period of my life, the two sunny years at Bonn sped rapidly by. They brought me an abundance of delightful and valuable experiences : the enjoyment of nature in a world full of beauty, youthful knowledge, attachment to select and clever men, Rhenish joyousness and the germs of much knowledge that ripened later into intellectual possessions.

Some amount of travel, undertaken during the vacations (in the late summer of 1901 through England and Holland) and, with my brother Eitel Fritz, at the close of my university career, also helped to widen my intellectual vision. The impressions afforded me I welcomed with an awakened and more receptive mind than ever before.

When I recall those travels, two figures particularly stand out before me as lifelike and undimmed as though not years but only days or at most weeks separated me from them. These are Abdul Hamid, the last of the Sultans of the old régime, and Pope Leo XIII. Strange as it may seem, these two men, who, in their natures and in their world, differed in the extreme both outwardly and inwardly, are inseparably united in my mind by circumstances from which I can scarcely detach myself. In the solemn completeness of the Vatican, seemingly so untouched by haste or time, and in the fairyland of the Sultan's court, so entirely remote from every occidental standard and law, there was revealed to me something utterly new and unsuspected, something into which I entered with astonishment. These men—the most remarkable Pope of the twentieth century (for whose spiritualized being I could not, for a moment, feel anything but the deepest awe) and the ruthless, almighty Padishah (in whose presence I quickly recovered my self-possession)—both had the same expression of eye. Penetrating, clever, infinitely pondering and experienced, they looked at you with their grey eyes, in which age had drawn sharply-defined white rings around the piercing pupils.

The picture that awaited my brother Eitel Fritz and myself as we arrived at Constantinople on board the English yacht *Sapphire* on a wonderful spring morning, was absolutely enchanting ; and the events of the few days during which we were guests at the Golden Horn deepened the impression that we were dreaming a dream out of the *Arabian Nights*.

Shortly after our arrival in the harbour, the Sultan's favourite son came to welcome us in the name of his father ; and towards noon the Estrogul Dragoons—excellent-looking troops on small white Arabs—escorted us to the Yildiz Kiosk, where the Sultan received us at the head of his General Staff and his court suite.

Abdul Hamid was an exceptionally fascinating personality—small, bow-legged, animated, a typical Armenian Semite. He was exceedingly friendly, I might almost say paternal, towards us.

We were quartered in a very beautiful kiosk of the enormous Palace buildings of the Yildiz. About half an hour after we had occupied our rooms, the Sultan came to pay us a return visit. He arrived in a little basket-chaise, driving the nimble horses himself and followed on foot by his entire big suite. This included many elderly stout generals, and as the Sultan drove at a trot and these good dignitaries were determined not to be left behind, their appearance when they got to the palace was anything but ravishing.

The rules of the country permitted Abdul Hamid to speak nothing but Turkish; consequently, our conversations with him had to be interpreted sentence by sentence and were excessively wearisome. Moreover, the old gentleman understood our French perfectly, and when I happened to tell him some humorous anecdote or other, it was most amusing to see him laughing heartily long before the dragoman, with the solemnity of a judge, had given him the translation.

In the evening a banquet was to be given in our honour. Where this was to take place no one knew at first, since the Sultan's fear of would-be assassins was so great that he took the precaution to keep the time and place of such festivities secret as long as possible. At the last minute, therefore, and much to the confusion of the marshals of his court, he issued the command for the dinner to be given in a great reception-room.

The Sultan and I sat at the head of an interminably long table. Every one else, including my poor brother, had to sit sideways so as to face the Padishah; there was not much chance of eating anything, but the sight of the Sultan is as good as meat and drink to a believing Mohammedan.

It struck me that my exalted host was wearing a very thick and ill-fitting uniform, till a sudden movement on his part revealed to me the fact that he had a shirt of mail concealed underneath it. In conversation he evinced great interest in all German affairs and proved to be thoroughly informed on the most varied subjects; we discussed naval problems, the recent results of Polar research, the latest publications on the German book market and, above all, military questions.

The days that followed were no less interesting than the first. We visited the sights of the city and its environs, and the old gentleman displayed a touching care for our welfare.

On the last day of our sojourn he invited us to a private dinner in his own apartments. The only other people present were my attendants, the German Ambassador and the Sultan's favourite son. The Sultan, who was very fond of music, had asked me to play him something on the violin. The Prince accompanied me on the piano, and we played an air from *Cavalleria Rusticana*, a cavatina by Raff, and Schumann's *Träumerei*. Then there followed an affecting incident. As a surprise for the old gentleman, I had practised the Turkish National Anthem with my army doctor, Oberstabsarzt Widemann; and as soon as we had finished playing it, the Sultan, who seemed to be deeply moved, flung his arms about me; then, at a sign from him, an adjutant appeared with a cushion on which lay the gold and silver medal for arts and sciences, and this the Ruler of all the Ottomans pinned to my breast. Then he showed us his private museum, containing all the presents received by him and his ancestors from other European princes. Here, among a great quantity of trash, were grouped a number of beautiful and valuable articles. Thus, I recall an amber cupboard presented by Frederick William I.

This meeting with old Abdul Hamid has remained for me one of the most interesting encounters that I have ever had with foreign princes.

In my twenty-second year I was appointed to the

command of the 2nd Company of the First Foot-Guards. The abundance of work involved by this responsible position for the next two and a half years brought me the greatest satisfaction. That I was entrusted with this particular company filled me with peculiar pleasure, as I had become acquainted with all my non-commissioned officers when a lieutenant. The heads of companies, squadrons and batteries form, in conjunction with the regimental commanders, the backbone of the army, inasmuch as, within the scope of their duties, the value of the individual as leader and trainer has a chance of making itself felt. But not much inferior to the personal importance of the head of the company must be ranked the personality of the serjeant-major, significantly dubbed in Germany the " company's mother." My own sergeant-major, Wergin, was a devoted and conscientious man who set an example to all in the company. Early and late his thoughts were occupied with the royal Prussian service, and he was, at the same time, continually busied about the welfare of his hundred and twenty grenadiers.

In themselves the labours which fell to us captains in the First Foot-Guards were light and gratifying. The corps of non-commissioned officers was complete and consisted throughout of thoroughly efficient men; while the recruits of each year were excellent, all of them being well-educated young fellows and representing, in many cases, the fourth generation of service with the regiment or even with the same company. On the other hand, there was a certain difficulty in the bodily dimensions of the men. The height of many of them was altogether out of proportion to their breadth, and it was necessary to exercise great care lest they should, at the outset, be subjected to over-exertion. Furthermore, my tall grenadiers could eat an incredible quantity of food! With my company and with the troops afterwards entrusted to me, I laid great stress upon smartness and discipline. Our combined movements and our drill as a whole were worth seeing, and the grenadiers themselves were proud of their unimpeachable form.

My general principles were short but very energetic spells of duty; for the rest, leave the men as much as possible unmolested; plenty of furlough, fun in the barracks, excursions, visits to the sights of the town and its surroundings, occasional attendance at theatres, a minimum of disciplinary punishments. My men soon knew that, when he had to punish them, their captain suffered more than they did themselves. I endeavoured to work upon their sense of honour, and that was nearly always effective.

Of course, in the foregoing, the duties and labours of a company's captain are anything but exhausted. Apart from all questions of military service, he must be a true father to his soldiers; he must know each individual and know where the shoe pinches in every particular case. Just this phase of the officer's calling gave me the greatest pleasure, and its exercise gained for me the confidence and the attachment of every one of my grenadiers. They came to me with their troubles both small and great, and I felt myself happy in their firm and honest confidingness. Some fine, charming young fellows have passed thus through my hands. Many a one I met again afterwards in the war; many a one now rests in foreign soil, true to the motto on the helmet of our first battalion: *Semper talis*.

Despite this passionate and devoted attention to my duties with the First Foot-Guards, in which regiment I made closer acquaintance with my two former adjutants and future lords-in-waiting—the conscientious Stülpnagel and the faithful Behr—I was not purely and solely a soldier during those years. The Bonn impetus continued active, and the living questions of politics, economics, art and technical science occupied even more of my leisure time than in the years that had opened my eyes to their importance.

Whereas, in the year of my lieutenancy, I had joined with a certain interest and curiosity in all the Court festivities that came in my way, an ever-increasing dislike for the pomp of these affairs began to develop within me as my judgment matured. The much too frequently repeated ceremonial, maintained as it was here in rigid form, appeared to me often enough to be an empty and almost painful anachronism. How many deeply reproachful or gently admonitory glances have I not received from the eyes of court marshals whose holiest feelings I had wounded! But here, as in so many other spheres, the exaggeration of the circumscribed, the "exalted," the congealed, had impelled me to a noticeable nonchalance—not by any means always intentional, often enough involuntary and as though a reaction was bound to take place of its own accord.

Court festivities! Thinking of them reminds me of a man for whom and for whose art I always cherished the greatest veneration, and the sight of whom on these occasions invariably filled me with pleasure and brought a smile to my lips. This was Adolf Menzel. His appearance was generally preceded by a tragi-comedy in his home and on the way to the Palace, for he was so deeply absorbed in his work till the last moment that no amount of subsequent haste in dressing could enable him to arrive in time. In his later years an adjutant of my father's was always sent to fetch him, and this messenger often enough had to help in getting him dressed. But it was all to no purpose; he still came late.

Indelibly imprinted on my memory is Menzel as I

saw him at the celebration of the Order of the Black Eagle. On this occasion, the Knights wear the big red velvet robes and the chain of this high order. The little man, whom none of the robes would fit, struggled wildly the whole time with his train, at which he kept looking daggers from his spectacled, but expressively flashing, eyes.

At the close of the ceremony, it was customary for the knights to defile, two by two, before the throne, to make their obeisance to the Kaiser and to leave the chamber. According to the order of rank, it always happened that the dwarfish Menzel was accompanied by the abnormally tall *hausminister*, von Wedel. When this ill-matched couple stood before the throne, the sight was in itself sufficient to fill one with a warm sense of amusement. But when, at the same time, the artist was aroused in Menzel's bosom, it was difficult to restrain one's hilarity. Menzel seemed to forget altogether where he was, and I have seen him, entirely captivated by the picturesqueness of the scene before him, give his head a sudden jerk, set his arms akimbo and stare long and fixedly at my father. Meantime old Wedel had delivered his correct court bow and was marching off, when, to his horror, he noticed his partner still planted before the throne.

I don't know which delighted me more at that moment, whether the perplexed and dismayed face of the *hausminister*, who felt himself implicated in an unheard-of breach of traditional etiquette, or the little genius, who, turning his head first one way then the other, gazed at the Kaiser, heedless of those waiting impatiently behind him for the space in front of the throne. In the end, Wedel took courage and plucked Menzel by the sleeve. This interruption greatly annoyed the seemingly very choleric master of the brush. If a look can foam with rage, it was the one that, with head thrown back, Menzel flung up into the eyes of his tall companion. Then, gathering up the skirts of his robe, he stumbled, angry and offended, out of the room. It was as though he seemed to be saying to himself: "Bah! What a gathering, where one may not even look at people for a bit."

Time and again have I stood and chatted with him at such court ceremonies. He was full of dry humour, sarcasm and criticism. Nothing escaped his notice; and since, little by little, people had ceased to expect from him a strict subordination to rules, he had come to regard himself as a species of superior outsider and perhaps felt fairly happy in the exceptional position, which certainly provided him with many an artistic suggestion.

For my part, as already stated, these festivities, in which everyone made a show of his own vain-glory, soon lost all attraction for me. Their rigid mechanical nature became dreary; their stiff pomp was like a mosaic made up of a thousand petty vanities set in consequentiality of every shade. I perfectly well recognized that ceremonial festivities necessitated a certain formality; but it appeared to me that they ought also to be animated by an innate freedom, and of this there was scarcely a trace perceptible.

In free and unconstrained intercourse with capable men of every category, with artists, authors, sportsmen, merchants, and manufacturers, I found greater stimulus than in these courtly shows. Moreover, as a lover of sport and the chase, I gave my physical frame its due share in cheerful exertion.

Withal, I felt the vexation of having continually to take into consideration my position as Prince. In everything that I undertook, I was surrounded by people who—with the best intentions, no doubt, but much to my annoyance—rehearsed, again and again, their two little maxims: "Your Imperial Highness must not do that," and "Your Imperial Highness must now do this." Any attempt to repulse these admonitions or to introduce the freedom of action of a free being into this fusty formalism met with a total lack of understanding. It was, therefore, best to let people talk and to do what seemed most simple and natural.

Only one person showed any sympathy with my chafing at restraint or any comprehension of my desire to be a little less "Crown Prince" and a little more of a contemporary human being. It was my dear mother. Ever and again, when I sat talking with her on such matters, I felt how much of her nature she had passed on to me—only what in my blood offered masculine resistance had ultimately accommodated itself and quieted down in her. For this self-resignation she undoubtedly drew never-failing energy from the deep religiousness of her nature.

To the strictly religious character of her ethical views is also to be attributed her urgent desire that we, her sons, should enter wedlock "pure" and untouched by experiences with other women. With this object in view, she and those around us whom she had instructed endeavoured to keep us, as far as practicable, aloof from anyone and every one who might possibly lead us astray from the straight paths of virtue. Undoubtedly my mother, in her thoughts and purposes, was inspired by the best intentions in regard to us and to our moral and physical welfare; and, whatever nonsense may have been early circulated about me, I, at any rate, cannot have greatly disappointed her.

CHAPTER III

MATRIMONIAL AND POST-MATRIMONIAL

June, 1919.

WROTE letters first thing. Then, after breakfast, two hours at the anvil in the smithy. Luijt told me that an American had offered twenty-five guilders for a horseshoe that I had forged. Might he give him one? These people are, after all, incorrigibly ready to inspire the likes of us with megalomania—even when we sit on a grassy island far from their madding crowd. At one time they used to pick up my cigarette-ends; and now, for a piece of iron that has been under my hammer, a snob offers a sum that would help a poor man out of his misery in the old homeland. It is not surprising to me that many a one, under the influence of this cult, has become what he is! No, we are not always the sole culprits!

I left Luijt and went down to the sea, stripped and plunged in. How that washes the wretchedness out of you for a while and makes you forget the whole thing!

About noon, I told my dear Kummer, who has been with me for some time, the story of the American. He is on fire with enthusiasm! " Twenty-five guilders, at the present rate of exchange! I'd keep on making horseshoes for those Johnnies the whole day."

After dinner, looked through the old notes of the battles at Verdun and worked at the subject for the book. Took a walk with Kummer.

And now it is evening again.

Another day passed. How long will it be now?

On a beautiful and memorable summer's day of the year 1904, in fir-encircled Gelbensande, the seat of the Dowager Grand-duchess Anastasia Michailovna of Mecklenburg, I was betrothed to Cecilie, Duchess of Mecklenburg. Not quite eighteen years of age, she was in the first blush of youth and full of gaiety and joyousness. The years of her childhood, in the society of her somewhat self-willed but loving and beautiful mother, had been replete with serene happiness.

On a bright June day of the following year, my beautiful young bride gave me her hand for life. She entered Berlin on roses; she was received by the welcoming shouts of many thousands; she started upon her new career upborne by the love and sympathy of a whole people. And as, on that day, I rode down the Linden with my 2nd Company to form the guard of honour, the warm-hearted participation of all that great throng touched me very deeply. Moreover, the city and the happy faces, the many pretty girls and the roses all over the place, presented an unforgettable picture. My grenadiers naturally felt that they quite belonged to the family and stepped out smartly.

A kind destiny permitted my choice to be free from all political or dynastic considerations. It fell upon her to whom my heart went out, and who gave me her hand as freely and whole-heartedly in return. Our union was the outcome of genuine and sincere affection.

Shall I take any notice of all the nonsense that has been talked and written concerning my wedded life? If the good people who have such "brilliant connections" and consequently such "intimate insight" and "reliable information" would but be a little less self-important! I can say this: whenever the newspapers printed such things as "The Divorce of the Crown Prince Imminent," my wife and I had a good laugh over the matter. What a craving for sensation possesses the public!

I can only thank my wife from the bottom of my heart for having been to me the best and most faithful friend and companion, a tender helpmate and mother, forbearing and forgiving in regard to many a fault, full of comprehension for what I am, holding to me unswervingly in fortune and in distress.

She has presented me with six healthy and dear children whom I am proud of with all my heart and for whom I feel a longing as often as I stroke the head of one of these flaxen-haired little fisher-lads here. May my four boys some day be brave German men, doing their duty to their country as true Hohenzollerns!

During the time of severe torment that followed Germany's downfall, my wife stuck to her post with exemplary faithfulness and bravery and, in a hundred difficult situations, proved herself to possess that strong, noble nature for which I love and revere her.

After all, "war" has made its way into our married life!

In 1915, the Crown Princess paid me a two-days' visit in my head-quarters at Stenay. At four o'clock in the morning of the second day, there began a French air attack manifestly aimed full at my house, which, at that time, had no bomb-proof cellar or dug-out. A direct hit would undoubtedly have meant thorough work. The attack lasted two hours. In that time, twenty-four aeroplanes dropped bombs around us and a hundred and sixty bombs were counted. Several of them landed only a few yards from the house, and, unfortunately, claimed a number of victims. It was the severest air attack that I had ever experienced, and was a test to the nerves in which my wife showed the greatest courage and calmness. The way in which she stood the strain was magnificent.

Following upon my captaincy in the First Foot-Guards, I was now to be appointed to the command of a squadron. Through the mediation of his Excellency, von Hülsen, I requested His Majesty to entrust me with a squadron of the Gardes du Corps. At first, His Majesty wished to appoint me to the Hussars. Ultimately, he gave way and placed me, in January, 1906, at the head of the *Leib-eskadron* of the Gardes du Corps, though, instead of the handsome uniform of that regiment, he ordered me, by special decree, to wear the uniform of the Queen's Cuirassiers.

In this new position, my love of horses found once more a wide field of activity, and I look back with great satisfaction to the delightful period during which I was attached to this proud regiment, whose glorious traditions are so intimately bound up with the history of the Brandenburg-Prussian State. That it was no mere parade troop was proved at Zorndorf and again in the gigantic struggle of the world-war. It was a bitter-sweet joy to me to receive, only a few days ago, a loving sign that the old and well-tried members of the body-squadron had not forgotten their former leader in his present misfortune: on my birthday, May 6, a small album containing the signatures of the officers and gardes du corps of the old squadron found its way to my quiet island. Of the officers and of the gardes du corps! How many names are wanting! East and west repose those whose names are not in the album. My thoughts wander in both directions to greet the brave dead.

Here, although it belongs to a later period, I would

MATRIMONIAL AND POST-MATRIMONIAL

say a word about my appointment to the third military weapon—the artillery. To render me familiar with it, I was appointed, in the spring of 1909, to the command of the *Leib-batterie* of the First Field Artillery. I felt particularly happy in this excellent regiment—excellent both from a military standpoint and in its comradeship; and I recall with sincere gratitude the assistance given me by my faithful mentor, Major the Count Hopfgarten, and his manifold suggestions in matters relating to artillery.

Even at that time, the mode of employing our field-artillery and, to some extent also, our mode of firing, struck me, in some points, as out of date when compared with French regulations. About five years later, the experiences of the war demonstrated that the French army really had gained a start of us in the development of this weapon. With us the technology of artillery had dropped behind the equestrology; the horse had obtained too many privileges over the cannon.

As personal adjutant, I asked and obtained the services of Captain von der Planitz. This excellent and well-trained officer, whom I shall ever gratefully remember as a sincere and noble man and as my long-standing and trusted companion and counsellor, fell as commander of a division in Flanders.

A report is being circulated by the newspapers which purports to come from an eye-witness of the murder of Tsar Nicholas, and to reveal, in all its horrors, his bloody end.

This description, whose ghastliness is only enhanced by its cold objectivity, I read this morning. Ever since, as the rain outside has continued to pour down ceaselessly, my thoughts have reverted again and again to this poor man, to him and those around him, on the two occasions that I came into closer contact with him—first, as his guest in Russia, and afterwards on the one occasion that he was our guest in Berlin.

Now, as I write these lines in recollection of him, it is night.

When I first met Tsar Nicholas at Petrograd in January, 1903, he was in the height of his power. I had been dispatched to take part in the Benediction of the Waters. The court and the troops formed an exceptionally brilliant framework to the celebration. But the Tsar himself, who was at bottom a simple and homely person and most cordial and unconstrained in intimate circles—appeared irresolute, I might almost say timid, in his public capacity. The ravishingly beautiful Empress Alexandra was, in such matters, no support for him, since she herself was painfully bashful, indeed almost shy. In complete contrast to her, the Dowager Empress Maria Feodorovna, embodied perfectly the conception of majesty and of the *grande dame*, and she exercised also the chief influence in the political and court circles of Petrograd. It was particularly noticeable how little the Tsar understood how to ensure the prestige due to him from the members of his family, i.e. from the grand dukes and grand duchesses. When, for instance, the company had met previous to a dinner, and the Imperial couple entered, scarcely a member of the family took any notice of it. An absolutely provocative laxity was displayed on such occasions by the Grand Duke Nicholai Nicholaievitch, who, by the way, did not hesitate, in conversation with me, to give fairly pointed expression to his dislike of everything German. In vain did I look for traces, in Petrograd, of the old friendship between Prussia and Russia; English and French were the linguistic mediums; for Germany no one had any interest; more often than not I even came across open repugnance. Only two men did I meet with who manifested any marked liking for Germany, namely Baron Fredericks and Sergei Julivitch Witte, who, a few years later, was made a count. With Witte I had a long talk upon the question of a new Russo-German treaty of commerce, in the course of which the politician, with his far-sighted views of finance and political economy, maintained emphatically that, in his opinion, the healthy development of Russia depended closely upon her proceeding economically hand in hand with Germany.

The fear of assassins was very great at the Court. Among the many precautionary and preventive measures which I saw taken everywhere, one that I met with on paying the Tsar a late evening visit made a deep impression upon me. In the vestibule of his private apartments, the Emperor's entire bodyguard of about one hundred men were posted like the pieces on a chessboard. It was impossible for anyone to pass; and my entrance created the greatest alarm and excitement.

Within the inner circle of his family, the Emperor was an utterly changed being. He was a happy, harmless, amiable man, tenderly attached to his wife and children. From the Empress, too, disappeared that nervousness and restlessness which took possession of her in public; she became a lovable, warm-hearted woman and, surrounded by her young and well-bred daughters, she presented a picture of grace and beauty. I spent some delightful hours there.

On the second occasion, my wife and I were invited to Tsarskoe Selo. Here I might have imagined myself on the country estate of some wealthy private magnate, save that, at every step, the police and military precautions reminded me that I was the guest of a ruler who did not trust his own people. Tsarskoe stands in a great park. Outside the palings was drawn up a cordon of Cossacks who trotted up and down night and day to keep watch. Within the park stood innumerable sentinels, while inside the palace one saw everywhere sentinels in couples with fixed bayonets. I said to my wife at the time that it made you feel as though you were in a prison, and that I would rather risk being bombed than live permanently such a life as that.

A distressing motor drive still remains vivid in my memory. The Tsar wanted to show us the palace on the lake-side. We started off in a closed carriage. It was the first time, for months, that the Emperor had left Tsarskoe. The drive lasted about four hours. The impression was cheerless and deeply depressing. Every place we passed through seemed dead; no one was permitted to show himself in the streets or at the windows—save, of course, soldiers and policemen. Weird silence and oppressive anxiety hung over everybody and everything. To be forced to conceal oneself like that! It was a life not worth living.

We also took part in a great military review. The Guards looked brilliant; and, true to their ancient tradition, they later on fought brilliantly in the war. An uncommonly picturesque impression was made by the bold-looking Don, Ural and Transbaikal Cossacks on their small, scrubby horses.

The reception in the family circle was as hearty as on my first visit. For hours we canoed about the canals, and discussed exhaustively many a political problem. These talks convinced me that the Tsar cherished sincere sympathy for Germany, but was too weak to combat effectually the influence of the great anti-German party; the Dowager Empress and

THE CROWN PRINCE'S ELIZABETHAN HOUSE, POTSDAM.

THE CROWN PRINCE'S RESIDENCE AT OELS.

the Grand Duke Nicholai—both pronounced opponents of Germany—possessed the upper hand.

Tsar Nicholas was not, in my judgment, the personality that Russia needed on the throne. He lacked resolution and courage and was out of touch with his people. As a simple country gentleman, he might perhaps have been happy and have had many friends; but he did not possess the qualities essential to lead a nation to the full development of its powers; possibly, indeed, his timid mind scarcely dared even contemplate the merest shadow of such qualities.

Deeply tragical appeared to us, even at that time, the weakly and continually ailing little heir-apparent, Alexis Nicholaievitch. Though already nine years old, he was usually carried about like a little wounded creature by a giant of a sailor. With anxious and trembling tenderness the parents clung to this fragile offspring of the later years of their wedlock, who was expected some day to wear the imperial crown of Russia.

All over! Gone in blood and horror this little wearily flickering life.

* * * * *

After I had completed another two and a half years of military service, I felt a lively desire to fill in the very considerable gaps in my knowledge of political and economic affairs. Wishes repeatedly expressed by me in the matter had hitherto been disregarded, which was the more remarkable as, in the history of our house, the ruler for the time being had always treated the timely preparation of the heir-apparent for his future career as a particularly urgent duty of the office conferred upon him. Consequently, I felt myself ill-used in being thus denied the opportunity to grasp and fathom subjects whose mastery was essential for me. Without exaggeration, I can say that I had to wrestle tenaciously and uncompromisingly for admission to an environment in which I might acquire this indispensable knowledge.

It was therefore with all the greater satisfaction that, in October, 1907, I welcomed the Kaiser's finally consenting to attach me to the bureau of the Lord Lieutenant at Potsdam, to the Home Office, to the Exchequer, and to the Admiralty. I was, however, to wait a while before being initiated into questions of foreign policy; these were treated as a trifle mysterious—and as though they lay within the sphere of some occult art. For the present, therefore, I was to have the opportunity of attending lectures on machine construction and electrotechnics at the University of Technology in Charlottenburg, where I might acquire a more extensive acquaintance with these subjects which had always aroused my peculiar interest.

Thus the obstacles that had heretofore stood in my way were now removed; doors that had been kept religiously closed to me at last opened to my hankering for knowledge.

My determination to acquire knowledge in the various ministries—greatly facilitated by my father's orders to supply me with every desired information—speedily led to my occupying myself busily with the great questions of the day and their international interdependence; and thus I soon found myself absorbed in the study of the German and the foreign Press.

The pulse of our life is the newspaper: in it beats the heart of the times; inertness and activity, lassitude and fever here both impress and express themselves, and, for him who has to care for the well-being of the entire national organism, they become, under certain circumstances, admonishing and warning voices. In that year of study which I devoted to the Press, my first modest gain was that I learned to estimate clearly the significance of the newspaper for those who are willing to hear, to see, and to recognize; yes, for those who will hear, see, and recognize, and are not blinded to the signs of the times by an ostrich-like psychology either imposed upon them or voluntarily adopted.

Of course, I had read the newspapers before, in the ordinary acceptation of the term. Mainly, I had confined myself to journals of the conservative type and colourless, well-disposed news-sheets; though I had, at any rate, read them unmutilated by anybody else's scissors. Now, I ploughed my way daily through the whole field from the *Kreuzzeitung* to the *Vorwärts;* and often an article marked by me found its way to the proper persons to give me the required explanations and enlightenment.

Consequently, in regard to particular cultural and political questions, I soon arrived at a point of view which showed me the problems from quite a different angle from that adopted by His Majesty on the ground of the press-cuttings and the reports presented to him. The humour of history was grotesquely inverted: the King was guided *ad usum delphini,* and the Dauphin drew his knowledge out of the fullness of life. By reason of this deeper insight into the driving forces of the masses and of the times, many of the fundamental notions kept to by the Kaiser in his method of government appeared to me to have lost their roots and to be no longer reconcilable with the spirit of modern monarchy with its wise recognition of recent developments and current phenomena.

Besides the German state organization, there was another which, at that time, aroused my special interest, namely, the British. I had been about a good deal in England, and, in many an hour's talk on this fascinating subject my great-uncle, King Edward, had lovingly instructed me concerning England's political structure, in which I recognized many a feature of value to our younger development. When I recall these memorable conversations, in which my part was that of a thoroughly unsophisticated young disciple of a successful past-master and fatherly friend, it strikes me that the King wanted to bestow upon me something more than a simple lesson in the conditions of England; it was rather as though this, in his own way, highly talented man recognized that the ideas which had governed the first two decades of my father's reign had been leading further and further from the lines along which the monarchy of Germany ought to develop, if that monarchy were to remain the firmly-established and organic consummation of the State's structure; it was as though he clearly and consciously meant to call my attention to this danger point, in order to warn me and to win me to better ways even at the threshold of my political career.

All that my old great-uncle imparted to me out of the fullness of his observation and experience I gladly accepted and developed, and doubtless it has had its share in forming my views concerning the Kaiser's maxims of government and in my feeling a strong inclination for the constitutional system in operation in England.

During this period of eager study, I received from Admiral von Tirpitz, the head of the Admiralty, some particularly deep and stimulating impressions. In him I found a really surpassing personality, a man who did not stare rigidly at the narrow field of his own tasks and duties, but who saw the effects of the whole as they appeared in the distant political perspective and who served the whole with all the comprehensive capacities of his ample creative vigour.

The great work of producing a German navy had

been entrusted to him by the Kaiser, and his life, his thoughts and his activities were entirely filled with the desire and determination to master the enormous task for the good of the empire and in spite of all external and internal opposition. How well he succeeded has been proved by the Battle of Jutland, which will ever remain for him an honourable witness and memorial—Jutland, where the fleet created by him and inspired by his mind passed so brilliantly through its baptismal fire in contest with the immensely stronger first navy of the world. Germany had then every reason to be proud of the glorious valour and exemplary discipline of her young bluejackets.

Only in one fundamental question did I, in that year of co-operation, differ from the Lord High Admiral. He held firm to the conviction that the struggle with England for the freedom of the seas must, sooner or later, be fought out. His object was the " risk idea," that is to say, he maintained that our navy must be made so strong that any possible contest with us would appear to the English to be a dangerous experiment because the chances of the game would then be too great—chances that could not be risked without involving the possibility of the English dominion of the seas being entirely lost. To the ideal principle underlying this defence theory I did not shut my eyes ; but, considering our political and economic position, it seemed to me that its form, which presupposed our being the sole opposing rival of England at sea, did not permit its realization. I was rather of opinion that the " risk idea " could only ripen into a healthy, vigorous and real balance of power at sea, if the counterpoise to England were formed in combination with another Great Power whose land forces for this purpose would not come into consideration, but whose navy in conjunction with our own would yield a force adequate to gain the respect and restraint aimed at. In this way, if the thing were at all feasible, not only could an immense reduction of our naval burden be effected, but it would be easier to overcome the great danger of the whole problem, namely, the smothering of our sea-forces before! their goal had been reached; for I always frankly maintained and asserted that the British would never wait until our "risk idea" had materialized, but, consistently pursuing their own policy, would destroy our greatly suspected navy long before it could develop into an equally-matched and—in the sense of the "risk idea"—dangerous adversary.

That, in point of fact, the will to adopt such a radical course was not wanting was further proved to me recently on reading Admiral Fisher's book. He states the matter with astounding candour in the following way: "Already in the year 1908, I proposed to the King to Copenhagen the German navy."

In consequence of our political isolation, all my doubts and considerations had to remain doubts and considerations. An ally whose navy came into consideration as an adjunct to ours we did not possess. Nor would an alliance with Russia, such as was aimed at by Tirpitz, have given us the help of such a navy.

When the various efforts to bring about an understanding over the naval question had all failed, the right moment and the last chance arrived for England to try conclusions with the German navy with some likelihood of success. The opportunity of war in the year 1914 offered that chance, and provided also an unexampled war-cry; there were binding treaties to be kept, and England could likewise appear as a spotless hero and the protector of all small nations.

In all this, too, it was naturally not the naval

problem *per se* which induced England to seize this opportunity of joining in a war against Germany. Sea-power is world-power; our navy was the protecting shield of our world-wide trade; it was not the shield, but the values which it covered, at which the blow was aimed, in the not over-willingly waged war. The motive forces which urged towards war, towards final settlement, across the Channel were the same that had previously effected our economic isolation; they grew out of England's struggle for existence with the vast development of German industry and German commerce. Her attempted strangling of these in pre-war years had failed; the German expansion continued. Hence England gave up the endeavour to avoid war; the final settlement must be faced. No one who knew the situation could doubt that England would make the utmost use of such an excellent opportunity as that provided by our treatment of the Austro-Serbian dispute. Only lack of political insight on the part of our statesmen could overlook all this and hope for the neutrality of England, as Bethmann Hollweg did.

And when we were once involved in war with England and problems of attack were presented to our navy in place of the defensive tasks for which it had been created, it was a fatal blunder to keep it out of the fray, or to deny a free hand in its employment to Grand Admiral von Tirpitz, who knew the instrument forged by him as no one else could. The parties who, at that time, had to decide concerning the fate of the navy failed to win that immortality which lay within their reach. Although it lay within arm's length of both von Müller and Admiral Pohl, neither of these men has succeeded in gaining immortality. Everybody clung to Bethmann's notion of carrying the fleet as safe and sound as possible through the war in order to use it as a factor in possible peace negotiations—an idea that was scarcely more sensible than, say, the idea of carrying the army and its ammunition intact through the war with a like purpose. People philosophized over distant possibilities and missed the hour for acting!

Admiral von Tirpitz was a highly talented and strong-willed man looked up to by the entire navy. His sense of responsibility and his resoluteness personified, as it were, for them the fighting ideal of his weapon, and I am still convinced that he would have turned the full force of the fleet against England as rapidly as possible. Such an attack, carried out with fresh confidence in one's own strength and under the conviction of victory, would not have failed. That such a view is not in the least fantastic and is shared by the enemy is evidenced by a passage in Admiral Jellicoe's book, in which he writes:

" With my knowledge of the German navy, with my appreciation of its performances and with a view to the spirit of its officers and its men, it was for me a great surprise to see the first weeks and months of the war pass by without the German navy having conducted any enterprises in the Channel or against our coasts. The possibilities of an immediate employment of the German forces succeeding I should not have underrated."

But, as Goethe says, enthusiasm is not like herrings; it cannot be pickled and kept for years; and the spirit of attack, patriotic pride and discipline cannot be preserved or bottled. In our navy, so proud and powerful at the outbreak of the war, these qualities withered and decayed because that navy was not allowed to prove its strength, was not used at the right moment.

Hence, the weapon which failed to strike when it

ought to have struck finally turned against our Fatherland and helped to bring about our defeat.

I have perused the sheets written yesterday. These jottings of mine will not constitute a regular and well-arranged book of reminiscences reproducing events in their exact order of time. I had intended to write of my initiation into the affairs of the Admiralty and of my work with Admiral von Tirpitz, so profitable to me; and, in the ineradicable bitterness of my recollections, I sped into the events of later years.

In mentioning the "risk theory" of Tirpitz, I touched upon our political isolation. On this subject there is perhaps much more to be said.

When, soon after the completion of my labours at the Admiralty, I penetrated further and further into the problems of the foreign policy of the empire, I repeatedly found confirmation of the fact that, as I had observed during my travels, our country was not much loved anywhere and was indeed frequently hated. Apart from our allies on the Danube and possibly the Swedes, Spaniards, Turks and Argentines, no one really cared for us. Whence came this? Undoubtedly, in the first place, from a certain jealousy of our immense economic progress, jealousy of the unceasing growth of the German merchant's influence on the world market, jealousy of the great diligence and of the creative intelligence and energy of the German people. England, above all, felt her peculiar economic position threatened by these circumstances. This was naturally no reason for us to feel any self-reproach, since every people has a perfect right, by healthy and honourable endeavours, to promote its own material well-being and to increase its economic sphere of influence. By fair competition between one nation and another, humanity as a whole attains higher and higher stages of civilization. Only ignorant visionaries can imagine that progress in the life of the individual, of the peoples or of the world can be reckoned upon if competition be barred.

But it was not alone jealousy of German efficiency that gained for us the aversion of the great majority; we had managed by less worthy qualities to make ourselves disliked. It is imprudent and tactless for individuals or peoples to push themselves forward with excessive noisiness in their efforts to get on; distrust, opposition, repulsion and enmity are thereby provoked. But this is the fault into which we Germans, both officially and individually, have lapsed only too often. The openly provocative and blustering deportment, the attitude adopted by many Germans abroad of continually wishing to teach everybody and to act as mentors to the whole world, ruffled the nerves of other people. In conjunction with the stupidity and bad taste of a similar character proceeding from leading personages and public officials at home and readily heard and caught up abroad, this attitude did immense damage, more especially, again, in the case of England, who felt herself particularly menaced by modern Germany.

In many a political chat, that was as good as a lesson to me, my great-uncle, King Edward VII—with whom I always stood on a good footing and who was undoubtedly a remarkable personality endowed with vast experience, as well as great wisdom and practicality—repeatedly expressed his anxiety lest the economic competition of Germany would some day lead to a collision with England. "There must be a stop put to it," he would say on such occasions.

Facing all these facts squarely, and remembering that England's forces had always been employed against that Continental Power which at any given moment happened to be the strongest, I felt

MATRIMONIAL AND POST-MATRIMONIAL

that, sooner or later, the German Empire would inevitably become involved in a war unless the opposition between it and England were removed.

Personally, I considered it desirable to strive for an understanding with England on economic, economico-political and colonial questions. I did not, however, entertain any illusions as to the difficulty of such an undertaking. I was quite aware that any such effort presupposed a thorough discussion both of the naval programme and of economic matters. The object appeared to me well worth the sacrifice, for the relaxation of the political tension to be followed ultimately by an alliance with England would not merely have secured peace, but would have provided us with advantages amply compensating for the concessions indicated. Prince Bülow, with whom I once talked about this delicate question, referred me to a saying of Prince Bismarck's, namely, that he was quite willing to love the English, but they refused to be loved. For an alliance with England, which, while not involving the sombre risk of war with Russia, would have been calculated to bind England really and seriously, he seemed at that time not at all disinclined. But as, according to him, Lord Salisbury, the British Prime Minister in the early years of the century, was not to be persuaded to such an alliance, he thought to do better, under the circumstances, by adopting a "policy of the free hand." Similar answers were given me by all the other leading statesmen of the realm to whom I opened up my ideas: an understanding with England, they said, was impossible; England would not have it; or, if a basis were found, we should lose by the whole affair. But their reasons failed to convince me. Why, a glance across the black, white and red frontier-poles showed that, all around us, political feats quite different from ours had been performed; but they had been performed by men who understood their profession and the signs of the times. Nor do I consider that, in the years to which I refer here, England was ill-disposed or could not have been won over, even though matters were no longer handed to us on a silver salver as they had been at the beginning of the Boer War, when Joseph Chamberlain quite openly tried to bring about an alliance between Germany, England and the United States. Yet the possibility of starting again where we had then failed was anything but irretrievably lost. Nevertheless, I had to accept the fact that Prince Bülow and his politicians were not to be persuaded to a serious, well-grounded understanding with England; they seemed thoroughly satisfied with the outwardly good and courteous relations, they considered the situation well tested and satisfactory, and saw no reason to regard it as so acute or threatening.

For the future, therefore, I endeavoured to think the matter over on the rigid lines laid down by the Wilhelmstrasse. Assuming it to be impossible to alter the antagonism with England or to bridge the rift started during the Boer War by the over-hasty Krüger telegram (the responsibility for which, by the way, has been quite unjustifiably laid upon the Kaiser), the only possible and profitable ally left for us in Europe was Russia. If we had an alliance with Russia, England would never risk a war with us; nay, she would have to be content so long as this alliance did not menace her Indian dominions. Consequently every effort should be made to re-knit the bond which, subsequent to Bismarck's retirement, had been broken by the denunciation of the re-insurance treaty; everything ought to be done to loosen the Franco-Russian Alliance and to draw Russia into co-operation with ourselves. This, too, was no easy task; but there was a prospect of succeeding, if we supported Russia's wishes in regard to the Dardanelles and the Persian Gulf.

I talked at the time with Turkish politicians about the matter, and found them anything but unapproachable in regard to the question of a free passage through the Dardanelles. Moreover, opposition to this solution was scarcely to be feared from our allies Austria-Hungary. Here, therefore, I seemed to see a suitable starting-point.

From all these considerations France was excluded, since, after the weakening of Russia by the war in the Far East, we had missed the opportunity of coming to a complete understanding with the well-intentioned Rouvier Cabinet in the early summer of 1905. In the meantime, by skilful cultivation of the idea of revenge against Germany, even the bitterness towards England caused by the Fashoda affront had been dissipated. The *conditio sine qua non* for any agreement would be the sacrifice of at least a part of the Reichsland, a thing which we could not even discuss in times of peace.

But, neither during Bülow's chancellorship nor Herr von Bethmann's was any energetic action undertaken or well-defined programme adopted by the Government to bring about an understanding with England or to link up our policy with Russia. People clung to the hope of sailing round any possible rocks of war; they wished to offend nobody and therefore conducted a short-term hand-to-mouth policy which had no longer anything in common with the clever and wide-spun conceptions of the Bismarck tradition.

As a consequence, very depressing misgivings often overcame me when I thought what notions our leading statesmen entertained concerning our political position. That they misconstrued the seriousness of affairs I refused to believe, for the fact of our isolation was sufficient to prove even to the most inexperienced observer with any sound common sense that with our peace policy of " niemand zu Liebe and niemand zu

Leide " (without consideration of persons) we were in danger, between two stools, of coming to the ground. Hence I was forced merely to look on at the incomprehensible calm with which our political leaders guided the realm through those times, while our opponents' ring closed tighter and tighter.

The game was an unequal one!

It was unequal in the personages that faced each other as exponents of the two sets of effective forces. On this side was His Majesty, who, down to the crisis of November, 1908, ruled with great self-confidence and a perhaps too assiduously manifested desire for power; beside him, and severely handicapped by all the various moods and political sympathies and antipathies of the Kaiser, stood Prince Bülow, whose place was taken the following summer by Theobald von Bethmann.

On the other side was King Edward VII, and beside him and after him half a dozen strong, clear-headed men who, misled by no sentiment, worked along the lines of a firmly-established tradition to accomplish the programme mapped out for England and England's weal.

I repeat it: the game was unequal.

I do not underestimate the great talents which, in the most difficult circumstances, enabled Prince Bülow, time and again, to bridge over rifts, to effect compromises and adjustments, and to disguise fissures. But he was not a great architect; he was not a man of Bismarck's mighty mould; he was not a Faust with eyes fixed on the heights and the far horizon; no, he was none of these, but he was a brilliant master of little remedies with which a man may save himself from an evil to-day for a possibly more bearable one to-morrow; he was a serious politician who had thoroughly learned his craft and exercised it with graceful ease; firm in the possession of this, he was therefore no charlatan;

he was a reader of character, too, who knew how to deal with his men—a personality.

Of all post-Bismarckian chancellors, Prince Bülow strikes me as far and away the most noteworthy; indeed, I would place him well beyond the limitations of this very relative compliment, which really does not say much. He understood perfectly how to defend his policy in the Reichstag; and his speeches, with their genuine national feeling, scarcely ever missed their mark. Moreover, he could negotiate, he showed skill and tact in personal intercourse with parliamentarians, foreigners and pressmen; and, like no one else since the first chancellor, he gave a due place in his calculations to the value of the Press and of public opinion. I look back with pleasure to my conversations with him. What a sprightly, supple intellect! What sound sense! What excellent judgment of men and of problems.

He was also, I consider, the best man at our disposal in the summer of 1917; and I greatly regretted, at that time, his not being called to the chief post after Bethmann's exit. His peculiar character would assuredly have understood how to bring about fruitful co-operation between the Government and the Higher Command; I believe, too, that this adroit diplomatist would have succeeded in finding a way out of the difficulties of the world-war, and that he would have effected a peace that would have been tolerable for our country.

On each of the two occasions when a fresh chancellor was to be appointed, I advised His Majesty to choose either him or Tirpitz—unfortunately, without success! The reappointment of Bülow as chancellor would not have been prevented by the aversion which the Kaiser had conceived for him during the events of November, 1908, if the proper influential parties had assiduously supported his selection. I was able to ascertain that, on both occasions, the necessary precautions had been taken to ensure Bülow's being passed over by the Kaiser.

Yonder stood the King.

I am aware that there is a tendency (not by any means confined to the general public) to impute to King Edward a personal hatred of Germany—a diabolical relish for destruction which found expression in making a noose for the strangling of our country. To my mind such a presentation of his character is totally lacking in reality. Among others, my father has never viewed King Edward without all sorts of prejudices, and has consequently never formed a just estimate of him. That trait which was so often to be observed in the Kaiser, of readily attributing his positive failures to the activities of individuals and of regarding them as the result of machinations directed against him personally, may here play some part. But there was doubtless always, as a matter of fact, what I might call a latent and mutual disapproval present in the minds of these two men, notwithstanding all their outward cordiality. The Kaiser may have felt that his somewhat loud and theatrical rather than genuine manner often struck idly upon the ear of King Edward, with his experience of the world and his sense of realities, that it encountered scepticism, was perhaps even sometimes received with ironic silence, that it met with a sort of quiet obstruction too smoothly polished to present any point of attack, yet easily tempting the Kaiser to exaggerate his manner.

As I knew King Edward from my earliest youth and had ample opportunity of talking with him on past and present affairs almost up to his death, my own conception of his character is a totally different one. I see in him the serene, world-experienced man and the most successful monarch in Europe for many a long day. Personally, he was, as long as I can remember, extremely friendly to me, and, as I have said before, he took a most active interest in my development. In the year 1901, just after the passing of the Queen, he invested me with the Order of the Garter; the ceremony took place at Osborne, and King Edward addressed to me an exceedingly warm-hearted and kinsmanlike speech; I was then on the threshold of my twentieth year, and my great-uncle seemed, from what he said, to feel a sort of responsibility for my welfare. His sense of family ties was altogether strongly marked; to see him in the circle of his Danish relatives at Copenhagen filled the beholder with delight; there he was simply the good uncle and the amiable man.

Often have we sat talking for hours in the most unconstrained fashion while he lay back in a great easy chair and smoked an enormous cigar. At such times, he narrated many interesting things, sometimes out of his own life. And it is from what he imparted to me and from what I saw with my own eyes that I have formed my picture of him—a picture that contains not a single touch of intrigue or trickery, a picture that reveals him as a brilliant upholder of his country's interests, and one who, I am convinced, would rather have secured those interests in co-operation with Germany than in opposition to her, but who, finding the former way barred, turned with all his energies to the one thing possible and needful, namely, the assurance of that security *per se.*

Owing to the great length of his mother's reign, Edward VII did not come to the throne till he was a man of very ripe age. As Prince of Wales he had enjoyed to the full his excessively long period of probation. On leaving his parental home with an excellent training and education, he rushed into life with an ardent thirst for pleasure and sport. In this way he passed through all circles and all strata of society— good, bad and indifferent—and nothing human remained alien to him. Just as an old mariner now at peace on shore talks of the voyages weathered in years gone by, so did King Edward speak to me of those experiences of his which had drawn from the public harsh and adverse judgments. Yet, for him and for his country, those restless years became fruitful. His clear, cool and judicial insight, and his practical common sense brought him an unerring knowledge of mankind and taught him the difficult art of dealing properly with differing types of humanity. I have scarcely ever met with any other person who understood as he did how to charm the people with whom he came into contact. And yet he had no vanity, he showed no desire to make any impression by his urbanity or his conversation. On the contrary, he almost faded into the background; the other person seemed to become more important than himself. Thus he could listen, interject a question, be talked to and arouse in each individual the feeling that he, the king, took a most kindly interest in his thoughts and actions—that he was fascinated and stimulated by him. In this way he gained the friendship and attachment of a great number of people— above all of those who were of value to him.

In his own country, his taste for sport secured him an enviable position. He owned a superb racing stud, devoted himself with great enthusiasm to yachting, and was perhaps the best shot in England. In his outward appearance and bearing he was the *grand seigneur* and finished man of the world.

It is thus that I see the King, and the qualities that

MATRIMONIAL AND POST-MATRIMONIAL

served him in carrying out his policy. An excellent reader of character and a cool tactician, he gained permanent successes wherever he interposed his personality. It was his influence that drew France into the *entente cordiale* with England in spite of Fashoda; and it was he, personally, who attracted the Tsar further and further away from Germany and won him for England, notwithstanding the great commercial rivalries of the Far East and in Persia.

And all this to what end ? To destroy Germany ? Certainly not ! But he and his country had recognized that, for some years, the curve of Germany's commercial, economico-political and industrial progress had been such that England was in danger of being outstripped. Here he had to step in. As an agreement could not be effected, commercial isolation became his instrument for curtailing our development. War with Germany the King, I believe, never wanted. I believe, too, that not only would he have been able to prevent the outbreak of war, but that he would in fact have prevented it. I believe so, because his statesmanlike foresight would have recognized both the revolutionary dangers and the risk run by the Great Powers of Europe of losing authority and influence in world-competition if—armed as never before—they tore and lacerated each other by war among themselves. I will go further, and assert that, with the acknowledged status enjoyed by him in Europe and in the world at large, King Edward, if he had lived longer, would probably not have stopped at the creation of a Triple Entente but would perhaps have built a bridge between the Entente and the Triple Alliance and thus have brought into being the United States of Europe. He, but only he, could have done it.

Those who came after him have placed the outcome of his labours at the service of Russia and France;

and therewith began the war, long, long before the sword itself was unsheathed.

In the face of all this and in sure and certain anticipation of this final settlement, it became the bounden duty of the German Empire to arm itself as thoroughly as possible and to demand a similar fighting-power from Austria, which country, under the influence of the Archduke Francis Ferdinand and the men selected by him, had become politically very active. This was the least we could do to ensure some prospect of an honourable and tolerable settlement. And that there was danger in the air was proved not merely by the general aspect of the political skies; the feverish and unconcealed warlike preparations of the Entente were clearly directed against us and showed that they meant to be ready and then to await the right watchword for a rupture. France exhausted her man-power and her finances in order to maintain a disproportionately large army; Russia, in return for French money, placed hundreds of thousands of peasants in sombre earth-hued uniforms; Italy turned greedy eyes on Turkish Tripoli and built fortress after fortress along the frontiers of her deeply-hated ally, Austria. England watched this activity and launched ship after ship.

In spite of these huge dangers, our own preparations were limited to the minimum of what was essential; and if proofs were required that we did not desire the war, it would suffice to point out that it did not find us prepared as we ought to have been. So far as my very circumscribed capacities and my feeble influence went in the years preceding the war, I persistently advocated, in view of the menacing situation, an augmentation of our military resources.

Not much was done, however. The last Defence Bill of 1913 had to be forced down the throat of the Imperial Chancellor von Bethmann Hollweg. The re-equipment of the field artillery could not be carried out before the outbreak of war, with the result that the superior French field-guns gave us a great deal of trouble for a long time.

* * * * *

I am speaking here of the Bethmann era, and yet I do not wish to pass from the period of Prince Bülow's chancellorship without dwelling for a little on one of the most perturbing incidents in the life of the Kaiser, namely, the conflict of November, 1908.

In the Reichstag sitting of the tenth of November—ten years to the day before everything came to an end in the journey to Holland—the storm began to howl and lasted throughout the following day. The causes are known.

What were the real facts of the case?

In the year 1907, while staying with the retired General Stuart-Wortley at Highcliffe Castle in the Isle of Wight, my father had entered into a number of informal conversations in which, undeniably, several unguarded and therefore injudicious remarks and statements escaped him. With the help of the English journalist, Harold Spender, these remarks were afterwards worked up by Wortley into the form of an interview to be published in the *Daily Telegraph*. The manuscript was forwarded to the Kaiser with a request that he would give his consent to its publication. In a perfectly loyal way, the Kaiser sent it on to the Imperial Chancellor and asked him for his opinion. The proceedings were consequently all absolutely correct; and nothing improper had occurred, unless the remarks themselves are to be characterized as such; and even then, one must give the Kaiser credit for having made them with the object of improving Anglo-German relations, just as General Stuart-Wortley, with the same intention, conceived the idea of making them known to a wider public.

The manuscript was returned to the Kaiser with the remark that there was no objection to its being published—only, unfortunately, through negligence and a number of unfortunate coincidences, none of the gentlemen who were responsible for this judgment had actually read the text with any care. And so the mischief began.

For two days the Reichstag raged at the absent Kaiser; two groups of representatives of almost every party poured out their pent-up floods of indignation; all the dissatisfaction with his methods and his rule that had been accumulating for two decades now burst forth in an unchecked torrent. And yet the man who was called upon by my father's trust to stand by his Imperial master, to cover and to defend him, that man failed, that man shrugged his shoulders and shuffled off with a scarcely concealed gesture of resignation. Nerves, it may be said. Possibly. The only man who, on that occasion, chivalrously rushed into the breach in defence of his King was the old and splendidly faithful deputy von Oldenburg. Considering the general indignation that had arisen, the task before which Prince Bülow stood was indisputably very difficult; but, on the other hand, it is perfectly comprehensible that the Kaiser—who, in this case, had acted quite correctly, and now saw himself suddenly, and for the first time, face to face with the almost universal opposition of the nation—was rudely torn out of his security and unsuspecting confidence and felt that he was deserted and abandoned by the Chancellor.

Meantime, the Press storm continued and produced day after day a dozen or two of accusing and disapproving articles.

My father had returned. Prostrated by these exciting

MATRIMONIAL AND POST-MATRIMONIAL 87

and violent events and still more by the lack of understanding he had met with, he lay ill at Potsdam. The incomprehensible had happened: after twenty years, during which he had imagined himself to be the idol of the majority of his people and had supposed his rule to be exemplary, disapproval of him and of his character had been quite unmistakably pronounced.

It was under these circumstances that I was urgently called to the New Palace. At the door, my mother's old chamberlain awaited me to say that Her Majesty wanted to see me before I went to the Kaiser.

I rushed upstairs. My mother received me immediately. She was agitated, and her eyes were red. She kissed me and held my head before her in both hands. Then she said:

"You know, my boy, what you are here for?"

"No, mother."

"Then go to your father. But sound your heart well before you decide."

Then I knew what was coming.

A few minutes later I stood beside my father's sick-bed.

I was shocked at his appearance. Only once again have I seen him thus. It was ten years later, on the fatal date at Spa, when General Gröner struck away his last foothold and, with a shrug, coldly destroyed his belief in the fidelity of the army.

He seemed aged by years; he had lost hope, and felt himself to be deserted by everybody; he was broken down by the catastrophe which had snatched the ground from beneath his feet; his self-confidence and his trust were shattered.

A deep pity was in me. Scarcely ever have I felt myself so near him as in that hour.

He told me to sit down. He talked vehemently, complainingly and hurriedly of the incidents; and the bitterness aroused by the injustice which he saw in them kept reasserting itself.

I tried to soothe and encourage him.

I stayed with him for quite an hour sitting on his bed, a thing which, so long as I can remember, had never happened before.

In the end, it was arranged that, for a short time, and till he had completely recovered from his illness, I should act as a kind of *locum tenens* for the Kaiser.

In exercising this office, I kept entirely in the background, and was soon released from the duties altogether, since, in a few weeks, the Kaiser was seemingly himself again.

Seemingly! For, as I have already said, he has never really recovered from the blow. Under the cloak of his old self-confidence, he assumed an ever-increasing reserve, which, though hidden from the outside world, was often more restricted than the limits of his constitutional position. In the war, this personal modesty led to his being almost completely excluded from the military and organizing measures and commands of the Chief of his General Staff. Those of us officers who had an insight into the business of the leading military posts could not but regret this fact, as we had unreservedly admired the sound judgment and the keen military perception of the Kaiser even in operations on a grand scale. During the war, I had frequent occasion to discuss the entire strategic situation with my father, and I generally received the impression that he hit the nail on the head.

July, 1919.

Bright midsummer days are now passing over the island in which I have lived for some three-quarters of a year.

Three-quarters of a year in which the closely circumscribed space and its inhabitants have become dear to me, in which the vast silence and the sky and the sea, the privacy and the seclusion have brought me much that I had never before possessed—change and ripening in my own nature, changes in my views and judgments on the things that lie behind, around and before me. It is not inactive reverie with me, for each day is filled up from morning till night with letter-writing, with my reminiscences, diaries, reading, music, sketching and sport.

I am not unhappy in my loneliness, and I almost believe that to be due to all the unstifled desire to produce which is still pent up within me and makes me hope in spite of everything—makes me hope that the future will somehow open up the possibility of my working as a German for the German Fatherland.

Anxieties as to the pending request of the Entente for my extradition? That is a question constantly repeated in the letters sent by good people at home and I can only repeat as often : No, that really will not turn my hair grey.

I have a longing for home, for my wife, for my children. Often it comes over me suddenly, comes through some accidental word, through a recollection, a picture. The other day, as I had just got out my violin and was about to play, I couldn't bring myself to do so, so strongly had this yearning taken possession of me.

And then at night! The windows are wide open, and one can hear the distant plash of the sea and often the deep lowing and bellowing of the cattle in the pastures. Heinrich Heine says somewhere : " Denk'ich an Deutschland in der Nacht, bin ich um meinen Schlaf gebracht."

In the June days just gone by, came the news that the Versailles " Diktat " had been signed. The Peace Treaty ! The word will scarcely flow from my pen, in consideration of this rod of chastisement, this birch that blind revenge has bound for us there, in consideration of this closely-woven network of chains into which our poor fatherland has been cast. Preposterous demands, that even with the very best intentions no one can fulfil ! Brutal threats of strangling in the event of any failure of strength ! Withal, unexampled stupidity —a document that perpetuates hatred and bitterness, where only emancipation from the pressure of the past years and new faith in one another could unite the peoples into a fresh and peacefully reconstructive community.

There remains only trust in the oft-tried energy and capacity of the German himself, who, time after time when gruesome fate has led him through darkness and the depths, has found the way up to the light again ; and there remains, too, the great truth of universal history, that folly in the long run wrecks itself.

Poverty-stricken, Germany and the German people go to meet the future. The wicked treaty, that rests upon the question of war-guilt as upon a huge lie, has torn from them colonies, provinces and ships. Workshops are destroyed, intellectual achievements stolen, competition in wide spheres of activity violently throttled. The treaty prepares for Germany the bitterest humiliation ; it purposes to strangle and destroy her in unappeased hate and unabated terror.

But, in spite of it all, Germany will persist and will flourish once more ; and a time will come when this enforced pact will be talked of only as an infamy of a bygone day.

I wish the homeland tranquillity and internal peace in which to get back to its wonted self, in which this earthly kingdom—exhausted by unheard-of sacrifices and damaged by the blows of fate—may recover its strength. And I should like to share in its new era! Yet, the only service I can render to my country is to stand aside and continue to bear this exile.

The short space of time during which I was entrusted with the task of acting as the Kaiser's representative gave me a deeper insight than at any previous period of my life into the mechanism of his work as head of the government, into the manner in which he was kept informed by the various officials and into the disposal of his time. Although, from years of cursory observation, I was fairly familiar with the outlines of this mechanism, I clearly remember that the closer acquaintance I now made with its framework filled me with the greatest amazement. That I speak of it here with unreserved candour is evidence that I do not regard my father as ultimately and solely responsible for the existing state of affairs. If you remove the mask of monarchy, the Kaiser is, by nature, simple in his character; and if he allowed these evils to arise around him, his share in them was due partly to the out-of-date upbringing caused by an old-fashioned conception of the royal dignity, and even more to his innate harmony with the settled forms of his environment and his renunciation of that simplicity and directness which would better have become his deepest nature. As a consequence, there developed, little by little, out of the zeal displayed by those around him for the pettiest affairs, a vast ceremoniousness that robbed the simplest proceedings of their naturalness, that removed every little stone against which the monarch might have struck his foot, and that was fain to drown every whisper that might be disagreeable to his ear. In the course of decades, this system deprived the Kaiser more and more of his capacity to meet hard realities with a firm, resolute and tenacious perseverance.

How can a man accustomed to expect as a matter of course the spreading of a carpet before his feet for every step he takes, sustain himself when he is suddenly confronted with really serious conflicts in which nothing can help him but his own resolution?

Time seemed to be no object in ceremonial affairs; and, while spent on them, it often could not be found for questions that demanded serious and calm consideration.

Not only for me but for many a minister and state secretary, it was often quite a feat to break through the protective ring of zealous gentlemen who wished to prevent His Majesty being " worried " with troublesome affairs and to save him from over-fatigue and annoyance. Even when the ring was penetrated, one had not, by any means, gained one's point; I remember many a case in which one Excellency or another who had come to report to the Kaiser on some burning question went away with an admirable impression of the animation, the vigour and the communicativeness of His Majesty, and possibly with enriched knowledge concerning some department of research or technology, but without having unburdened himself on the burning question with which he came. Anyone who failed to proceed, more or less unceremoniously, with his report might well find himself listening instead to a report of the Kaiser's on the subject in hand based upon preconceived notions; the would-be adviser would then be dismissed without ever having found an opportunity of stating his own views.

I have already hinted that the Imperial Chancellory prepared for the Kaiser a filtered version of public opinion in the form of press-cuttings. The preparation of this material appeared to me to be too much inspired with the desire to exclude the disagreeable and even the minatory—to be pleasant rather than thorough. Many things, therefore, that ought to have come under the Kaiser's eyes, even if they were not exactly gratifying, were never seen by him. In much the same plane lay the consular reports. They were often nothing more than amusing chats and serial stories. When these " political reports " passed through my hands in 1908, I missed any clear judgment of the situation, any clear, sharply-defined presentation or positive suggestion.

A favourable exception among the communications sent in by our representatives abroad was to be found in the reports of the naval officers in command. They were evidently drawn up by men whose eyes had been trained to look broadly at the world, to see things as they really are and to form a just estimate of the whole; they were filled with calm and practical criticism, and furnished cautious and far-seeing suggestions.

August, 1919.

The last few days have brought me again one or two welcome visitors from the homeland—above all, excellent Major Beck, to whom I am attached by so many hard experiences shared in the army. Hours and hours were spent in taking long walks and sitting together—sometimes talking, sometimes silent. And during those hours, the prodigious struggle of the past came vividly before me again—especially the last anguish that followed our failure at Rheims, the unceasing decay of energy and confidence, and then the end.

A few Dutch families have also been to see me; and Ilsemann came over from Amerongen, and had much to tell me about my dear mother; she suffers severely, is physically ill, and will not give way, knows only one thought, namely, the welfare of my father and of us all, has only one wish, which is to lighten for us what we have to bear.

But the best visit is still to come. My wife and the children are to spend a short time with me here in the island. How we shall manage with such limited room and such a lack of every accommodation I don't know myself—but we shall do it somehow. It was touching to see the ready proffers of help that were made on the mere report of my expecting my wife and children. Not merely in the island—where every one now likes me and where the Frisian reserve has long given place to hearty participation in my joys and sorrows—but from yonder on the mainland also.

In a day or two Müldner, my untiring and faithful companion in this solitude, is to go to Amsterdam for some shopping and other errands. In one of the rooms, the wall-paper is to be renewed; all sorts of household utensils need replenishing; and Amsterdam friends are going to lend me furniture. The parsonage is to become more respectable; in its present condition, it would really be quite impossible for it to lodge a lady. These excellent people of mine are working feverishly.

* * * * *

But to get back to my subject. I stopped at my recollections of our foreign policy in the years prior to the war. Closely connected with it were our home politics. Here, too, we suffered from the same lack of resolution, firmness and foresight. People fixed their eyes upon the things of to-day instead of on those of to-morrow. Hence only half-measures were taken, and everybody was dissatisfied.

Ever since I began to concern myself with politics I have become more and more convinced that our home policy should develop along more liberal lines. It was clear to me that one could no longer govern on the principles of Frederick the Great—still less by outwardly imitating his manner. Just as little could I sympathize with the continually yielding and generally belated manner in which our liberal reforms were carried out. The almost systematic method of first refusing altogether and then finding oneself obliged to grant a part of what was demanded appeared to me doubtful and dangerous. A foresighted and well-timed liberal policy ought to have been able to reject inordinate demands from whatever quarter they came, and thus to maintain a just balance of forces for the welfare of the whole. Such government would also have been able to reckon with a certain constancy of parliamentary grouping. But after the collapse of the Bülow *bloc*—which certainly, in itself, presented no very great attractions—the only policy we had was Bethmann's " governing over the heads of the parties " with its convulsive beating-up of majorities for each case as it arose and its silencing of the minorities.

In so far as they could be fitted into the historically determined development of the State, the political and economic aims of the social democratic party, as representing a large section of organized labour, ought to have been taken into consideration unequivocally and without any misconstruction or suppression of what was possible ; though the Government had no reason and no right to allow themselves to be pushed or driven on every question.

In its ideological endeavours to entice the social democrats away from their policy of negation into the sphere of productive co-operation, and in its misconception of the fact that, for purely tactical reasons, the social democrats of that period would not give up their policy of opposition within the then existing constitution, Bethmann's Government allowed itself to be exploited and weakened by the extraordinarily well managed and well disciplined social democratic party. To the other parties little attention was paid. Moreover, the fact was altogether overlooked that, in their humane and progressive spirit, social legislation and the care for workmen in Germany were already a very long way ahead of all measures of the kind in other countries and that this great work had been ardently promoted by the Kaiser. As in its attitude towards the opposition, so upon the questions of Poland and Alsace-Lorraine, the policy of the Government was uncertain and almost invariably harsh where it ought to have been yielding and yielding where it ought to have been firm. Absolutely nothing was done in the way of economic mobilization to meet the eventuality of war, although there could be no doubt that, if an *ultima ratio* ensued, England would at once endeavour to cut us off from every oversea communication and that, in respect to food-stuffs and raw materials of every kind, we should be thrown on our own stocks and resources.

As in all problems of foreign policy, so again in this question, the only man in the Government who showed any understanding for my fears and anxieties was Admiral von Tirpitz.

In the eight years' chancellorship of Herr von Bethmann Hollweg, I over and over again took the opportunity of talking to him about the attitude of the Government towards foreign and home affairs. Here, in one and the same sentence in which I write that I always found him to be high-principled in thought and action and a man of irreproachable honour, I wish to say that we were not friends and that an impassable chasm lay between his mentality and my own. In the post for which we ought to have sought for the best, the boldest, the most far-sighted and the wisest of statesmen, there stood a bureaucrat of sluggish and irresolute

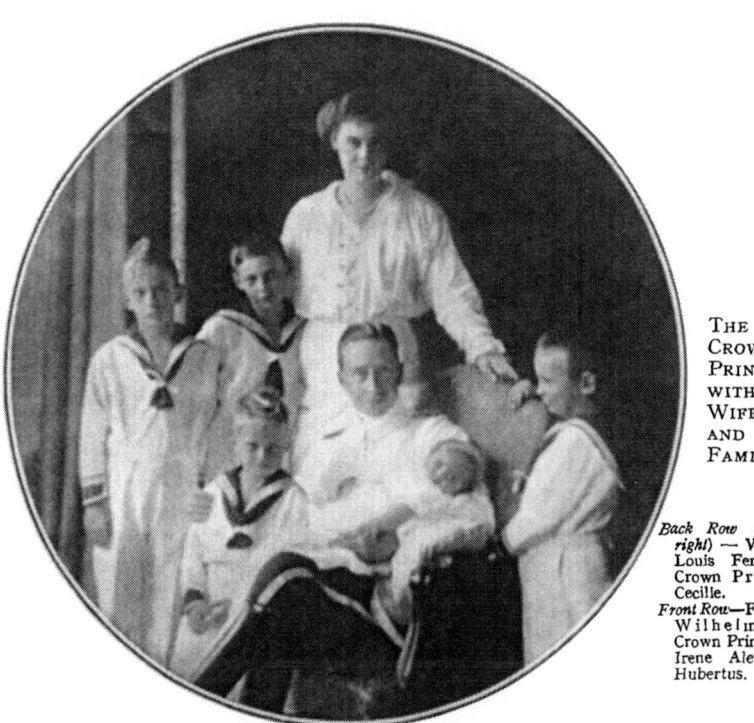

THE CROWN PRINCE WITH HIS WIFE AND FAMILY.

Back Row (left to right) — Wilhelm, Louis Ferdinand, Crown Princess Cecille.

Front Row — Friedrich Wilhelm, the Crown Prince with Irene Alexandra, Hubertus.

Back Row — Prince Joachim of Prussia, Duchess of Brunswick, Duke of Brunswick.

Second Row — Prince Oscar of Prussia, Princess August Wilhelm of Prussia, the Crown Prince, Prince Eitel Friedrich.

Front Row — Princess Eitel Friedrich, the Crown Princess, Prince Adalbert, and Prince August Wilhelm of Prussia.

character, his mind in a reverie of weary and resigned cosmopolitanism and tranquil acceptance of unalterable developments. People liked to call him the "Philosopher of Hohensinow." I never succeeded in discovering a trace of philosophic wisdom in the languid nature of this man, who dropped so easily into tactless fatalism and who qualified even every upward flight with the parrot cry of "divinely ordained dependency." His hesitating heart had no wings, his will was joyless, his resolve was lame.

This man, eternally vacillating in his decisions and overborne by any contact with natures of a fresher hue, was certainly not the proper person, in the years prior to the war—least of all in the three that immediately preceded its outbreak—to represent German policy against the energetic, resolute, quick-witted and inexorable men whom England and France had selected as exponents of their power.

Even in the days when I was attached to the various ministries for purposes of study, many people of excellent judgment told me that it was easy to discuss questions with Bethmann, but the disappointing thing about it was that one never reached any conclusive result; for, whatever the seemingly final outcome might be, he had—after musing for a while, one more sentence to utter, and that sentence began with the word "nevertheless." This word "nevertheless" stands for me like a motto above Herr Bethmann Hollweg's political career.

On one single occasion I allowed myself to be swept into a marked demonstration against him before the whole world, and I readily admit that this public utterance of my opinion would have been better left unspoken. It will be remembered that, in the Reichstag sitting of November 9, 1911, I gave clear expression to my approval of the speeches hurled against

Herr von Bethmann's and Kiderlen-Wächter's policy in the Morocco affair, at first aggressive and afterwards retracting, which had brought us a severe diplomatic check. At the time, the Press of the Left hastened to stigmatize me as a battering-ram of extravagant and bellicose pan-German ideas. Nothing of the kind! The case was quite different! The drastic methods of Kiderlen, the wanton provocation implied by the dispatch of the *Panther* to Agadir, was just as disagreeable to me as the hasty retreat which followed Lloyd George's threats in his Mansion House speech : both bore testimony to the groping uncertainty of our leadership, a leadership which failed to see what an unhappy effect was produced on the minds of the other side in the dispute by the first step, and how much the second impaired our prestige in the eyes of the world. Thus, it was from the feeling that political tension had risen to fever heat that, on that 9th November, 1911, I spontaneously applauded those speeches which were directed against the feeble and oscillating policy of the Government.

What a curious part coincidence plays in our affairs! Once again the 9th November stands marked in the book of my remembrances—three years after the great Reichstag storm over the Kaiser interview in the *Daily Telegraph*, and seven years to the day before the last act of the collapse in Berlin and Spa! A discussion of the incident speedily followed. On the same evening, as a matter of fact.

To begin with, the Kaiser admonished me. Very well.

Then I gave vent to my thoughts and feelings ; and I blurted out all my fears for the future, my wishes for the suppression of a shilly-shally policy. I spoke without the slightest reserve ; and once more I was forced to take note of the fact that the Kaiser was incapable of listening.

In the end we dined together in a not particularly talkative mood.

Then, at His Majesty's request and in his presence, Bethmann, who, withal, was once again highly interesting and to the point, gave me, the "Frondeur," a long lecture which did not succeed in convincing me.

Politics, even high politics, are not an occult science. The times are dead and gone in which they could be conducted with Metternich-like ruses. They can nowadays dispense with aperçus of speech and with the *jabot* of the Congress of Vienna just as well as with the monocle of a later epoch of development. But they presuppose, besides all the things that are obvious and the things that can be learned, a few such things as practical common sense to reduce all their problems to the simplest formulæ, knowledge of human character, and an eye for the general mentality of the peoples with whom one has to reckon.

Herr von Bethmann Hollweg—who, by the way, knew scarcely anything of foreign countries—possessed none of these things; and neither Kiderlen-Wächter nor Secretary of State Jagow was the man to fill the gap with his intellectual talents.

True, there were, in our diplomatic service, men of quite another category, who thought broadly and saw clearly; but people were content to know that they filled posts abroad where their voices could be heard, but where their influence upon the conduct of foreign politics was bound to remain very slight. I have not the least doubt that such men as Wangenheim and Marschall— even Mont and Metternich—would have understood how to give a timely turn to our foreign policy so as to guide it into the proper and the constant way.

Just this very Herr von Kiderlen used to be praised by Bethmann as the great political light from the East. Personally, too, I myself liked this agreeably unaffected and courageous Swabian, despite his panther-like leap into the china-shop of Agadir. But I was not impressed with his special suitability for the highly important post of Foreign Secretary, the more so as he entirely lacked the most important quality for such a position, namely the capacity to see things from other people's points of view. He not only utterly failed to consider the mentality of France and England, but he did not even appreciate the political tendencies of Roumania, the country in which, for ten years, he had had charge of Germany's interests.

That sounds almost like a bad joke, and it is, after all, only an example of what a poor reader of character the Chancellor himself was and how limited was the horizon of his staff at the Foreign Office.

But it is incumbent upon me to furnish evidence for my views as to Herr von Kiderlen's knowledge of Roumania. On returning from my Roumanian travels in April, 1909, I told my father I had received the impression that there was only one person in Roumania who was friendly to us, namely King Carol himself. The leading political circles, who were only waiting for the decease of the aged King, were thoroughly and firmly under French and Russian influence. The sympathies of the Crown Princess were directed towards England, and the Crown Prince was very much under her influence. Consequently, I could not help thinking that, in the event of war, Roumania would fail her allies, even if she did not go over to the other party altogether. His Majesty sent me to the Secretary for Foreign Affairs in Wilhelmstrasse to report my impressions. Herr von Kiderlen-Wächter listened with complaisant superiority, and smiled. He thought I must be mistaken; believed I must have had a bad dream; the whole of Roumania, with which he was as familiar as with his own hat (" wie sei' Weste' tasch ") was, to the backbone, our sterling ally. " Sozusage' mündelsicher ! " Soon afterwards, we had to face the trend of events that followed upon King Carol's death.

But, after all, what is the false estimate of Roumania in comparison with the erroneous conception formed by Herr von Bethmann Hollweg and his Excellency von Jagow concerning the attitude of England ? They remained hoodwinked in the matter until, in August, 1914, Sir Edward Goschen tore the bandage from the Chancellor's dismayed and horror-struck eyes.

Because—be it said to his credit—he had repeatedly made mild and inadequate attempts at a *rapprochement* with England without encountering any fundamental opposition, and because he knew that England had repeatedly stated in Paris that she desired to avoid a provocative policy and did not wish to participate in a war set on foot by France, Bethmann imagined that the *rapprochement* had thriven to such an extent as to preclude England's joining in war against us at all. But the last effort made in the year 1912 by inviting Lord Haldane, the Minister of War, to come to Berlin, had also been a failure. It had failed because, meantime, the relations of England to France and thereby to Russia had become too intimate ; so that even the great sacrifice which Admiral von Tirpitz declared himself prepared to make in the question of the Navy Bill in exchange for a British neutrality clause was ineffective. England was determined to maintain her " two keels for one " standard under all circumstances. Sir Edward Grey declined to enter into any engagement on account of " existing friendship for other Powers " ; and thereupon matters became clear to anyone who had eyes to see.

Nor did Haldane make any secret of England's attitude in the event of war with France and Russia ; as the Kaiser told me himself later, Haldane informed our ambassador, Prince Lichnowsky, in a visit concerning political questions, that under the suppositions stated and irrespective of which side might set the ball rolling, his Government could not agree to a defeat of France by us and a consequent domination of Germany on the Continent. They would intervene in favour of the Powers allied with England.

One finds it difficult to understand that, in spite of this fact, the gentlemen at the Foreign Office and above all the Minister responsible for our foreign policy continued to live on calmly and self-complacently in their world of dreams during those perilous and menacing times. The ears of our politicians had caught up the voices from Paris in which they heard England's desire for peace and they allowed themselves to be misled by the alluring idea that England would maintain peace in Europe in any circumstances; they assumed that the serious, warning words spoken by Lord Haldane in London were intended solely to prevent a breach of peace on the part of Germany.

* * * * *

I have again run off the track of my story; it seems that I cannot even make a chronicle of the affairs. But I must try to take up the thread again.

Down to the year 1909, I had visited, sometimes alone and sometimes in my father's suite, England, Holland, Italy, Egypt, Greece, Turkey and a few districts of Asia Minor. My stay in these countries had always been relatively short, but had sufficed to provide me with valuable opportunities of comparison and to convince me of the necessity for seeing more of the world.

It was, therefore, a great satisfaction to my desire for further knowledge when, in 1909, my father consented to my undertaking an extensive tour in the Far East. My wife accompanied me as far as Ceylon and then went to Egypt; while I proceeded to travel through India. The British Government had prepared for my journey in the most friendly way; so that I really obtained a great deal of information. In every detail and everywhere I went, I met with the greatest hospitality. I recall with special pleasure Lord Hardinge, Sir Harold Stuart, Sir John Hewett and Sir Roos Keppel. The Maharajah of Jaipur and the Nizam of Hyderabad also provided me with a splendid reception.

In India my love of hunting and sport was satisfied to my heart's content. The magnificence of Indian landscape and of Indian architecture opened up a new world to me. The profusion of experiences of all kinds offered to me I welcomed with all the susceptibility and power of enjoyment natural to my youth; I wished to devote myself unrestrictedly to all that was great and novel, and I sometimes forgot, perhaps, that I had to fill a ceremonial rôle, that people expected to find in me the son of the German Emperor and the great-grandson of the Queen.

Of all the impressions I received the greatest and most lasting was that made upon me by the organizing and administrative talent of the English. It struck me, too, as a noticeable peculiarity, that, in the various branches of administration, comparatively very young officials were employed, but that they were energetic and were invested with great independence and responsibility. Extensive and healthy decentralization prevailed generally. Everywhere I was impressed by the vast power of England, whose greatness the German people, before the war, frequently and grossly undervalued, intoxicated as they were with their own rapid rise.

But it became just as clear to me how enormous was the competition which Germany created for the

British in the markets of the Far East. Thus, many an English merchant told me, in confidential talk, that it could not go on like this—England could not and would not allow herself to be pushed to the wall by us. I myself, during the sea-voyage, noticed that we met about as many German merchant vessels as British ones. Moreover, the muttered curse, " Those damned Germans ! " occasionally reached my ear.

Omens of a gathering storm !

When, later on, I talked of these observations to the responsible parties at home, the warning was treated very light-heartedly. That some English shopkeeper or another swore when we spoiled his business for him didn't matter in the least ; the man should give up his " week-end " and work as our people did, then he would have no need to swear. Besides, we really wanted to live in peace with those gentlemen. " And your Imperial Highness has seen for yourself how you were received there." Thus, there was not much to be done. I, for my part, knew that the " shopkeeper " was England herself, that no one over there was willing to sacrifice his week-end, and that my reception was an act of international courtesy and nothing more. The will to live at peace with others has significance only if one knows and adopts the means by which that peace may be realized.

After my return and in pursuance of His Majesty's commands, I visited with my wife the courts of Rome, Vienna, St. Petersburg, and St. James's, the last on the occasion of the coronation.

Everywhere we met with the most friendly personal reception ; but everywhere, too, appeared warning signs of the conflict and danger which were gathering ominously around Germany.

The journey to England we performed on board the new and heavily armoured cruiser *Von der Tann*.

AN ANTELOPE HUNT.

WITH HIS FIRST ELEPHANT.

THE CROWN PRINCE IN INDIA.

This excellently-constructed vessel aroused the utmost excitement in England. During the great naval review in the Solent, it was interesting to observe the British naval officers and sailors devoting the greatest attention to our *Von der Tann*. For the war vessels of other nations they displayed not the slightest interest. Their judgment was expressed in unbounded praise of the wonderful lines of the ship and of the practical distribution of her guns.

During the coronation festivities in London, the reception accorded to me and my wife by all classes of the population was exceptionally cordial. The English Press also welcomed us warmly; and during those days we noticed nothing of the hatred of Germany. But if an eloquent illustration were needed of how misleading it is to draw conclusions from the signs of sympathy shown towards princes and heirs-apparent, such an illustration is to be found in an experience of our own. It has remained as a *signum vanitatis* in my memory.

As King George and Queen Mary at the close of the coronation ceremony left Westminster Abbey, spontaneous cheers rose from the assembly. Immediately afterwards, the foreign princes moved down the gigantic church, and, as the Crown Princess and myself reached the middle of the nave, the same spontaneous cheers that had greeted the King and Queen were accorded to us. Afterwards I was told by English people that I might be " proud of myself " ; for never before in the history of England had a foreign princely couple received such an ovation in Westminster Abbey. Four years later we were at war ; four years later, the man whom they then cheered had become a " Hun."

Here I should like to mention an incident in my London sojourn which casts a light on the ideas of a leading English statesman of that day. The Foreign Secretary, Sir Edward Grey, was introduced to me, and, in the course of the thoroughly animated conversation which ensued, I made the incautious remark that, in my opinion and with a view to a certainty of peace, it would be far and away the wisest thing for Germany and England, the two greatest Teutonic nations—the strongest land Power and the strongest sea Power—to co-operate; they could then, moreover (if it must be so), divide the world between them. Grey listened, nodded and said: " Yes, true, but England does not wish to divide with anybody—not even with Germany."

In Vienna, the then heir-apparent, Francis Ferdinand, spoke with me very earnestly and very anxiously about the dangerous Serbian propaganda; he foresaw an early European conflict in these intrigues that Russia was fanning. I had, for a long time, been watching with discomfort the growing dependence of our Near East policy upon the ideas of the Vienna Ballplatz; consequently, the remarks of the Archduke raised in my mind grave doubts concerning this shifting of our political focus from Berlin to Vienna; these doubts continued to worry me from that day onwards, but the unreserved expression I gave to them, both in the Foreign Office and in the presence of individual representatives of our diplomatic service, was all in vain. The fears that Germany would some day become fatally dependent upon the superior diplomacy of Austria-Hungary, as expressed with such anxious prescience by Prince Bismarck in his last memoirs, seemed to me to have long ago found their fulfilment. In the Vienna Belvedere, under the influence of the strangely suggestive words of this dangerously ambitious Archduke, who was prepared to act an anything but modest part and who was as clever as he was ruthless, the definite feeling came over me that, as a result of this too great dependence, we should sooner or later become involved in a conflict brought about for the purpose of promoting the ambitions of the Austro-Hungarian dynasty; the Archduke was putting out feelers and developing ideas which should enable him to see what he might expect from me. Destiny took the game out of the hands of that undoubtedly remarkable man, and made of him the spark which was to kindle the great conflagration. But, after bringing him to a bloody end, it spared us none of the bitter effects of our dependence and subordination; the results of the excessive Viennese demands upon Serbia involved us in the war against our will. On July 28, 1914, when Serbia had accepted almost all the points of the Austrian ultimatum, my father annotated thus the telegram which brought the news of Serbia's submission: " A brilliant performance within a limit of 48 hours. That is more than one could expect. A great moral success for Vienna; but with it disappears every reason for war, and the Austrian minister, Giesl, ought to have remained quietly in Belgrade. After that, I should never have given orders for mobilization." I quote this telegram and its marginal notes, because they prove irrefutably the peaceful desires of Germany and the Kaiser. They prove our goodwill, in spite of which our destiny—bound to the policy of the Vienna Ballplatz to the extent of vassalage—moved on its fated path.

In Russia, where, as already stated, I sojourned with my wife after my Indian travels, I received the impression that the Tsar was as friendly to Germany as ever, but that he was less able to put his friendliness into action. He was completely enmeshed by the Pan-Slav and anti-German party of the Grand Duke Nicholai Nicholaievitch and powerless to oppose that prince, who quite openly displayed his hatred for Germany.

CHAPTER IV

STRESS AND STORM

September, 1919.

THE beautiful, happy days are passed which I was able to spend here with my dear wife and the boys, the days in which we all wanted to enjoy the brief pleasure like simple rustic holiday-makers, and in which I purposely tried to forget that my nearest and dearest were staying for only a short sojourn with a voluntary exile.

By nature and upbringing I am not sentimental, and I will not lose myself in sentimental emotions; but I can honestly say that the island is more desolate than ever, now that I have to go my walks between the pastures, along the irrigation canals, up the shore and through the villages without my wife and without the boys. In their childish way, the little fellows found everything that was strange and new to them here incomparably delightful, thought it all a thousand times finer than the best that they had in our own Cicilienhof at Potsdam or at Ols. Everywhere I now miss those boys, miss the inquiring remarks of those youngest ones who really made their first acquaintance with their father here in the island, miss continually the kind, wise and understanding words of the wife who has so many sorrows and worries of her own to bear and who yet never loses courage. Over there, at Hippolytushof, we stowed the little fellows in the house of the ever-ready Burgomaster Peereboom—for we had no room for them in my parsonage—and there they were soon the friends and confidants of all the lads anywhere near their own age. In our Oosterland cottage, quarters were found only for my wife and her companion. Everything now seems empty, since it is no longer filled with her fun at the primitive glories and makeshifts of our " bachelor's household."

On her way home she stayed at Amerongen.

It is depressing to read what she writes about things there. Our dear mother suffering, and yet untiringly occupied with the Kaiser, with my brothers, my little sister and her grandchildren; my father bitter and not yet able to release himself from the ever-revolving circle of brooding about the things that have been.

It is a very different thing whether the will and vital courage of a man of thirty-six years are to withstand the test of such a terrible strain of destiny, or whether a man of sixty is to see shattered before him his life's work that he had regarded as imperishable.

In the last few days, my thoughts have reverted to him over and over again.

* * * * *

At the time that I was about to start on my Indian tour, my military career had reached the point where I was to receive the command of a cavalry regiment. It was a matter of great moment to me; and, considering the political situation, I did not wish to be too far away from the centre of government, from those men who had to cook the broth in the serving out of which I was at the time so interested.

In this matter of the army I could not approach the Kaiser directly. My appointed intermediary was the *chef du cabinet militaire,* General von Lyncker. I discussed the affair with him and asked for the Gardes du Corps. Herr von Lyncker, who treated my request quite impartially and without any prepossession, entertained great doubts; he told me that His Majesty would almost certainly not consent; rather than raise this " problem " again, they would prefer to drop my suggestion. From the trend of the conversation, moreover, it was observable that the inner circle of His Majesty's advisers and certain government offices did not passionately share my wish that I should remain near the centre of government.

I therefore asked for the King's Uhlans in Hanover or the Breslau Life Cuirassiers; and Herr von Lyncker said that this would not create any difficulty, and he would advise His Majesty accordingly. I was content; after all, Hanover and Breslau did not lie quite beyond the world and one might keep fairly in touch with things from either place.

Such was the situation, when I left for India. But at Peshawar I read in an English newspaper that His Majesty had appointed me to the command of his First Life Hussars at Langfuhr by Danzig.

My prime feeling was one of disappointment, not only because my wishes had been once more totally pushed aside, but because it seemed to be a sort of principle to refuse the fulfilment of the wishes of us sons in military matters. Nor was this all. The remote position of Danzig and the bleak climate, which I feared especially on my wife's account, were not particularly alluring. Contrary to my expectations, everything turned out capitally, and, but for my worries about the general situation of affairs, the two years and a half spent in Danzig became the happiest time of my life.

We lived in a small villa which scarcely afforded sufficient room for my already considerable family.

But we made ourselves very comfortable and led a happy and peaceful life.

It was for me an honour and a pleasure to be the commander of that fine old regiment. The officers were all young—a companionable mixture of nobles and commoners. The serious and faithful character of my old regimental adjutant, Count Dohna, I recall with particular pleasure. Most of the officers were the sons of landed proprietors in East and West Prussia whose fathers and grandfathers had worn the Black Attila and the Death's Head of the Body Hussars. Similarly, the regiment recruited its non-commissioned officers and men almost exclusively from among the young countrymen of East Prussia, West Prussia, and Posen, tip-top soldiers who brought with them from their homes a love of horses and an understanding of how to look after them. Finally, the horses themselves were excellent; and we were the only white-horse regiment in the army.

The love for riding which had been in me from childhood could now have full sway. In accordance with the convictions gained by experience, I limited riding-school drill to the minimum, and laid chief weight upon cross-country work and jumping, in which really first-class results were obtained. Great stress was laid upon foot-practice and firing, more perhaps than was then customary with many a hardened out-and-out cavalryman. The war showed that this training is, even for cavalry, a thing that should not be in any way neglected.

I did my best to maintain a love and liking for the service among my Hussars. I had a nice commodious casino installed for the use of the non-commissioned officers, as well as comfortable quarters for the men. The men who had been in the ranks for a year or more were lodged separately from the recruits to prevent possible difficulties. In the leisure hours there were plenty of outdoor games. Towards the end of my time, we had a well-trained football team in which the officers took part.

It was during this period of my life that *Deutschland in Waffen* was published, a picture-book for young Germans. The preface which I wrote for it has been unjustly taken to indicate that I had ranged myself among the firebrands of war. Nothing was ever further from my thoughts; nor can an impartial perusal of my paragraphs discover such a meaning in them. The preface was written in consequence of the increasing dangers that threatened us; it was directed against sordid materialism and pointed out to the youth of Germany that it was their duty and honour to fight, if necessary, for their country. It was the admonition of a German and a soldier to the rising generation of Germans, whose young energies and whose patriotic spirit of self-sacrifice we could not dispense with in the hour of need.

Since my demonstration against Bethmann Hollweg's Morocco policy, I was labelled as a war-inciter by every blind pacifist in Germany and by their friends abroad whenever I came before the public. So it was in the case of this little dissertation on our army: people sought in it evidence of the character unjustly ascribed to me. Similarly they imagined they had pinned me tight when, a short time afterwards, I came forward in another public affair, namely the Zabern incident, which obtained such unfortunate notoriety.

Our policy in the *Reichslanden* (Alsace-Lorraine) had for years caused me great anxiety. My visits to these provinces, as well as the reports of many of my comrades in the garrisons of the west frontier, and the honest descriptions given me of conditions there by those familiar with them, had opened my eyes to the realities of the situation. Sugar-plums and the whip had prevailed ever since 1871. The results corresponded to the tactics. The last period had been one of sugar-plums, and the *reichsländische* constitution had been its culmination. French propaganda now had it all its own way and did whatever it pleased. The pro-French notables set the fashion and called the tune for the civil administration. The military were, in a sense, merely tolerated by the irredentist circles. Just one example to illustrate the pre-war conditions in the German *Reichslanden* and the attitude of the government authorities. Two of my flying-officers told me one day that, in the year 1913, a great French presentation of the colours took place, and they —the military—were advised not to show themselves in the streets on that day lest the sight of their Prussian uniform might irritate the French. Under such conditions it was that the conflict arose. The civil population had heckled the Prussian military, the officer had defended himself, and then the whole world suddenly howled at Prussian militarism. At this moment, at a time when foreign countries and the never-wanting sophistical advocates of absolute justice in our own poor Germany were doing everything to discredit our last and only asset, our army, in the eyes of friend and foe, I readily and " without the proper reserve," as it was said, took my stand by my comrades who were so hard pressed by the attacks of public controversy. I wired to General von Deimling and to Colonel von Reuter. That is all true. But that I sent the colonel a telegram containing the words, " Immer feste druff " I learned from the newspapers, and thanks to the falsifying imagination of those peace-lovers who, with this invention, sought perhaps to strengthen the great longings for peace all around us. In truth I had telegraphed to Colonel von Reuter as a comrade that he should take severe measures, since the prestige of the army was at stake. If Lieutenant von Forstner had been condemned, every hooligan would have felt encouraged to attack the uniform. An untenable situation would have been sanctioned, doubly untenable in the *Reichslanden*, where, in consequence of the lax attitude of the civil authorities, the military already found themselves in the most difficult circumstances. I should like to have seen what would have happened in England or France, if an officer had been provoked as Lieutenant von Forstner was.

But we were in Germany. German public opinion had once more a pretext for busying itself with me in conjunction with the events described; the old talk about a *camarilla*, about the war firebrand and the *frondeur* of Langfuhr were dished up again in the leading articles of the scribblers. If they were to be believed, I had once again made myself " impossible." The highest dignitaries wore the doubtful faces prescribed for such occasions of national mourning, and His Majesty was highly displeased.

Schiller says in *William Tell* : " The waters rage and clamour for their victims " ; and another passage runs : " 'Twas blessing in disguise ; it raised me upwards."

Out of the blue and with great suddenness everything happened. His Majesty took my regiment from me and ordered me to Berlin, so that my overgrown independence might be curtailed and my doings better watched. I was to work in the General Staff.

In this way a circle was completed : the desire not to have me too near the central authorities had sent me to Langfuhr by Danzig ; the desire to have me within reach brought me back again ; in both cases, a little indignation and a little annoyance played their part.

At any rate, among the incorrigible pacifists who wished to disperse with pretty speeches the war-menace already hanging above the horizon, indignation was aroused by my farewell words to my Hussars. I had called it a moment of the greatest happiness to the soldier "when the King called and March! March! was sounded." According to them I ought doubtless to have told my brave comrades some pretty fairy tale.

When I rode for the last time down the front of my fine regiment and the farewell shouts of my Hussars rang in my ears, my heart became unspeakably heavy. It was as though a still small voice whispered that this was the farewell to a peaceful soldier's life which I was never again to know. What I was now to leave had all been so beautiful, so happy and so replete with honest labour.

In foreign soil, sleeping their eternal sleep, now rest many—too, too many—of the bright and capable young comrades of my beloved and courageous regiment of Hussars whose uniform I was delighted and proud to wear throughout the war. Among them lies my cousin, Prince Frederick Charles of Prussia, a particularly undaunted rider and soldier. My memory will be with them all in grateful sadness as long as I live.

*   *   *   *   *

Perhaps I ought to have torn up the sheets I wrote yesterday and to have re-written them in a different style. When I read them through to-day, I found in them a note of irritability that I would prefer not to introduce into my memoirs. But I shall let them remain as they are; they bear witness to the bitterness which still possesses me when I recall that last year before the war and the absurdity of our "ostrich" policy. What a sorry humour comes over me when I remember how they dubbed me the instigator of a "fresh, free, rollicking war" because of my warning: "Then preserve at least your last for the grave day and keep yourselves armed for the struggle that is surely coming!"

The truth is that I was clearly conscious of the terrible seriousness of our position, that I neither was nor am a Cassandra filling the halls of Troy with verses of lament, but a man and a soldier. Yet people in our beloved homeland took it very ill that I was the latter, and they do so still.

For the winter 1913-14 I was ordered to the Great General Staff for purposes of initiation and study. My instructor was Lieutenant-General Schmidt von Knobelsdorf, who became afterwards my Chief of General Staff in the Upper Command of the Fifth Army. In matters of military science I owe much to His Excellency von Knobelsdorf. He was a brilliant teacher in every domain of tactics and strategy. His lectures and the themes he set for me were masterpieces. His chief maxim was: clearness of decision on the part of the leader; translation of the decision into commands; leave your subordinates the widest scope of personal responsibility.

My appointment to the General Staff gave me an exhaustive insight into the enormous amount of work it performed. I was able to penetrate into the superb organization of the whole, to become acquainted with the maintenance, the recuperation and the movements of the army, and to form an opinion concerning the defensive forces of other nations. In the operations department I heard lectures on the proposed concentration of the armies in the event of war.

From the lectures and discussions concerning a possible world war, I obtained the impression that the British army and its possibilities of development in case of war were treated too lightly. People seemed to reckon too much with the disposable forces of the moment, and too little with the value of what might be created under the pressure of war and resistance. I knew something of the English and their army from my various visits and from personal observation, and I knew, too, their great talent for organization as well as their skill in improvising. If a conceivable war were carried through successfully before these talents could be brought into play, the estimates of our General Staff might prove correct, but not otherwise. The Russian army I also considered not to have been always rated at its full significance.

In regard to our western neighbour and presumably immediate adversary, I have only to recall that France, at that time, despite her considerably smaller population, maintained an army almost as large as ours. To do so, she levied eighty per cent. of her men, whereas we contented ourselves with about fifty per cent.

The general view of the peace strength in the event of a war such as that which actually occurred may be put thus: For Germany not quite 900,000 troops and for Austria-Hungary about 500,000—together, roughly 1,400,000 men on the side of the Central Powers. On the other hand, Russia alone provided the Entente with well over 2,000,000 soldiers, to whom were to be added those of France and Belgium. Thus, even at the outset of the war, we were outnumbered in the ratio of two to one. Reckoning the quality of the German as high as you please—and to place him very high was quite justifiable—the odds were too great.

With all that, we had, in 1914, an army that, in every way, was brilliantly trained; and consequently, in the summer of that year, when the die was cast, we took the field " with the best army in the world."

But, so far as provision for war was concerned, we had unfortunately not, in our peace preparations, attained the maximum of striking energy. We were far from having exploited all our resources of strength in people and land or mobilized them in time. That the Great General Staff had repeatedly expressed urgent wishes in this matter I can, myself, testify. The fault did not lie there. Nor did it lie with the German Reichstag, which, in consideration of the menacing seriousness of the situation, would not, despite its party differences, have refused to provide the German sword with all possible force and keenness, if the responsible Ministers had used all their weight to this end. But it seemed then, as it had done in peace time, as though all communications, suggestions or inquiries issuing from military quarters and especially from the General Staff, fell on barren ground. Close co-operation was, under such circumstances, impossible.

In that very year 1914, a question arose which was viewed from totally different standpoints by the two parties. The Russians began to make a comprehensive redisposition of their troops. Quite evidently the centre of gravity was being shifted towards the German and Austrian frontiers, which felt more and more the pressure of these amassments. From the interior of Russia, also, the General Staff received news of curious troop movements. How were these proceedings to be explained? The military view that they gave us good reason to be prepared for any event was met by the watery explanation that the affair was only a test mobilization; and, in stupid anxiety lest a definite clearing up of the matter might "start the avalanche," the political gentlemen adopted the attitude of "Wait and see."

* * * * *

Subsequent to the 'summer visit of the General Staff to the Vosges under the leadership of its chief, von Moltke, I received a few weeks' furlough, which

I spent in West Prussia. Early in July, I joined my family in a charming little villa presented to us by the town of Zoppot. It was a magnificently brilliant summer, and the days went swiftly by in such recreations as swimming, rowing, riding and tennis. Zoppot was filled with strangers, including many Poles.

In the midst of this serene peacefulness, I was startled by the gruesome telegram which brought me the tidings of the Archduke's assassination. That this political murder would have serious consequences was obvious. But this gloomy conviction remained, for the moment, confined to my own bosom; not a soul among our leading statesmen thought it necessary to hear my views or to inform me of those of our Ministers. Neither from the Imperial Chancellor, nor from the Foreign Office, nor from the Chief of the General Staff, did I learn a thing about the course of affairs.

The Kaiser was cruising in Norwegian waters, which I had to take as an indication that nothing unusual was to be anticipated. Only the newspaper reports strengthened my belief that serious developments were on the way. From Danzig merchants who had just returned from Russia I also received news indicating that an extensive westward movement of Russian troops was taking place; though, naturally, I had no means of checking the correctness of this information.

It was also from the Press that I gleaned my first information concerning the Austrian ultimatum. Its wording left the door open to every possibility, according to the political attitude adopted towards it by our Foreign Office. To me it seemed quite self-evident that the Wilhelmstrasse ought to assume an independent position and certainly ought not to allow itself to be drawn once more, as unhappily had previously been the case, into the wake of a pronounced Austrian policy.

To these days, in which the world faced such tremendous decisions, belongs an interlude, a painful one for me, that was once more to reveal to me, just before the eleventh hour, the chasm between my own conception of things and the Imperial Chancellor's. It was my last peace conflict with Herr von Bethmann—in reality a matter of no consequence and one of which I speak here only because, at the time, it was dragged into the newspapers and capital made of it to my detriment.

I had given expression to my interest in the utterances of two Germans who, like myself, saw the gathering storm and raised their voices in warning. The one was the retired lieutenant-colonel, D. H. Frobenius, who had published a political pamphlet called *The German Empire's Hour of Destiny*; the other was Professor Gustav Buchholz, who had delivered a speech on Bismarck at Posen. The wording of my telegram to Frobenius ran : " I have read with great interest your splendid brochure ' Des Deutschen Reiches Schicksalsstunde ' and wish it the widest circulation among the German people.—Wilhelm Kronprinz."

These " bellicose manifestations " (" Kriegshetzerischen Kundgebungen ") Herr von Bethmann considered calculated to " compromise and cross " (" kompromittieren und kontrekarrieren ") his firmly established policy; and he found time, on July 20, to address personally to His Majesty a long telegram complaining of my action and requesting him " to forbid me by telegram all interference in politics." Thereupon, in a telegram from Balholm dated July 21, the Kaiser, appealing to my sense of duty and honour as a Prussian officer, reminded me of my promise to refrain from all political

STRESS AND STORM 121

activity; accordingly and without any discussion as to whether, in my telegram quoted above, anything more could be found than the thanks of an interested and approving reader, I wired to His Majesty on July 23: "Commands will be carried out." At that moment I had other matters to worry about than disputes with Herr von Bethmann over the limits of my right to thank some one for a book that had been sent me.

The next thing I learned touching the great problem was that the Kaiser had arrived at Kiel on board the *Hohenzollern* on the morning of the 26th, and that he had proceeded immediately to Potsdam. That was comforting, since, if there were any prospect of maintaining peace, he would exert himself to the utmost to do so.

Then silence again. Then, in the newspapers, which we seized eagerly: "Grey has suggested to Paris, Berlin and Rome concerted action at Vienna and Belgrade—the crown council in Cetinje has resolved upon mobilization."

Distinctly and clearly, as though it were but yesterday, I still recall the 30th of July. My adjutant Müller and I were lying in the dunes sunning ourselves after a delightful swim, when an urgent telegram was brought me by special messenger. It contained His Majesty's orders for me to come at once to Potsdam. We now saw the full seriousness of the situation.

I started immediately.

On the 31st there was a supper at the New Palace, at which my uncle, Prince Henry, was also present.

After supper, His Majesty walked up and down in the garden with myself and Prince Henry. He was excessively serious; he did not conceal from himself the enormous peril of the situation, but he expressed the hope that a European war might be avoided; he himself had sent detailed telegrams to the Tsar and to the King of England and believed he might anticipate success.

Some difference arose between my uncle and myself through my asserting that, if it came to war, England would most assuredly take the side of our adversaries. Prince Henry contested this. Thus I found here the same optimism that had clouded the views of the Imperial Chancellor, who, to the last moment, held firm and fast to his belief in England's neutrality. His Majesty was in some doubt as to the attitude which England would adopt in the event of war.

My last conversation on this question with the Imperial Chancellor, von Bethmann Hollweg, took place at the Palace in Berlin on August 2. It is stamped into my memory—sharp and indelible; the impressive hour in which it occurred enhanced the depth and significance of the effect, which, with final and terrible clearness, once more revealed to me, on the threshold of war, that our only prospect of success lay in the strength of the German army.

On that 2nd of August, I had just taken leave of my father to join the army. My car stood ready. As I was about to leave the little garden between the palace and the Spree, I met the Chancellor coming in to report to His Majesty, and we spent a few minutes in talk.

Bethmann : Your Imperial Highness is going to the front ?

Myself : Yes.

Bethmann : Will the army do it ?

Myself : Whatever an army can do we shall do ; but I feel constrained to point out to Your Excellency that the political aspect of the stars under which we are entering the war is the most unfavourable that one can imagine.

Bethmann : In what way ?

Myself : Well, that is clear : Russia, France, England on the other side ; Italy and Roumania at most neutral—though even that is improbable.

Bethmann : Why, that is impossible. England will certainly remain neutral.

Myself : Your Excellency will receive the declaration of war in a few days. There is only one thing to be done : to find allies. In my opinion, we must do everything to induce Turkey and Bulgaria to conclude alliances with us as soon as possible.

Bethmann : I should consider that the greatest misfortune for Germany.

I stared at him puzzled, till I perceived the connexion between his remark and what had gone before. In his incomprehensible ideology he meant that, by such alliances, we might forfeit the friendship and the certain neutrality of England—friendship and neutrality that existed only in his own head.

As soon as I grasped this, our conversation was at an end. I saluted him and drove off.

There was only one hope, one support, on which we could lean ; that was the German people in arms, the German army. With that we might perhaps succeed in our task despite our diplomatists and despite the naïve imaginings of this Chancellor, who was so spiritually minded that he was almost completely out of touch with mundane realities.

The incredible conception of our political situation, as revealed by Herr von Bethmann Hollweg in the conversation just cited, is apparent also in the report of the British Ambassador, Sir Edward Goschen, on his decisive interview with the Chancellor the next day. According to that report, Herr von Bethmann, now that he was at last bound to see before him England's true face, admitted with emotion that his entire policy had collapsed like a house of cards.

Since those fateful summer days of the year 1914, I have thought much and often about these incidents; and here in the solitude of the island I have pondered more and more over the matter. The blue, the red and the white books of the various countries have furnished me with many a hint as to the actual proceedings of the weeks immediately before the war. And I find myself obliged to formulate a judgment in even more severe terms than before: in those fateful days Bethmann Hollweg's policy and the Foreign Office failed more completely than might have been looked for from the example of preceding years.

That, in a war between Austria and Serbia, Russia would back Serbia and France Russia, and so on, was known to every amateur politician in Germany. Instead of critically examining Austria's action and saying categorically to the Ballplatz: "We shall not wage war for Serbia," people did as I had feared; they allowed themselves to be completely taken in tow by Austria. That is what happened, and, in my opinion, none of the other representations of the case by the Foreign Office go to the root of the matter. The totally incomprehensible attitude of the Foreign Office placed us in quite a false light; so that the Entente, adducing the outward appearance as proof, assert that we declined the mediation of England because we wished to go to war.

Withal, this Foreign Office was so sure of itself that it allowed the Kaiser to proceed to Norway, the Chief of the General Staff to stay at Carlsbad, and His Excellency von Tirpitz to remain on furlough in the Black Forest.

Thanks to an incredibly blind management of our foreign affairs, we just blundered into the world war.

So remarkable was the incompetence of our responsible authorities that the world refused to believe us, refused to regard such simplicity as possible, took it to be a cleverly chosen mask behind which was hidden some particularly cunning scheme.

When the Kaiser returned from Norway, it was too late to accomplish anything. Destiny took its course.

Middle of July, 1920.

For considerably more than half a year I have not had in my hands these sheets on which I had set down a review of my life and of my immediate surroundings down to the outbreak of war and, at the same time, my impressions and reminiscences of the events which led up to it. Not that I had given up the idea of sketching the incidents of the war in a similar way, but because, in the progress of the work, it soon appeared necessary to lift these out of the scope of personal reminiscences and to mould them into the form of an historical presentation of the events of the war.

Consequently, from October of last year till now, my task has been the recording of the purely military happenings which from the day we took the field I shared and experienced in common with the troops entrusted to me, during the long days of the war as leader of the Fifth Army and as Commander-in-Chief of the " Kronprinz " group of armies.

All the great events that took place in those years and all the sufferings that I had to wrestle with and to endure I have conscientiously noted down. In this way there has been laid the foundation of a presentation of the tremendous military performances of that fellowship whose members stood as comrades under me and with me in the field. It is a presentation which, the more I occupied myself with it, tempted me more and more to make the utmost use of the copious material in my possession; I was attracted, too, by the thought of erecting to my faithful fellow-soldiers a chaste and simple monument in the shape of a straightforward and unadorned story of their doings.

The account that I have given in it, as a soldier, of those bloody and yet immortally great four and a half years, will not fit into the framework of what I have already recounted in these pages. It is military technical writing in the strictest sense of the word, and is to take the form of a separate and complete volume.

These considerations have led me to decide upon lifting the picture of the military enterprises and battles bodily out of these present memoirs and to proceed, as before, with the frank and free description of my most personal impressions and experiences and my attitude towards the most weighty problems brought before me by the war and into which I was swept by the general collapse and ruin.

But before returning to my memories of that more remote past, I should like to say something of the eight or nine months which have elapsed since I wrote of them last in this manuscript.

If anyone had said to me last autumn: When the New Year comes, and spring, and summer, you will still be in this island and far from your home, I should not have believed him, should scarcely have been able to bear the thought of it. Thus the never-failing hopes of a progressive restoration of our homeland to fresh order and tranquillity, coupled with the work which—alongside of everything else brought by the days, months and seasons—I have never interrupted for any length of time, have helped me over this period. Friends also, who have visited me in my solitude and brought me a kind of echo from the world, have helped to lighten my sequestered lot; so, too, have the good simple people around me, who, since they made the acquaintance of my wife, have grown doubly fond of me; finally, there is my faithful comrade, Major von Müldner, who, in self-sacrificing devotion, shares with me this solitude and, ever and again, takes upon himself a thousand and one troubles and worries in order to spare me the burden.

Who were all the people that came? In autumn there was that fine editor, Prell, a thorough German, who conducts the *Deutsche Wochenzeitung* in the Netherlands, accompanied by his colleague, Mr. Rostock. This German-American gave me some interesting descriptions of anti-German war propaganda in America. He also brought with him a propaganda picture which is said to have met with great success over there; it represented me armed as an ancient Teutonic warrior fighting women and children in the attack on Verdun. Another visitor was Captain König, the famous commander of the *Deutschland* submarine. Then there were Mr. Kan, the Secretary General to the Home Office, a strictly correct Dutch state official, to whose truly humane care I owe so much—and His Excellency, von Berg, formerly Supreme President of East Prussia and afterwards Chief of the Department of Home Affairs, who has proved one of the best and most unerringly faithful advisers of our House in fortune and misfortune; he belongs to the distant "Borussia" days of Bonn, was a friend of the Kaiser's in his youth and is one of the men who, with deep human comprehension, have remained true to the lonely ageing man at Amerongen.

The winter has set in with comfortless and sombre severity. The anniversary of my landing in the island was shrouded in greyness and mist, like the day itself. Leaden clouds lay heavy over the sea and over the little island; and, day and night, tempests swept across the dykes and scourged the unhappy country. A few days' work with Major Kurt, my former clever and indefatigably active intelligence officer, constituted a welcome respite.

Shortly before Christmas, Müller, my old adjutant and chief of staff, arrived with Christmas presents from home—presents sent by relatives and touching tokens of affection from modest unknown persons. For the German children who, at the time, were staying with good people in the island to recuperate from the gruesome effects of the famine blockade, I arranged a Christmas feast in the little Seeblick Inn at Oosterland, with a Christmas tree and all sorts of presents and old German carols.

On December 23, the small and intimate circle of my household celebrated Christmas in the parsonage; and next day Müldner and I, accompanied by two gentlemen appointed by the Dutch Government, crossed over to the mainland and proceeded to Amerongen to keep Christmas with my parents in the hospitable home of Count Bentinck. A few months before—in October —I had seen my father for the first time since that 9th of November of the previous year, on which day, after grave talks, I had left him in Spa under the assured conviction that, in spite of all opposition, he would remain with the army.

Ineffaceable is the image left to me of that man with silver grey hair standing in the light of the many candles on the tall dark-green tree; still there rings in my ear the unforgettable voice as, on that Christmas Eve, he read the Gospel of the first Noël: " Glory to God in the highest, and on earth peace, goodwill toward men."

On the 27th I travelled back to Wieringen.

The New Year came, and its days resembled the

days of the year gone by. " Peace on earth " ? Hatred and revenge more savage than ever before! The unbroken determination to destroy on the part of France, who cannot pardon us the mendacity of her theses on war-guilt! The newspapers once more full of inflammatory comments on the extradition question! And, very amusing for me, the wild rumours of my approaching or even accomplished flight in an aeroplane, a submarine or God knows what! On one occasion two American journalists actually appeared in my cottage and asked permission to assure themselves of my presence here with their own eyes. I willingly consented to their request.

In the beginning of February, the official extradition list was made known—nine hundred names, with mine at the head. On that occasion, for the first time, I interrupted the aloofness of my life here in this island, and addressed a telegram to the Allied Powers offering to place myself voluntarily at their disposal in lieu of the other men claimed. This step, a simple outcome of my feelings, evoked no reply from any one of the Powers and was extensively misinterpreted both at home and abroad.

Buoyed up by the reports in the various newspapers, I lived on into March in the hope that, despite all the after-effects of the revolution fever and party strife, our homeland was on the road to internal tranquillity and consolidation. This belief was suddenly crushed by the news of the Kapp *putsch* and its important consequences. Over and above the pain caused by this relapse into sanguinary disturbances, the incident meant for me a bitter disappointment of my hopes that, at perhaps no very distant date, I might venture to return to my place within my family and on German soil without risk of introducing fresh inflammable matter into the Fatherland. Events had clearly shown that the hour of my return had not yet come, that possibly it still lay in the distant future. Considering the mentality manifested by the homeland, I was forced to fear that I might become the apple of discord among opposing parties, to fear that—hold aloof from all political affairs as I might—my return would be made the countersign for fresh struggles for and against existing conditions by one party or another without any consideration of my wishes in the matter. The reasons which, on November 11, 1918, had decided me, with a heavy heart, to go to Holland, proved to be still valid; hence, if I were not to render my sacrifice null and void by failure halfway to its completion, I had still to remain and to endure.

I frankly concede that those March days, in which, with intense bitterness, I struggled through to this conviction, held some of the hardest hours of my life. The fifteen months spent on my island in primitive surroundings and far from every intellectual stimulus and from all culture had been rendered tolerable by the belief that the end of my solitude and the re-entrance into the circle of my people and into the life of German labour were within measurable distance of being accomplished. The goal had seemed to be attainable in perhaps a few months. This open outlook had enabled me to endure really very great hardships with courage, and the thought that it was now only a little while longer had been my best solace. In this way everything acquired the character of the transitory and provisional.

It would have been stupid self-deception for me to try to maintain this confidence after those days of March. The old wounds that had been ripped open again could not be healed in months; it would take years for that.

It is strange how small external aids of nature often give us sudden strength to overcome the severest mental conflicts that have lasted for days and nights together. I quite clearly see a day at the end of March. I smell the keen sea-breeze and the vapours rising from the soil as the earth awakened in the early spring. From the study in my parsonage a small verandah, bitterly cold in winter, communicates with the vegetable garden—long and narrow like a towel and not much bigger. On the day in question, I was standing in the doorway of the verandah and looking pensively across the desolate winter-worn garden. In the previous spring we had let everything grow as rank and wild as it pleased. Why not? We should be gone in three months or so. But now, at the sight of the tangled and unkempt beds, the raggedness of the shrubs, and the paths weather-worn by frost and rain, I felt suddenly the impulse to do something here. Against a little kennel-like shed attached to the house there leaned a spade. I snatched it up with an ardent will, and set to digging. I went on and on till my back ached. The work of that hour was a relief from the inner burden I bore. I would not let the time pass in vainly waiting for the hour of my return home. Strive for the attainment of your wishes and your longings, but accept the hardships of the times and so live that they, too, may help to determine the future. Since that morning, I have worked daily in our little garden. It is restored to order. Some one will reap the fruits—I or another.

That was in the days of the Kapp *putsch*. I must say something more about this unhappy episode. Feeling and believing that a monarchical government, which stands above all party differences, best suits the peculiar political and complex conditions of our homeland—of the German country and the German

people—I should not be true to my convictions if I did not frankly state that I can understand the temptations and allurements which enmeshed so many excellent, experienced men of high ideals in this mistaken enterprise. That they lacked a proper comprehension of the new situation created by the collapse of Germany and consequently had not the necessary strength to withstand the temptation of the moment I deeply regret. To reckon with facts, even when the facts do not respond to our wishes, is more essential for us Germans than ever, because our prime and weightiest duty towards ourselves and our successors is first to rebuild our demolished house, and every particle of strength squandered in pursuing other aims is lost to the main object. So soon as that house stands once more grand and firm on the soil of our home, our disease-stricken and debilitated German national feeling will find its strength again in its pride over what has been done.

What more have I to report? A mild spring has come—my second spring in the island. My parents have removed to their new residence.

* * * * *

In his "Memories," published towards the end of 1919, Lord Fisher says with blunt candour:

"The essence of War is Violence."

"Moderation in War is Imbecility."

"It is the duty of the Government—of any Government—to rely very largely upon the advice of its military and naval counsellors; but in the long run, a Government which is worthy of the name, which is adequate in the discharge of the trust which the nation reposes in it, must bring all these things into some kind of proportion one to the other, and sometimes it is not only expedient, but necessary, to run risks and to encounter dangers which pure naval or military policy would warn you against."

If we admit the correctness of these maxims of Lord Fisher—and, for my own part, I do not hesitate to subscribe to them—we find in them a keen criticism of the attitude of our Imperial Government, since, throughout the war, there was no such co-operation between them and the Higher Command, and, above all, there was no such preponderance of the Government. The Imperial Government, which ought to have uttered the final and decisive word in all matters touching the sphere of politics, played much too passive a part. In critical moments, when events clamoured for decision and for action, little or nothing was done. At the best, the Government " weighed considerations," " made inquiries," swayed between the " to be sure " of their discernment and the " but nevertheless " of their fear of every activity, so that the right moment was allowed to pass unseized. So it came about that the Higher Command occasionally interfered more in questions of home and foreign policy than, according to its province, it ought strictly to have done. It is this which now forms the principal accusation against General Ludendorff. But the Higher Command did so, because it was forced to do so ; it did so in order that something, at any rate, might be undertaken for the solution of pressing questions, that things might not simply disappear in sand. If, therefore, the public blamed General Ludendorff, and still blame him, for having ruled like a dictator inasmuch as he meddled with all political affairs, and with problems of substitutes of every kind, food, raw materials and labour, no one acquainted with the actual circumstances and events is likely to deny that there is a grain of truth in the assertion. He will have to point out, however, that General Ludendorff was compelled to interfere by the inactivity and weakness of the authorities and personages whose right and whose duty it was to deal with the tasks arising out of the matters in question. I could not contradict Ludendorff when he used to say to me: "All that is really no business of mine; but something must be done, and if I don't do it, nothing will be done at home"—meaning, by the Government. In such moments, my heart well understood this energetic and resolute man, albeit my reason told me that there was too, too much piled upon his shoulders. Every man's capacities have their limit; and no day has more than 24 hours. Hence it was impossible for one man, even one of our best, to supervise and direct both the enormous machine of our Higher Command and also every department of our economics and of our home and foreign policy. The necessity of adapting himself to such excessive tasks was bound to cause some detriment to the powers of the most highly gifted person.

The unfavourable issue of the Battle of the Marne in September, 1914, frustrated the prospects of Schlieffen's programme of first rapidly prostrating France and then dealing with Russia. That we were faced with a war of indefinite duration now seemed probable, and, personally—in the year 1915—I came to the conclusion that, in the event of an excessive prolongation of the war, time would be on the side of our adversaries. It was bound to give them the opportunity of mobilizing the immeasurable resources of the world which lay like a hinterland behind their fronts. It would give them the chance of marshalling these against us, while our mewed-up Central Europe had to confine itself to the exploitation of its own raw material which, moreover, had not been supplemented by any systematic pre-war preparation. Time, too, would afford our adversaries opportunity to levy and train enormous armies and to reduce to a minimum the calls made upon the individual fighter; whereas we should be forced to demand from every German the sacrifice of his last ounce of energy, thus, in the end, exhausting our strength by the inequality of the terms imposed.

From the moment that this was recognized, it became the duty and task of the leading statesman, the Imperial Chancellor, continually to consider political steps for the conclusion of the war more or less independently of the plans and views of the military leadership. Whatever successes were achieved by the army, were they never so brilliant, the far-sighted politician ought to have made use of them solely and simply as footholds and rungs for him to climb by; on no account ought he to have been dazzled by them; on no account ought he to have adopted towards the Higher Command the attitude: " Finish your work first; then it will be my turn, for the present there is nothing for me to do." But had Herr von Bethmann Hollweg the least capacity either to will vigorously or boldly to dare anything? Had he survived the terrible collapse of his "England theory" or the political hara-kiri of his declaration of August 4, 1914, as a man psychically unimpaired? Be that as it may, our political destiny continued to remain entrusted to this man, whose hands had been palsied by ill-starred enterprises and whose eyes had acquired the lack-lustre of resignation. When I seek for any energy in Bethmann Hollweg, there occurs forcibly to my mind an episode told to me, with every guarantee for its veracity, by a Hamburg shipowner in the summer of 1915. Ballin, he said, had called on the Imperial Chancellor and, out of the wealth of his knowledge concerning world affairs, had urgently talked to him about the general situation. When he stopped, Bethmann heaved a deep sigh, drew his hand across his forehead and said : " I only wish I were dead. . . ." In order to rouse him out of his lethargy, Ballin, with an attempt to laugh, replied : " I dare say you do. No doubt it would just suit you admirably to lie in your coffin all day long and watch other people working and worrying."

Quite certainly it would have been no easy matter, and for that discouraged heart it would have been impossible, to detach one of our enemies from the alliance and come to a separate understanding with him ; but that it would have been useless, as the Foreign Office assumed, to make the attempt, I failed to see during the war, and I fail to see still. Separate peace might, I conceive, have been concluded perhaps with Russia, say in the early summer of 1915, immediately after our break through at Gorlice. Still the difficulties of negotiating with Russia at that time were very great. Nicholai Nicholaievitch and the entire Russian war party were at the helm of affairs, the Entente agreement to conclude no separate peace was still quite young, and Italy's entrance into the war dated only from May. But, for all that, it is impossible to say what attitude Russia would have adopted towards proposals on our part if they had included the preservation of her frontier-line of August 1, 1914, and a big financial loan or the guarantee of her financial obligations towards France.

In any case, the chances of a separate arrangement with Russia were excellent in the latter part of the summer of 1915, when Russia was in very serious military difficulties and the Tsar had appointed the admittedly pro-German Stuermer to the premiership. I considered it, at the time, an unmistakable sign of willingness to negotiate, and I urged our leaders to grasp the opportunity. As a matter of fact, in the course of the summer and in the early autumn, numerous deliberations of a general character were carried on and terms considered; but all this took place privately among German diplomatists or extended only to conversations between them and the Higher Command. Practical deductions which might have resulted in the inauguration of relations with Stuermer were not discussed. We got no further than empty lamentations and futile complaints that the war had completely cut us off from all possibility of communicating with people across the frontier, that we could not join them, " the water was much too deep."

If it be contended that it is all very easy, now that the war has been lost, to come forward and say, " I always told you so ; if you had listened to me, things might have turned out differently," I would meet such not altogether unjustifiable arguments by quoting some thoughts and suggestions from a memorial drawn up and addressed by me to all persons concerned on December 18, 1915, that is to say, at a time when such ideas might have borne fruit. In this memorial, I maintained that we ought to strain every nerve to achieve a separate peace with one of our opponents. Russia appeared to me to be the most suitable. At the end of the memorial I wrote :

" What our people have accomplished in this war will only be properly valued by historians of a future date. But we will not flatter ourselves with any complaisant self-deception. The sacrifice of blood already made by the German people is enormous. . . . It is not my office here to marshal the figures ; but a series of very grave indications ought to make us consider how long we can continue to fill up the gaps in our army. I am quite aware that, if we were to drain our national energy in the same way as France, the war might be continued for a very long time. But this is just what ought to be avoided. Every one who is at all in intimate touch with the front is deeply saddened when he sees what children now find their way into the trenches. We ought to consider that, after the war, Germany will need forces to enable her to fulfil her mission. I will not speak here of the financial situation because I am not in a position to form a competent opinion. In an economic sense, Germany has adapted herself to the circumstances of the war most admirably; but still, in this domain also there should be the desire not to prolong the war unnecessarily, as that would cause too heavy a loss. Moreover, despite all the wise measures of the Government, the progressive rise in the cost of living continues to weigh upon the poorer classes of the population, and there is a great lack of fodder in the country. All this, with all that it involves, makes a curtailment of the war very desirable; so that the answer to the question 'What can we attain?' is simply this:

"If we get a separate peace with Russia, we can make a clean sweep in the west. If this is impossible, we ought to endeavour to bring about an understanding with England. Only in one of these ways is it, I believe, feasible to bring the end within sight; and an end must be made visible, unless we are to fight on till our country is utterly exhausted.

"Our present favourable situation makes it possible to proceed on the lines suggested."

That is what I wrote and advocated before Christmas, 1915. It had no effect whatever; I might as well have shouted to the winds.

Similar circumstances came about in the following year; but it was not until the autumn of 1916 that the Imperial Chancellor had carried his meditations to the conclusion that there was no prospect of a separate peace with Russia : Russia, he said, was under the dictation of England, and England was for continuing the war.

Meantime we had truly gained a success which was bound to exclude all possibility of an amicable understanding with Tsarist Russia: we had created the Kingdom of Poland and, in the summer of 1916, we had drafted a Polish programme that could not but be like a blow in the face to the Tsar and to all Russia. Stuermer fell; and, in the early spring of 1917, the Tsar was swept off the throne by the waves of the revolution which the Entente had been promoting. During the months which followed the outbreak of that revolution, the East front was quiet. It was not until the last day of June that the Russians attacked again under Brussilov. A fortnight later, our counter-attack pierced their lines at Tarnopol and a great victory was gained over the already decaying Russian army.

At about the same time, namely on July 12, Bethmann resigned. In the main, the Chancellor's remarks in his second volume concerning my share in the proceedings are correct, and I have nothing of moment to add to them. Herr Michaelis, a man of unproven political possibilities and concerning whose capacities or incapacities no one, at that time, was able to express a convincing judgment, took over the inheritance. According to what I heard, Valentini, wringing his hands and crying, "A kingdom for a chancellor," stumbled, in his search, across this official, who within the scope of his previous sphere of activity had certainly merited well. I myself had never yet met Dr. Michaelis. He was now introduced to me as an exceptionally capable man to whom one might apply the proverb: " Still waters run deep." This was in July, 1917, just before his presentation to the Kaiser; and when, at the command of His Majesty, I was to negotiate with the party leaders at Schloss Bellevue in connexion with the Bethmann crisis, the conversation turned upon the burning question of the situation created by the action of Erzberger in the Reichstag Committee, and still more upon the bad impression made upon the enemy by the matter and form of the peace resolution, whose drafting was so impolitic, unwise and clumsy that it had seriously injured our interests. Instead of being the expression of a genuine desire for peace on the part of an unbroken combatant, this resolution looked like a sign of military weakness and waning resistance. Only the reverse of the desired effect could be expected. I found Michaelis in general quite of my own opinion; but I could not induce him, in this short interview, to disclose his own ideas, and consequently I could form no image of the plans he carried in his pocket for grappling with the exceedingly difficult task which was to fall to him as Bethmann's heir. But, in Dr. Michaelis, the best of intentions coupled with pious confidence was recognizable. That was not exactly a great deal; but I said to myself: "He is about to present himself to His Majesty, he knows your antipathy to the policy prevailing hitherto and does not know how much he can venture to say to you; you must wait and see." In any case, the change of Chancellors appeared to provide the right moment for me to risk raising my voice once again and to place my view of things before the deciding authorities. I was induced to take this course by the conviction that, after all the criticism which I had expressed upon the Bethmann Hollweg Government, a judgment upon a system which, with Bethmann's exit, had come to a certain formal close, should not exhaust itself in rejection and negation; I felt that he who claimed the right to criticize assumed the duty of proposing something better and of defending it both in the present and in the future.

Consequently, in the summer of 1917, while we were fighting in Russia, I worked out another memorial and laid it simultaneously before the Kaiser, the Imperial Chancellor and the Higher Command. It came into being in the days when, as leader of my army, I had just gained on the Aisne and in Champagne an extensive defensive victory against an attempt of seventy-nine French divisions to pierce my lines; and I will gladly leave it to public opinion to decide whether, in this memorial, the " war fanatic " and " victor " is speaking or whether it is a witness to my desire for an honourable peace. This memorial was written after a conversation with the clever and politically far-seeing Dr. Victor Naumann, but only those paragraphs referring to our foreign policy have any significance for my then attitude towards the peace question in the East. I quote here the principal passages, because, taken together as a whole, they show my attitude at that time towards many other important questions connected with the war :

" The change in the leadership of the empire, with which is to begin a new era in German and Russian policy, will naturally necessitate the drawing up of a balance concerning the past, in order to find a more or less reliable basis for future plans. In my opinion, therefore, the following points must be determined:
1. What stocks have we of raw materials of every kind?
2. What is our maximum capacity for working up these materials?
3. What stocks of coal do we possess?
4. What stocks of food and fodder have we?
5. What is the position of our transport facilities?

" When this has been determined, it will be necessary to decide how many military recruits Germany can call up and train next year without imperilling her absolutely essential economic capacity.

"But this is not all. We must also consider moral values, the mood of the people; and in testing these, one may with tolerable certainty predict that the longing for peace in the masses of the population has become very strong. The enormous sacrifices of blood during the three years of war already endured—sacrifices which have cast almost every German home and every German family into mourning—the prospect of further heavy losses of valuable human life, the mental depression caused and augmented by privations of every kind, the dearth of food and coal—all these things combined have awakened a dissatisfaction in wide circles of the people (and not by any means only among the social democrats) which is as hampering to the prosecution of the war as it is disintegrating to the monarchical idea.

"If it be added that the assured hope of a rapid conclusion of the U-boat warfare has not been fulfilled, this serious mood ceases to be surprising.

"We ought to construct, from the best available data, schedules of the resources of our allies parallel with those drawn up concerning our own; for only so can we learn what we have to expect and what we can accomplish.

"All this information in regard to ourselves and our allies having been collected, we shall have to obtain an approximately accurate knowledge of the forces and reserves of the enemy. Without exposing oneself to the reproach of being a pessimist, one may say at once that a comparison of the schedules will scarcely turn out favourable to ourselves. The natural deduction is that, even at the best, an attack on our part is no longer to be thought of, but only a maintenance of our position coupled with intensive prosecution of the U-boat warfare for a certain period. If this expires without having brought us any hope of a cessation of hostilities, we must seek the peace which our diplomatists will meanwhile have been preparing. This duty is all the more incumbent upon us inasmuch as we must say to ourselves that our chief ally, Austria-Hungary, by reason of her economic and, still more, her political conditions at home, will be unable to prosecute the war for more than a moderate length of time. I need scarcely add that in Turkey also the situation is anything but rosy.

" Now I do not for one moment overlook the fact that our adversaries also find themselves in a difficult position or that they dread another winter campaign extremely. Yet, there are two factors which have recently brought about a certain change of feeling. The first is America's entrance into the struggle, and the hopes which it has awakened; the second is the over-hasty action of the Reichstag (the peace resolution), which in enemy and neutral countries is regarded as an absolute declaration of bankruptcy. To-day, in London and Paris, and even in Rome, people believe that they may wait for us to lay down our arms, since it is now only a question of time.

" Now, what are we to do so that we may continue with honour and, if possible, with success, despite all these things? First, what are we to do at home? We must have maintenance of the lines of demarcation between the individual offices of the empire without prejudice to united action. Although, therefore, the leading Minister bears the full responsibility for our home and foreign policy, wholesome co-operation with the Higher Command, the Admiralty, etc., is indispensable. The larger federal States must also be kept informed as to our situation. Serious attention must continue to be paid to the regulation of our coal and food supplies.

" *Foreign Policy.*—Here again only one will can

dominate, but it must be supported by the mutual and candid information of the directing offices, e.g. the Foreign Office, the Higher Command, the Admiralty. Candour towards our allies is a duty. So far as possible we must spare the neutrals and defer to their wishes.

"Every idea of seeking peace via England is to be given up, and a resolute endeavour made to obtain peace with Russia. There is hope that, with the repulse of the present attack, a change of mood will take place in Russia; then we must seize the right opportunity. We may also advise the neutrals that, in general, we are not averse to peace on the basis of the *status quo ante;* they will let the other side know. Simultaneously, deft negotiators must use persuasion with the Russians.

"It is almost certain that the West will decline. On the other hand it may be hoped that Russia will seek peace. In this case, we shall have created a situation which will render England—already groaning under the effects of the U-boat privations—somewhat dubious as to whether she and her allies shall fight on or, within a reasonable time, enter into negotiations with us. Should Russia not give way, then we can come before the people and say: 'We have done everything to bring about peace. It is now demonstrated that our enemies wish to destroy us; therefore we must strain every nerve to frustrate their aim.' Possibly such action may bring us unsuspected help out of the ranks of the people. In any circumstances, it is our duty to work for a not too distant peace; for, unless the U-boats shall have brought England to reason within the next few months, their further employment will not have the same effect as heretofore. Distress with us will increase, and the replenishment of our reserves of men will become more difficult from day to day.

The vital energy of our people will be diminished by further blood-letting; in the interior, strikes and revolts may occur; a failure in the production of ammunition may render us defenceless. The financial burden of the empire will swell to gigantic proportions; our allies will possibly seek a separate peace; the neutrals may be forced to join the enemy.

" To carry out a policy properly one must have the courage to look facts in the face. A danger recognized is a danger half surmounted. Just now the preservation of the dynasty, the maintenance of the German Empire, and the existence of the German people, are all at stake. If our enemies dictate peace, the last syllable of Hohenzollern, Prussian and German history will have been written. It dare not come to that; and therefore, it is our duty, if it so must be, to obtain a peace of compromise. Such a peace would truly be a disappointment; but an indefinite prolongation of the war might see us, in the spring of 1918, facing the whole world alone, deprived of our allies, bleeding from the cruel wounds of a three and a half years' war and threatened with destruction.

" If we conclude an early peace with our eastern adversary, Russia will lie open to us as a domain for economic expansion. If that peace comes too late, then we come too late, because the Americans will have gained a firm footing in that vast realm. But we must also remember that, with an early peace, we should have financially won the war.

" One thing is certain : if we but maintain ourselves in this war, we shall be the real victors, because we shall have fought the whole world without being destroyed. This will procure us after the war an unexampled prestige and an enormous increase of power. Our position resembles that of Frederick the Great prior to the Peace of Hubertsburg. He stands rightly recorded in history as the victor, because he was not defeated.

(Signed) " WILHELM,
" Crown Prince of the German Empire and of Prussia."

In March, 1918, roughly three-quarters of a year after the drafting of my memorial, we concluded a peace with revolutionary Russia. What a peace! On the one hand with the dominating demeanour of the victor who dictatorially imposes his will—on the other hand yielding and accommodatingly trustful in questions that concerned our very vitals. Joffe was permitted to come to Berlin and circulate his roubles in Germany for the world revolution. Once more the old half-and-half methods.

No, so far as I can see, the Government did not make a sufficiently earnest effort to supplement the work of the sword with vigorous, prompt and adequate political measures.

In quoting the memorials addressed by me, in December, 1915, and in July, 1917, to the Kaiser, the Higher Command and the Imperial Chancellor, I have demonstrated that, during the war, I urgently advocated preparing the way for a peace by compromise. Of course the drafts referred to were only two of the many efforts which I made in the same direction. It would vastly exceed the limits proposed for these memoirs if I were to give chapter and verse for all that I undertook, subsequent to the Battle of the Marne, for the carrying out of my idea, which I never recanted, that the indefinite prolonging of the war would be intolerable, both for those at the front and those at home, as well as the urgent need for a compromise, and how advantageous (even though it might appear scarcely beneficial at first) this compromise would be compared with a similar agreement reached after complete exhaustion. Besides this, from my own knowledge gained in personal contact with soldiers and civilians, I made attempts to correct the erroneous and all too optimistic ideas entertained in certain high quarters about the privations of the people at home, the powers of endurance of the troops at the front, who had been overburdened during the past year, and about many similar questions. To all these things I may refer later on.

"But," many will say, "in public and especially to the troops, the Crown Prince, more than once, both by word of mouth and in writing, expressed and demanded determination to conquer and confidence of victory. He wished to prevent certain German journals, which tended to shake this confidence, from reaching the front."

Yes, most assuredly I did! And, in doing so, I fulfilled my duty as an officer and a soldier, just as I fulfilled my duty as a politically thinking man and as Crown Prince of the German Empire and of Prussia, when I endeavoured to induce the proper authorities to face unwelcome facts and to strive for a peace by compromise. I am unhesitatingly of opinion that each of these actions, apparently so opposite, was perfectly justified and indeed complementary. What I regret is simply the fact that, as an adviser without political responsibility, I possessed neither the means nor the power successfully to influence the persons politically responsible, and that I had to look on while political resolutions and irresolution were, as I believed, determining adversely the destiny of Germany.

I referred just now to my suggested prohibition at the front of various journals which systematically injured our prospects of winning the war. At that time the Democrats talked with great indignation about a deliberate gagging of the Press and of the public if the idea were carried out—at that time, forsooth, when it was essential to guard for its one single task the army on whose fighting powers everything depended and to shield it from any deteriorating or disintegrating influences. As a matter of fact, nothing was done; the evil was permitted to continue its work of corrosion.

Only with the support of a people determined to win and convinced of victory could the Government risk steps to bring about a separate peace—an understanding with one or another of our adversaries. Every effort in this direction was futile, nay, pernicious and damaging, when we gave the impression of being unable to continue the war and of urgently needing peace. Useless and senseless, therefore, were the offers of peace publicly trumpeted out to the world—offers which also gave no clear notion of what we really wanted. These offers—as any statesmen ought to have foreseen—only served to strengthen our enemies' hopes of an early collapse of our country, to increase their confidence and their determination to hold on till the " knock-out blow," all to our detriment, all to our doom.

Determination to win and confidence of victory sufficient to last out the war and bring it to a happy issue could only be maintained in the nation or in the army if there stood at the head of affairs not merely vigorous and bold military leaders but also an equally capable Government, which, during the bloody struggle on land, at sea, in the air, should not for one second lose control of the numberless threads of its foreign policy and which should never allow the slightest favourable movement of events in the war-fevered world to escape the grasp of its ever-ready hand—a Government that, with keen foresightedness, yet with wise

STRESS AND STORM

recognition and consideration of what was possible, was able to see before it the road along which it could lead the country as rapidly as possible to a happy and honourable peace.

* * * * *

The only Government that could be a sure guide to satisfactory peace was one that, by means of a wise home policy, had under complete control all the various elements, classes, members and parties of the entire people.

That it was particularly difficult to concentrate into one dynamic entity the variety of opinions, wishes and impulses of a people so inclined to internal differences and quarrels as the Germans is quite true. The sense of nationality that, in such countries as England and France, fused all parties into a single will for the whole duration of the war, unfortunately underwent manifest disintegration among us Germans by reason of the multiplicity of party views which soon began to be active, and through which the idea of a party truce was undermined and our vigour of attack weakened. Nor was it, by any means, only among the parties of the left that such sins were committed against the great idea of unselfish patriotism. By leaving to the war-speculator unlimited independence and unbounded opportunities of profit and by not organizing properly the industries essential to the existence of the struggling State, our mistaken economic policy was responsible for the early reappearance of the old social and economic animosities, which soon became very bitter. Moreover, an absolutely morbid tendency to a mistaken objectivity at all costs repeatedly drove a large section of our German people, even during the war, into extensive discussions and to self-examination that bordered upon mental penance. This was done openly before the whole world, and ultimately made the world believe that the conscientious amongst us doubted the justice of our deeds and aims. In England, all parties had only one principle for every programme and every action of their Government, the strong principle of a firmly-established nation, the principle of " right or wrong—my country."

A miserable hero of such mistaken objectivity, a man in whose heart the bright flame of the greater idea could never blaze up, was the first War Chancellor. His Reichstag declaration on August 4, 1914, concerning our advance into Belgium, is the great and bitter classic example of his incapacity to understand either the soul of his own people or the mentality of our adversaries. On that 4th of August, 1914, before a single shot had been fired over yonder, we Germans had lost the first great battle in the eyes of the world.

And blind he remained to all the events and developments around him throughout the long years of the war during which we had to put up with him.

Thus, he stressed again and again the special merits, as he called them, of the social-democratic party in offering to co-operate at the outset of the war. As though, at that time, the working masses would not simply have swept away their leaders if they had dared to pronounce against co-operation! At that moment the entire German people were unanimous in their deep conviction that we were entering upon a war forced upon us, an unavoidable war from which we could find deliverance only by resolutely and victoriously struggling through to an assured peace. That many a leader of the extreme left never, in his heart of hearts, desired a complete German victory, seems to have remained long hidden from the Chancellor's perception. At any rate, he did nothing to combat their efforts to undermine the confidence of the masses in the German cause.

General Ludendorff complains bitterly in his war memoirs that the Government at home did scarcely anything to keep alive the "will to victory" in the German people, or to combat energetically the tendency to *defaitisme*. I, too, could not resist the impression that, during the war, the proper authorities permitted these tendencies to grow without adopting energetic counter-measures. *Defaitisme*, which, regardless of every other consideration, was rigorously crushed in France, England and America, as a principle adverse to the necessities of the hour and opposed to the interests of the State, was allowed to run riot with us. Our Government were powerless to cope with it, yet believed themselves able to silence and neutralize anti-national conduct by weakly indulgence. Nervelessly they let things take their course, seemingly reluctant to picture to themselves the fatal end to which, sooner or later, it all must lead.

Wherever difficulties and impediments arose, recourse was had to small remedies, to half-measures, to extravagant concessions flung down with both hands or to a hesitating and belated compliance. They made shift with patchwork until no more patching was possible and everything fell to pieces. Civil dictators, conscious of their path and with eyes fixed on victory, like Clemenceau and Lloyd George, were altogether wanting among us. The longer the war lasted, the more autocratic and severe became the government of the hostile countries and the more vacillating and yielding our own. The munition workers at home were granted fabulous wages to keep them in a good temper. The only effect was that their cupidity was increased, a higher premium put upon shirking, the soldier at the front irritated and deprived of his willingness to fight. Why was not every calling of importance to the war made compulsory? Why were not the men called up for work at home placed in the same category as to wages and rations as those under the colours? People talk *ad nauseam* of the dutiful home warriors! " War " employer and " war " employee ought both to have been swept up by the organization of " war ' industry.

For the organization of industry at home, the Auxiliary Service Act (Hilfsdienstgesetz) was ultimately adopted. But it was due to the initiative of the Higher Command, whose business it was not; and when it came, what a mutilated thing it was!

Irresolute and somewhat unfortunate was likewise the attitude of the Government towards the Prussian Suffrage question during the war. The Social Democrats, making a watchword of the idea, carried on a vigorous propaganda and—while our armies were engaged in the severest struggles and their welfare depended upon the smooth working of the industrial mechanism at home—even did not hesitate to throw out threats of a strike.

Two courses were open to the Government. One was to say that war time was unsuitable for dealing with changes of the constitution, especially as the best part of the people were then under arms at the front and consequently unable to take part in the reorganization; but then they would have had to pull themselves together and ruthlessly repress every agitation aimed in a different direction. The other course was for the Government to decide upon a revision of the Suffrage Act, but in that case they ought not to have hesitated to arrange for a speedy dissolution of the House of Deputies, and should have resorted to every possible means to carry out their purpose.

The Government once more adopted the fatal method of half-measures.

When His Excellency von Valentini, the *chef du cabinet civil*, brought me the so-called " Easter message " in 1917, I expressed to him my astonishment at this patchwork, and pointed out to him that such a decree would satisfy nobody, that the Government would before long be forced to grant direct suffrage and it would be better to do it straight away as a spontaneous act of His Majesty. Valentini replied: " The direct secret ballot is out of the question ; what is proposed is a plurality vote similar to the Belgian arrangement." Count von der Schulenburg, Chief of the General Staff of my army, was present at this conversation.

August, 1920.

Since I last had these sheets in my hand, our parents and we children have suffered a heavy blow : my brother Joachim, utterly broken down, has passed out of this life. Immediately on receipt of the news, I travelled to Doorn, in order to be with my mother in, at any rate, the first and severest hours of her sorrow. What a mountain of suffering destiny has heaped upon our poor ailing mother's heart!

At the beginning of the month, my brother Oscar, who had arrived at Doorn just after me, came to see me here in the island. Eitel Friedrich was also here ; and so, little by little, they are all making acquaintance with the small plot of earth on which I have lived for over twenty months. I can imagine that, when they happen to have good weather here for their short stay, the place will not seem so very dreadful to them. It was a great pleasure to me to receive a visit from my old and trusted Maltzahn, who, when he came to see us at the front, shared with me many an anxiety concerning our internal situation. At the end of the month my wife is to come here again—this time with all four boys.

In these personal recollections of mine, I feel impelled to say a few words about the two men whose names enshrine, for the whole German people, their idea of military leadership, namely Field-Marshal von Hindenburg and his First Quartermaster-General, General Ludendorff.

It is superfluous to say much here of what our country owes to these two men. Suffice it to call to mind the great victories at Tannenberg and at the Masurian Lakes. At that time, the names of these two were in everybody's mouth, and both at home and at the front arose the wish that the leadership of the entire German army might be placed in their hands. We commanders-in-chief shared fully this general desire to see Hindenburg and Ludendorff in the most responsible positions, and we received, with joy and hope, the ultimate decision of His Majesty to place them there. Never have I seen any other two men of such different character furnish the exact complement of one another so as to form one single entity as did these two. In all questions that arose during their period of co-operation, the weal of the Fatherland and the happiness and honour of the army were, for them, the common basis for their deliberations, their plans and their resolutions.

If I were to describe the Field-Marshal General as he appeared to me in the years of his zenith, I would say that the greatest impression was made above all by the simple energy and composure of his reserved personality. It was a composure that communicated itself to every one who came into contact with him, convinced every one that the fate of the armies was safe in that calm firm hand, watched over by those earnest and yet ever-friendly eyes. If he spoke, the effect was heightened: one was then impressed not merely by the statuesqueness of his tall, broad-shouldered figure, but by the depth and timbre of his voice and the easy flow of his measured, thoughtful, and deliberate speech; the conviction was confirmed that the speaker was absolute master of the situation and expressed views that could be thoroughly relied on.

This feeling was not confined to the individual addressed, it extended to the masses when the Field-Marshal General appeared before them. Furthermore, a scarcely definable peculiarity of manner seemed to efface the dividing line between his professional and his human interest in people, problems and things.

The great and emancipating victories in the East were soon invested with almost mythical features; with these as a background, Hindenburg's personality became, for the nation and the army, a symbol of German victory and of rescue from the exigencies of war. That unrevealed something which has its roots to a great extent in the judgment of the heart and the feelings, which creates the hero for the multitude and which never appeared in such men as Falkenhayn or Ludendorff, soon fashioned a halo about Hindenburg and made him the ideal leader in the eyes of the Germans. At home and at the front, I have heard this confidence, so touching in its primitive simplicity, expressed over and over again in the words: " Our old Hindenburg'll manage it "; the utterance was, as it were, a refuge from the pressure of the time, and remained so later, when, for us leaders, who had long since been stripped of our optimism by our knowledge of the true state of affairs, the only reply possible was dead silence.

Even more now than during the war, there is a very widespread belief that, as Field-Marshal General, Hindenburg played little more than a decorative part beside General Ludendorff, who has been regarded as the real *spiritus rector* of the Higher Command. My insight into the admirable relations between these two leaders fully justifies me in characterizing such a view as mistaken; in no case could it be said of the era in which the Field-Marshal General was in unimpaired enjoyment of his physical strength and energy. That even a Hindenburg—who, though in full possession of his mental and bodily vigour, was nearly sixty-seven years old when he entered the campaign—could not help feeling the effects of his increasing age after three or four years of excessive work, worry and responsibility, may be safely asserted without fear of detracting in any way from the imperishable services of this venerable commander and estimable man. As, in the course of time, some relief became necessary, the indefatigable energy of the so much younger friend and close collaborator took over a portion of the burden; and their admirable unity remained a strong and resolute will without any bargaining about the intellectual share of each. How much aid Hindenburg received from his comrade became bitterly evident when the unity was broken by the retirement of Ludendorff, and his place was filled by one whose inadequacy despaired all too soon at the thought of keeping the leaky ship above water and bringing it safely to port through all storms and with its old flag still flying. The character of this new man was such that he struck the flag with an indifferent shrug just as coolly as he flung away as empty " ideas " the things that till then had been sacred to the German people; the energies of the same successor, exerted in a different direction, became the strongest forces shaping the peculiar development of the events of November 9 in the Great Head-quarters at Spa.

Owing to the nature of my tasks and duties, I came much more into contact with General Ludendorff than with the Field-Marshal General. I can conscientiously say that I always felt a strong sense of being in the presence of a personality of steely energy and keenly sharpened intellect, of a Prussian leader of the traditional glorious type in the best sense of the term. In his bright office-room, in which were focused the rays from every front of the foe-girt Fatherland, I have, on countless occasions, discussed with him the questions and problems of the war and especially the situation of my own troops. Whereas, on the one hand, in talks with the Field-Marshal General, one felt, as I have already hinted, that his grave and easy speech was the outcome of the deepest assurance, on the other hand one seemed, in conversation with General Ludendorff, to be in the glittering workshop where only the greatest mental wrestling succeeded in regaining this assurance from day to day by an unceasing struggle with untold antagonisms, hostile principles, obstacles, difficulties and shortcomings of every kind.

It has already been stated that this mass of affairs brought before him for settlement tasks and problems which did not properly belong within the traditional scope of his post. He took them upon himself because their solution was of the greatest significance for the military situation, and because without his intervention they would have remained undealt with. Successful and deserving of thanks as many of his performances in these domains that lay outside his own proper sphere certainly appear to me, still, I believe I may say, without in any way giving a wrong impression of his strong personality, that his essential importance and greatness lay in the provinces of strategy, tactics and organization. In these fields and so long as the troops and material lay intact in his hands, his brilliant mastery of the whole theory of war, his wealth of ideas and marvellously exact intellect, solved with the most astounding certainty military problems of the most difficult character and won for him and for the German arms imperishable fame. His keen and complete analysis of a situation, his unfailing conversion of theory into command and act, his accurate knowledge of the value of the forces employed, with which he could reckon as though they were invariable mathematical quantities—all these things contributed to win for him the great victories at Tannenberg, Lodz and the Masurian Lakes. Afterwards, when he had taken over the gigantic tasks of the Higher Command, they secured him successes of imperishable strategic significance during the struggle for the German Line down to the spring of 1918—successes whose lustre is perhaps still dimmed by the lack of ultimate effect and the shadow of the miscarriage in the final combat, but which the just verdict of the future will unquestionably range with the greatest military performances of all time.

His great and bold ideas were only impaired when the units which he fitted into his structure were no longer capable of satisfying the demands which, according to tradition, he believed himself justified in making upon the troops—when the normally accepted fighting value of the units had been too much exposed to physical and psychic trials, and thus the uncertainty and brittleness of the material introduced factors of error, which rendered it impossible to make exact calculations as to the capabilities of the machine.

The successful designer of battles and calculator of victories, who, ever since he led his first men as a little lieutenant, had been accustomed to regard the concepts of discipline, punctuality and fighting courage as things of iron-like rigidity, the practised strategist, who, ever since he first donned red-striped trousers as a young officer of the General Staff, had combined with the idea of a battery or a division definite striking values and calculable effects, now suddenly saw himself compelled to query all these notions. Enterprises which, assuming the reliability of the individual factors, held every promise of success, broke down in the execution because the machine, partly overstrained and partly rusty, failed to perform its task. The last German attacks, i.e. from March 21, 1918, down to the decisive turning-point of the war—the irruption of the enemy at the Forest of Villers-Cotterets on July 18 —were, notwithstanding some brilliant initial successes, nothing but a series of bitter examples of this fact.

Both as a man and as a soldier, General Ludendorff suffered severely under these conditions and bore them with a heavy heart. Like, doubtless, every other commander, I sympathized with him in this torture. All of us, who had passed through the iron school of the grand old army and had breathed the air of the Military Academy in Königsplatz, had been equipped in that famous building with the firmest confidence in the unflinchingness of the great army which was the embodiment of the strength and pride of the German people; and this palladium we now saw tottering.

For my part, I had, at an early period, been unable to shut my eyes to these cracks, rents and flaws; and I dutifully laid my observations and suggestions before the Quartermaster-General. Even yet, when I recall those conversations, I am filled with gratitude by the remembrance of the friendliness and attention with which General Ludendorff listened to the views and wishes of one so much younger than himself and did all he could to meet the demands which he recognized as justified.

It is true that, especially in the later period of our increasing exhaustion of man-power, food-stuffs and war-material, he was only too often obliged, with a resigned *ultra posse*, to decline what he would certainly have gladly conceded had he been able. As I learned to know him in years of mutual labour for the same end, General Ludendorff was never a dazzler or a " thruster." To his upright and stern soldierly character it would be as alien to seek the favour of individuals or to fear their disfavour as it would be to court the approval or dread the disapproval of the masses. For his decisions he knew only one criterion ; that was their practical fitness for the attainment of his great aim ; and that one aim was to carry the Central Powers and especially Germany out of the war into a firm peace which would leave us room and light for our further natural development. With absolutely passionate devotion and creative energy, he threw the whole of his abundant personality unreservedly into the accomplishment of his military tasks, never seeing in this immense self-sacrifice anything more than the fulfilment of the obvious duty owed to the Fatherland by every German, whether civilian or soldier. This admirable and robust conception of duty and of unflinching perseverance, coupled with a high estimate of the inherent moral worth of the German at the front and the German at home, inclined him, particularly in the last periods of the war, to assume and presuppose such vigour and virtue as a reliable basis for military operations and for demands upon the homeland, even when privations and disappointments as well as disintegrating influences and anti-moral forces had already enfeebled and corroded the original soundness. Filled by the strongest sense of national honour, he found it bitter to have to believe in the decay of this vigorous moral stamina of the German people, when no eye could any longer remain closed to the painful fact. For a long time he refused to recognize the reality of the situation, and strove to preserve within himself the proud image of the German immutably true to Kaiser and empire. This high estimation of the masses caused him for a long time to regard the disintegrating forces as merely pernicious, exceptional phenomena ; it was also, perhaps, the ultimate reason of his attention being turned so late to the agitators and their victims—too late, indeed, for any energetic action to be taken. In regard to the moral fighting value and physical capacity of the troops, which constituted the most important factors in calculating the chances of an early and fortunate conclusion of the war, our views differed more and more as time went on, and the difference became very wide in the latter half of the war. Neither would I conceal my opinion that in the choice of his immediate co-operators, General Ludendorff was not always happy, nor always open to representations as to the incompetence of such individuals, or willing to consider statements that ran counter to their reports. Severe views of fidelity towards painstaking subordinates who gave him the best assistance of which they were capable induced him to leave posts inadequately filled for a longer time than was consistent with the best interests of public affairs.

While anything but an uncritical upholder of General Ludendorff's views or a mute admirer of all his acts, I nevertheless account him to be a surpassingly great German commander, characterized by the strongest patriotic energy and faithfulness—a man who stood at the head of the German army like a symbol of its traditions and of its conscience. For his enemies to feature him as a " gambler " and " *hasardeur* " is to circulate an untruth. Would to God that we had had, among the political leaders of the realm, experts of equal capacity, of the same thorough deliberation and equally conscientious daring ; would to God it had remained possible for each and every individual to turn to good account all his energies in the sphere of his own most special calling.

In the chapter on Rome, in Count York von Wartenburg's *Weltgeschichte in Umrissen*, which I have recently been reading, I came across a passage the other day concerning the Battle of Cannæ and steadfastness in defeat which has imprinted itself upon my memory as particularly applicable to our own times. Referring to epochs subsequent to the days of Rome, York speaks of the disgraceful manner in which the Prussian people heaped contempt and contumely upon the army for having suffered defeat at Jena, when "it was neither the only culprit nor even the principal one." Further he says: "If a people desires victoriously to survive a Cannæ, it must never dare to lose its regard completely for its leaders and its standard."

From the bottom of my heart I long for the resurrection and the new greatness of our German fatherland and its people. But only when the vast multitude, now blinded by the ranting agitation of false prophets, has recovered its vision for past greatness, will it be able to understand and appreciate the old that was and to labour indomitably for the new that is some day to be.

CHAPTER V

PROGRESS OF THE WAR

October, 1920.

AT the beginning of the month I spent a few days on the mainland. I had to visit a dentist in Overveen named Schaefer. I could never have believed it possible for anyone to enjoy so much the modest little pleasures a dentist can provide with all his small instruments of torture. I felt thoroughly comfortable as I leaned back in his swivel-chair—a rather different kind of furniture from our Wieringen appointments. The trip was the first interruption for a long time to the persistent quiet and solitude of the island; and just at present, when the advance of autumn is robbing the drab landscape of its last few charms and the equinoctial gales are beginning to rage, it helped me to surmount the prospect of another long, hard and sombre winter in this seclusion and in the restricted accommodation of this little dwelling, so far from my home and my loved ones. Moreover, in Schaefer's delightful little villa near Haarlem, we found high-minded, amiable and well-educated people whose hospitality it was a pleasure to enjoy. On the way back, we called at Burgomaster Peereboom's and spent an hour or two with that old friend, who now lives at Bergen, his place at Wieringen having been taken by the equally excellent and ever-helpful Mr. Kolff. This new burgomaster and his wife, who is of German origin, do everything in their power to render my life more bearable.

* * * * *

Among the letters from home that awaited me on my return was one from a war-comrade. It spoke of a hundred matters, and touched upon the silly twaddle that is circulating among those who are better informed than anybody else in the world about my conduct as commander of the Fifth Army. So, then, I am said to be answerable for the disastrous retreat ordered by the Higher Command after the Battle of the Marne in the year 1914. These excessively clever people know that with unerring certainty. Perhaps, therefore, it will not altogether be out of place if I state what I know of this battle that formed the turning-point of our destiny—more particularly since what has so far been said on the subject by serious and critical observers tells very little concerning the doings of the Fifth, Sixth and Seventh Armies.

What I intend to write here is not a description of the military developments and the operations of my Fifth Army in those bitter days; for that I have made other arrangements; I propose here only to sketch in broad outline the circumstances which, at that time, led the German army to desist from its victorious advance and to start a tragic retreat. The blame mine? Only mean malice could invent such an idea, only unbounded stupidity could believe it!

As commander-in-chief of the Fifth Army, I led my army in the advance of August, 1914; I saw the decisions and notices that were issued, and was present at the scanty discussions with the General Higher Command and with the adjacent armies; finally, I had the best of opportunities to watch and study hour by hour the development of affairs during the Battle of the Marne. My impression is that it was an unfortunate combination of many circumstances that led to this pernicious result. Besides the unquestionable incompetence and the consequent moral and physical collapse of General von Moltke, there was the unfortunate and rapidly discouraged leadership of the Second Army by General von Bülow and the absolutely disastrous doings of an officer of the Headquarters Staff, who, oppressed by a sense of responsibility and personal pessimism, assumed a verbal order given to meet a particular emergency as conferring full powers upon him, and so occasioned a retreat of the two victorious armies on the wings before a decision had been reached.

Whenever I think of the senseless and incomprehensible flinging away of the successes gained at that time, whenever all the horror of that insensate folly comes before me, I see the tragic figure of a man who ought to have led, but who was no leader and who broke down when the rising pressure of events broke down the traditional scheme : that figure is the figure of Lieutenant-General von Moltke. I knew the general well, I sincerely revered him as a man and I feel deeply the tragedy of a fate which, in its purely human features, seems to me to have a certain intrinsic resemblance to the fate of the unfortunate Austrian, Benedik. General Moltke was a thoroughly high-minded man and a devoted friend of my father's. When, on the urgent recommendation of his most intimate advisers, the Kaiser in 1906 called him to the chief position in the General Staff, von Moltke earnestly begged His Majesty to excuse him, as he did not feel competent to fill the post. When, however, the Kaiser insisted upon his decision, the Prussian officer obeyed. He subsequently endeavoured, with inexhaustible diligence, to master the enormous detail of the work of the General Staff. There was something shy in his character; he seemed occasionally to have but little confidence in himself, and so he soon became totally dependent upon his collaborators. The great personal amiability and ardent human cordiality which he possessed made it difficult for him to gain that authority which is so essential to the Chief of a General Staff. During my service with that staff, it was mentioned to me as typical that even the quartermasters-general used to report to the old and inexorable Schlieffen with a certain feeling of nervousness, whereas everybody liked appearing before General von Moltke.

General von Moltke was never robust. When the war broke out, he had just completed two drastic cures at Carlsbad. He entered the war as a sick man. The direction of the various armies by the Chief of the General Staff was a very loose one. His head-quarters in Luxembourg were much too far distant from the scene of battle; and, at such a distance, he could not follow events with the necessary accuracy—could not supervise them with the necessary clearness; possibly, too, the eye for the essential and the requisite rapidity of resolve failed him at the crucial moments of the battle. In any case, the great imperfections of means of communication at that time gave rise to difficulties, so that there was occasionally a complete lack of connection with the advancing army. This destroyed the unity of leadership; ultimately, the armies, when they had once started their advance and knew their allotted path, waged war more or less independently, each communicating with its neighbour as occasion required. Immediately after the Battle of Longwy, I was called to the Great Head-quarters in Luxembourg. I took the opportunity of talking quite unequivocally with Moltke's right-hand man, Lieutenant-Colonel Tappen, concerning the loose control of the armies by the Higher Command, and I demanded the appointment of permanent liaison officers between the General Higher Command and the Higher Command of each army. The proposal was smilingly shelved with the remark that no change was necessary, as everything was working excellently as it was.

When the situation of the First and Second Armies became acute, the Chief of the General Staff sent Lieutenant-Colonel Hentsch as intelligence officer of the General Higher Command on a tour of inspection to the Higher Command in each army. As General von Kuhl once told me, the decision as to the course the battle was to take was laid in his hands.

At the beginning of his round, Hentsch appeared first at Varennes in the Higher Command of the Fifth Army on the afternoon of September 8. He gave us a sketch of the entire situation as far as it was known in Luxembourg. For a cool and impartial judge, these details constituted anything but an unsatisfactory picture, although indeed it was clear that the hitherto rapid and victorious advance had come to a standstill. On leaving us, Hentsch proceeded along the whole front to obtain a personal opinion concerning the Fourth, Third, Second and First Armies. Here began the unfortunate influences at which I have already hinted. Quite possibly, Hentsch really did receive some very bad impressions, especially from the Higher Command of the Second Army; maybe his nerves gave way; at any rate, instead of encouraging the Higher Command of the Second Army to unflinching resistance, he agreed to their retreating. The description which he gave of the dissolution of the Second Army and the use made of his supposed authority to order the retreat of the armies ultimately induced the First Army to fall back upon Soissons, though it did so with great reluctance and only because it had itself lost direct touch with the Second Army.

In these critical days of Hentsch activity, my Higher Command attacked without success along the line Vavincourt—Rembercourt—Beauzée and St. André, and prepared a night attack for September 10, whose object was to procure us more freedom of action, since we were closely confined between Verdun and the trackless Argonne region. The General Higher Command, which had manifestly been more and more disquieted by Hentsch's reports, at first disapproved of this plan for a night attack, in which the XIIIth Army Corps (with the 12th Cavalry Division) and the XVIth Army Corps were to participate; however, after repeated representations had been made, permission was finally given.

The attempt was therefore promptly undertaken and succeeded brilliantly. The army gained the line Louppy le Petit to the east of the Rembercourt heights and the north-east of Courcelles-Souilly; Sarrail's army giving way to the extent of about twenty kilometres.

On this day, September 10, Lieutenant-Colonel Hentsch returned via Varennes from his tour. Since he had first visited us, his view of the general situation had become pronouncedly pessimistic. He expressed himself hopeless as to the condition of the right wing, and demanded from me the immediate withdrawal of the Fifth Army. From his description, the First and Second Armies were now only fleeing remnants; the Third Army was maintaining itself with difficulty; the Fourth was in passable order.

I told Lieutenant-Colonel Hentsch that an immediate retreat of the Fifth Army was out of the question, since neither the general situation nor the position of the army mperatively called for it; further, that before

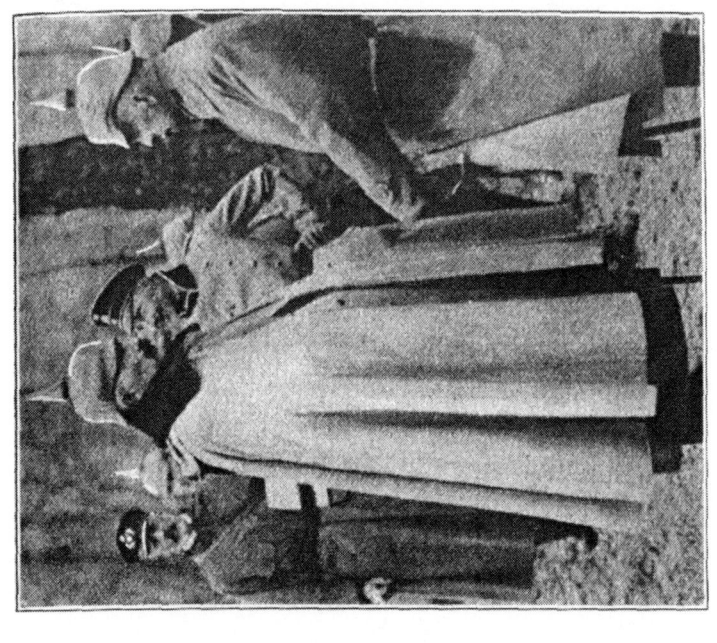

THE KAISER AND PRINCE HENRY OF PRUSSIA VISIT THE CROWN PRINCE AT HIS HEAD-QUARTERS IN FRANCE.

GERMAN GREAT HEAD-QUARTERS.
THE CROWN PRINCE WITH GENERAL VON HINDENBURG.

the idea could be even entertained, the removal of all my wounded from the territory just gained would have to be assured. As Hentsch, despite these objections, became importunate, I asked him for his authority in writing. He could produce none; and I thereupon informed him that we were not in a position to comply with his wishes.

With the retreat from the Marne, Schlieffen's great plan was frustrated. It was based on the rapid subjection of France. I shall never forget the terrible impression made upon me on September 11 by the sudden appearance in my Varennes and Argonne Head-quarters of General von Moltke accompanied by Lieutenant-Colonel Tappen. The general was completely broken down, and was literally struggling to repress his tears. According to his impressions, the entire German army had been defeated and was being rapidly and unceasingly rolled back. He explained that he did not yet know where this retreat could be brought to a standstill. How he had formed such a senseless conception was for us, at that time, beyond comprehension.

He was astonished at the calm and confident view of the situation taken by the Higher Command of the 5th Army. But he was not to be converted to a more optimistic opinion, and he demanded—as Hentsch had done the day before—the instant withdrawal of my army. As no imperative reasons for such a hasty step were even now perceptible, a lively controversy ensued which ended in my declaring that so long as I was Commander-in-Chief of my army I bore the responsibility for that army and that I could not agree to an immediate withdrawal on account of the necessary removal and proper transport of my wounded. With tears in his eyes, General von Moltke left us. From a human standpoint, I felt the deepest sympathy with the utterly crushed man, but, as a soldier and leader, I was unable to understand such a physical breakdown.

During the afternoon of September 11, Colonel von Dommes brought me the further instructions of the General High Command. My army was to fall back to the district east of St. Menehould. The colonel suggested retaining the southern edge of the Forest of Argonne. The Higher Command of the Fifth Army decided, however, to go as far back northwards as the line Apremont—Baulny—Montfaucon—Gercourt, since it did not appear advisable to remain in a more advanced position than that of the rest of the army (already retreating in compliance with the orders of the General Higher Command), especially as the liberated enemy forces were now in a position to advance from Verdun in any desired direction and thus threaten, not only the communications of the Fifth Army, but also those of the entire western army.

Only after the removal of all its wounded did the Fifth Army withdraw. The retreat was carried out in perfect order from the 12th to the 15th of September and the new positions were taken up with a strong sense of superiority. There was no molestation on the part of the enemy; Sarrail did not dare to attack us; and if he had, it would have been a bad thing for him. From the heights just to the north of Varennes, I watched the rear of the XIIIth and XVIth corps leave their trenches, and I can assert that, save for some cavalry patrols, no enemy forces followed our troops anywhere.

In the course of the war I had the opportunity of talking over the fatal incidents of the first Battle of the Marne with hundreds of officers of all grades and with hundreds of the rank and file. What I heard was always the same: we had completely repulsed the French counter-attacks and had ourselves successfully attacked again, when the incomprehensible orders to retreat arrived.

My brother Eitel Fritz commanded at that time the First Regiment of Guards. Later on, he described the day to me with honest wrath. " We were in full assault upon the French position," he said, " after having repulsed various French counter-attacks. Our men were, it is true, very fatigued ; but they advanced courageously and determinedly. Everywhere the French were to be seen in full flight. We had victory in our hands, when suddenly an orderly officer appeared with that damned order to stop the attack at once and start the march back." He told me that it was the most agonizing experience of his life to have to go back with his brave men over the road that they had won with such a severe struggle and to see the wounded, who were now certain to fall into captivity. Our famous grenadiers refused to believe it all and kept on asking : " Why must we fall back ? We have beaten the French ! "

And they were right. The German army was not defeated at the Marne ; it was withdrawn by its leaders. The battle was lost because the Highest Command gave it up as lost ; in spite of the numerical superiority of the enemy—in the ratio of two to one—that Highest Command might have led its armies to victory, if it had clearly perceived the situation and had acted adequately and resolutely.

It is not wisdom after the event, but the expression of a view borne in upon me at the time, when I say that, by a vigorous concentration of our right wing for united action and by strengthening it with easily available reinforcements from the left wing, a dispersal of the threatening danger might have been achieved without any serious difficulty.

General von Moltke I saw only once afterwards. It

was in the Head-quarters at Charleville. He had already been removed from his command; I found him aged by years; he was poring over the maps in a little room of the prefecture—a bent and broken man. It was a most touching sight; words seemed impossible and out of place; a pressure of the hand said all that I could say.

I was told later, on credible authority, that the unfortunate man sank into a morbid search after the reasons for his evil fate, that he tried to discover exonerations and justifications for his failure and lost himself in all kinds of barren mysticism.

In the end he died at Berlin of a broken heart. With him passed away a real Prussian officer and a high-minded nobleman. That he was faced with a task that was beyond his capacity, that, with a mistaken sense of duty, he undertook it against his will and with a consciousness of his own inadequacy, proved fatal to him and to us.

End of October, 1920.

In this second half of this month, I have been over to the mainland again. It was on the 22nd, the anniversary of my mother's birthday. They were quiet, sad days in Doorn; for it cannot escape the eye of anyone who loves her that my mother's strength is declining, that sorrow is eating her up. The wound made in her maternal heart by the death of my brother Joachim has never healed; he was the weakest of us boys and claimed a greater share of her motherly care.

On the birthday itself she had to keep her bed. I could only sit beside her, hold in mine her hand that had grown so fleshless, and talk to her. I told her a number of amusing and harmless little anecdotes about my island household; and it was a pleasure to see a faint smile light up her kind features every now and then; but it was only a short flicker of sunshine, that was gone again almost instantly. And when she is up and walks through the rooms and her tired eyes wander caressingly over all the old furniture and mementoes of her Berlin and Potsdam days, it is as though she were bidding them all a silent farewell.

My uncle, Prince Henry, was also at Doorn, and came over to Wieringen for a day on his way back.

Müldner is to make another trip home in November to hear and see how things stand. These journeys of his make me feel like Father Noah, " who sent forth a dove from him, to see if the waters were abated from off the face of the ground." When will he return with the olive branch?

Our old friend, the ever faithful and helpful Jena, is to take his place while he is gone, and to keep me and my two dogs and my cat company.

* * * * *

A few weeks ago I endeavoured, in these sheets, to refute the silly twaddle which connects my name with our failure at the Battle of the Marne. I should like now to explode a second fable.

Among the many untruths disseminated about me by spite or stupidity, is the assertion that I am answerable for the losses at Verdun and the ultimate failure there. The persistence with which this legend crops up again and again makes an explanation of the facts necessary.

The order to attack Verdun naturally did not proceed from me: it originated in a decision of the General Higher Command. This decision and the General Higher Command's reasons for the enterprise find expression in a report to the Kaiser by General von Falkenhayn, as head of the commander-in-chief's

General Staff, at Christmas, 1915. This report contains the following passage: " Behind the French section of the western front, there are, within range, objects for whose retention the French are compelled to risk their last man. If they do so, the French forces, since there is no option, will be bled white, whether we reach our objective or not. If the French do not risk everything, and the objective falls into our hands, the moral effects upon France will be enormous. For this local operation, Germany will not be forced seriously to expose her other fronts. She can confidently face the diversion attacks to be expected at other points, nay, she may hope to spare troops enough to meet them with counter-attacks." Soon afterwards, the General Higher Command issued orders for the advance on Verdun. The General Higher Command was unquestionably influenced by our numerical inferiority and a desire to anticipate an expected attack by the enemy with their maximum strength at some spot unsuitable to ourselves. British organization had by this time become effective; the French had been relieved. In the spring of 1916, the enemy troops in the west outnumbered our own by more than a million; according to General von Falkenhayn's own figures, the Germans totalled 2,350,000 against 3,470,000 of the Entente, and we were also inferior as regards munitions.

In judging of the plan, the Higher Command of the 5th Army took the view that both sides of the Meuse must be attacked simultaneously and with powerful forces. Such a proceeding was vetoed by the General Higher Command. The attack on the east bank only was carried out under the direct instructions of the General Higher Command; and it would probably have succeeded, but for the intervention of untoward circumstances.

PROGRESS OF THE WAR

The preparations for the attack had quite escaped the notice of the French. The concentration of the artillery had not been interfered with in any way; the attacking infantry had suffered scarcely any losses in the initial assault. Everything had been brilliantly prepared. Then, on the eve of the day originally selected for the attack, storms of rain and snow set in, which prevented every possibility of the artillery seeing their objective. From day to day, the attack had to be postponed, so that it actually took place ten days later than originally arranged. The Higher Command of the 5th Army passed an agonizing time; for, as things stood, every hour lost meant a diminution of our prospects of speedy success. As a matter of fact, in that period of waiting, our purpose was betrayed by two miserable rascals of the Landwehr who deserted to the French.

Nevertheless, it was no longer possible for our enemies to carry out their counter-measures quickly enough. The attack began on February 21, 1916; and the huge successes of the first three days are well known. The infantry of the IIIrd and XVIIIth corps, and the VIIth reserve corps, performed marvels of courage. The taking of Fort Douaumont crowned everything. Indeed, we should, after all, have succeeded in rushing the entire east front of Verdun if the reserves promised us had arrived to time. Why they failed to do so is not within my knowledge.

I was told by Captain von Brandis, who stormed Fort Douaumont, that, on the fourth day, he had observed a complete absence of Frenchmen in the whole district of Douaumont—Sonville—Tavannes. But our own troops had exhausted their strength; the weather was horrible, and rations could not everywhere be brought up as needed. That it would have been quite possible to take the entire east front of

Verdun by pressing the attack without respite is clear from the fact that the local leaders of the French had already given orders for evacuation. Only later was this order countermanded by General Joffre. But, from the statements and descriptions which I have recently seen in a report by a French officer who fought at Verdun, it is evident that on the third day the defence of the east front there was actually broken. Moreover, the great danger of the position for the French on February 24 has been described by General Mangin in the *Revue des deux Mondes*.

The fatigue of our troops after a tremendous military feat and the lack of reserves despoiled us of the prize of victory. I bring no accusation; I merely record the fact.

From that day onwards, surprises were no longer possible; and the early impetuous advances by storm gave place to a gigantic wrestle and struggle for every foot of ground. Within a few weeks, I perceived clearly that it would not be feasible to break through the stubborn defence, and that our own losses would ultimately be quite out of proportion to the gains. Consequently, I soon did everything in my power to put an end to the attacks; and I repeatedly gave expression to my views and the deductions to be drawn from them. In this matter I stood somewhat opposed to my then chief of staff, General Schmidt von Knobelsdorf, and my representations were at first put aside; the orders ran: " Continue to attack." That, in consideration of the high moral values attaching to a continuance of the enterprise, a contrary opinion had to overcome enormous opposition, and that the General Higher Command was bound to look at the struggle for Verdun from a different standpoint than that of the Higher Command of the Fifth Army, must be unconditionally conceded. Still, even looked at

The Kaiser and the Crown Prince at Verdun.

PROGRESS OF THE WAR

from that superior standpoint, I believe my suggestions to have been correct.

When, later on, the situation became so acute that, in view of the futility of the sacrifices, I felt unable to sanction the continuation of the attack, I reported personally to the Kaiser and made written representations to the General Higher Command; whereupon the Kaiser adopted my view and gave the desired orders to break off the attack. After the resignation, on August 29, of General Falkenhayn, the head of the Commander-in-Chief's General Staff and of the Operations Department, the orders to cease attacking were issued by Field-Marshal General von Hindenburg on September 2, 1916, together with instructions to convert the lines that had been reached into a permanent position.

Regrettable as the final result may be, it should not be forgotten that, although the attack on Verdun cost us very heavy losses, the French suffered even more than ourselves. About seventy-five French divisions were battered to pieces in the devil's-cauldron of Verdun. Hence, the force of the French onslaught at the Somme was very greatly diminished by Verdun; and it is impossible to say what the effects of the Somme advance might have been had not the Battle of Verdun reduced and weakened the resources of France in men and in material.

I feel that I cannot close my remarks concerning my attitude towards the struggle for Verdun without a reference to the cowardly and slanderous contumely cast upon me during the past two years by those German newspapers which prefer to make use of a cheap cry rather than allow truth to prevail.

Even during the last few days, I have read it once more : " The Crown Prince, the laughing murderer of Verdun."

Gall and wormwood in the little light left me on this

island, which, for three hundred out of the three hundred and sixty-five days of the year, is wrapt in fog and storm.

"The laughing murderer of Verdun!" So that's what I am, is it? One might almost come to believe it true, after hearing the calumny so often. It cuts me to the quick, because it concerns what I had saved as my last imperishable possession out of the war and out of the collapse. It touches the unsullied memories of my relations to the troops entrusted to me; it touches the conviction that those men and I understood and trusted each other, that we had a right to believe in one another, because each had given his best and done his best.

What was to be told of Verdun and my part in the contest for the fortress I have already told. It remains for me to say something about my relations to the troops and about my laughter.

It goes rather against the grain to say much concerning the former point. I will say only that, in the untold fights which took place, I had grown as fond of my brave and sturdy troops as though they were my own children; and I did everything in my power to ensure them recreation, quiet, rations, care and rewards in so far as these were at all possible in the hard circumstances of the war. Whenever feasible —that is, whenever my duties permitted me to leave the Higher Command of my group for any length of time—I joined my fighting troops in the fire-zone to see with my own eyes how things stood; and, wherever it could be managed, I personally saw that something was done to relieve their hardships.

In the Argonne it was the same as at Verdun or in the chalk pits of Champagne; and, among the many hundreds of thousands who came under my command in the course of the terrible war, there can be very few indeed who did not see me in their sector. Therefore, I can dispense with many words, and boldly call upon all my brave officers, non-commissioned officers and men of the old Fifth Army and my Army Group to testify to my relations with them. The knowledge that they repaid my love with incomparable soldierly qualities, with fidelity and with courage, that they were personally attached to me, is for me to-day a source of happiness that has remained to me out of the past, and that no unscrupulous vilifier shall destroy with his mendacious attacks.

"The Crown Prince, the laughing murderer of Verdun!" So then, now for my laughter! Indeed and indeed, in my youth I was wont to laugh. I was never a moper or a lie-by-the-fire. I was fond of laughter; for I found life gay and generous, and laughter was for me, as it were, an expression of gratitude to destiny for letting me rejoice in my strength with freshness, health and faith.

Even in the war, despite all its bitter trials, I never completely lost my capacity for laughter. Every one who went through it manfully must have experienced, in precisely the most terrible times, the desire to be rid of all that unheard-of horror, of all that death and destruction, must have felt an almost greedy impulse towards every sensation and every assuring expression of his life that hangs between the present and the undoubtedly better hereafter. And so, at that time also, I made no histrionic mask of my face for the benefit of the recording public, but showed myself as I was.

That, even at the time, at home and perhaps behind the lines, my laughter aroused adverse censure here and there I know perfectly well. "The Crown Prince," people said, "always looks happy; he does not take things very seriously."

Oh, you dear, kind, captious critics, what could you know about it? If I had troubled half as much about you then as you did about me, my laughter would no doubt have vanished. But I troubled myself only about one thing—about the men entrusted to me, the men who were bearing the brunt of things. And if those old warriors of mine, who were then the care of my heart and whom I look back to still in love and comrade-like attachment, if they had objected to my laughter, then I would admit you people to be in the right! But they understood and thanked me. For their sakes I really did many a time laugh and smile even when I felt in anything but a laughing mood.

Pictures of those bitter days rise before me.

I recall a review of the recruits. Last year's batch of young fellows have just completed their training and are to leave for the front. Six hundred dear bright German lads, scarcely out of their boyhood, stand there. They are really still much too young for their difficult task. Their bright eyes are turned expectantly and feverishly upon me: what is the Crown Prince going to say to them? I feel a lump in my throat, and my eyes are inclined to get dim; for I had seen only too many go and too few return, and these are scarcely more than children! Dare I let these lads see what is passing within me? No! —I pull myself together and smile; then I say to them: "Comrades, think of our homeland; it must be; it is hard for me to let you go, but you will accomplish your task. Show yourselves worthy of the comrades at the front. God bless you!" And they cheer and start confidently on their way.

A big battle is in progress. Serious reports are arriving from the front; the enemy have penetrated into our lines at a dangerous spot. I am sitting in the room of my Chief of Staff with the map before me and the telephone at my side. We have brought up the reserves; the artillery and the airmen are in action; and we await reports. The telephone rings, and I snatch up the receiver. Report from Army Higher Command: " The breach has widened, but we hope to halt in lines A to B." The weightiest cares press upon the Chief of Staff and the Commander-in-Chief. There are no more reserves at our disposal; the last man and the last machine-gun have been sent in. Now the soldiers must do it by themselves. Will it go well?

I walk out to step into my car, and motor to the neighbourhood of the attack. Hundreds of soldiers fill the road; their inquiring eyes are bent anxiously upon me. The difficulties of the situation up at the front have got about; it looks very much like a disposition to panic here. I get up and call out to them: " Boys, there is heavy fighting going on, but we shall manage it, we must manage it, and you must help me!" I smile at them. They doubtless say to one another: " It's a tough job, and it may cost us a lot. But he trusts to us, and he keeps a good heart himself; it'll be all right."

And, in place of the ominous silence that met me when I came out, loud cheers of encouragement follow me as I drive off.

Another picture. It is after the severe struggle on the Chemin des Dames. I drive to a regiment that has just returned from the fighting to recuperate for a few days on the Bove Ridge. The men have quartered themselves in shell-holes and in old French dugouts. I talk with many of them; they are utterly fatigued. In one of the shell-holes a party of corporals are playing the card-game of *skat*. I sit down with them and add three marks to the pool. Their tongues are loosed. They are all thorough-bred Berliners. Most of them know me. At first they grumble at the length of the war, but they add: " Well, we'll pull through somehow." Soon, I have to leave for other troops. An old fellow stands up—a man of quite forty-five—and holds out his horny hand to me saying: " You're our ole Willem, and we shan't forget your comin' to see us 'ere; when we goes back to the front, we'll think o' you, and you shan't 'ave no cause to complain o' us." A thunder of hurrahs echoed over the blood-soaked Chemin des Dames.

So much for my laughter then; and I can only confess it—I am still able to laugh. In spite of all the blows of fate, in spite of all vexations, reverses and loneliness, I still often feel it welling up in me; and I thank God that He has left me that! I felt it only yesterday while playing with the fisher-children over there in Den Oever; and I felt it the other day while talking with the smith's man.

December, 1920.

Müldner has come back.

How does the passage about Noah run in the Bible? " But the dove found no rest for the sole of her foot, and she returned unto him into the ark, for the waters were on the face of the whole earth: then he put forth his hand, and took her, and pulled her in unto him into the ark.

" And he stayed yet another seven days."

So there is nothing for it but to take one's heart in both hands and to enter the third winter on the island.

One great delight I have had: a visit! My little sister has been with me for a few days on her way home from Doorn. Anyone who could know what we have been to one another from childhood (the little sister's " big brother " and *vice versa*) would understand and appreciate how much this reunion after such a long time meant to us two.

Scarcely was the little duchess gone, when the storms burst across the sea—wild and ceaseless by day and by night. They almost carried away the roof of the parsonage from over our heads. Winter has rushed upon us this time in a big attack—with a sudden fall of the temperature, with snow-blizzards and hard frosts and masses of ice in the Zuyder Zee. It is worse than even the first bitter winter that we spent here two years ago.

A biting north-easter and driving ice in the sea make communication with the mainland almost impossible. Added to this is a telephone breakdown, so that we are quite cut off from the world.

And the latest news from the sick bed of my mother was so very grave that the worst is to be feared. When I think of it, there comes to me as it were a prayer: "Not now—not in days like these."

By three o'clock, or at the latest by four, it is night. Then I seat myself beside the little iron stove with the paraffin lamp and my books and papers before me.

When my eyes wander over the bookshelves, I think to myself: "What a lot you have read and ploughed through in the past two years! More than in all the thirty-six that preceded them."

During the war, the Higher Command of my 5th Army and my Army Group often received visitors from the homeland and from neutral countries. Of these visits I propose to say something here.

The German federal princes frequently came to see their troops, and I was able thoroughly to discuss, with some of them, the whole situation and the position of affairs at home; often enough their warnings were directed towards trying to find some possible opportunity for an arrangement with the enemy, a view which I heartily shared. It is to be regretted that the German federal princes were not oftener heard by the Imperial Government; many of them foresaw the catastrophe clearly. The federal character of the German Realm (so carefully guarded by Bismarck) was only too often relegated to the background during the last fifteen years of the Empire by reason of the excessive centralization at Berlin. People overlooked the fact that it was precisely the more local and tribal pride of the different States which best helped to cement them together into a realm.

Of the prominent personages who visited me from allied and from friendly States I would like to mention Enver Pasha, Crown Prince Boris of Bulgaria, Count Tisza, Kaiser Karl, and Sven Hedin. Count Ottokar Czernin was with me twice. We had some exhaustive political talks; and I received the impression that the Count was a high-minded, upright and clever statesman who surveyed the actual situation clearly and wished to reckon with facts. In the summer of 1917, he came to see me at Charleville; we discussed thoroughly the highly critical condition of things, and he was of opinion that the Dual Monarchy was on the point of exhaustion, that it only kept itself going by means of stimulants and that we, also, had passed the zenith of our military power. He foresaw the coming collapse and wished to prevent it by comprehensive and tangible concessions to the enemy. A peace by agreement on the basis of surrender and sacrifices on the part of the Central Powers was his aim; and his remarks disclose a certain conviction that this aim might be achieved provided the necessary steps were taken. We ought to relinquish Alsace-Lorraine and to find compensation in the east, where the annexation of Poland and Galicia to Germany should be worked for.

Austria, on her part, was prepared, not merely to relinquish Galicia, but also to cede the Trentino to Italy. Knowing only too well the difficulties of our position, I could not turn a deaf ear to his suggestions; but I pointed out to him that any such proposals as those he was now putting forward were bound to meet with strong opposition in Germany. People at home saw our victorious armies standing far advanced into enemy territory; the majority believed thoroughly in our chances of success; they would not be amenable to the idea of giving up old Imperial territory just to get peace, just to have kept the defence unbroken. Notwithstanding my recognition of these difficulties and my utter scepticism concerning the idea of compensation in the shape of Poland, I carefully weighed the sacrifice required from us by Czernin's scheme against the incalculable disaster into which I believed we should glide if the war were continued; and I told the Count that I would do all in my power to support his views, especially with the leaders of the army. The steps thereupon taken by Count Czernin himself failed. The Imperial Government seemed to consider the sacrifice expected from us to be too great. Unless I am mistaken, Bethmann Hollweg appeared particularly scared by the problem: " How am I to acquaint the Reichstag and the people with the truth ? " Still less amenable to the Count's proposals was the General Higher Command; as General Ludendorff explained, they regarded it as incomprehensible, with the armies unbeaten, that we should talk of giving up ancient German territory which had been so long under foreign domination and had been regained with German blood. I give due honour to all the arguments put forward by General Ludendorff in defence of his standpoint: they are to be found in his memoirs, and proceeded from the optimistic heart of a fine soldier, not from the mind of a cool and judicial statesman. On my side, I endeavoured to see the problem in its simplest form, namely: " Prestige in the French portions of Alsace or the existence of the realm ? " Hence, I advocated an attempt on the lines suggested by Czernin. But my sole success was that I was said to have " got limp " and to have gone over to the political " bears."

Dutch, Swedish, Spanish and, at the beginning, American military missions were frequently our guests. Among them, there was many an excellent and sympathetic officer.

Several times, too, German parliamentarians found their way to me. There came, for instance, von Heydebrand, Oldenburg-Januschau, Kämpf, Schulze-Bromberg, Trimborn, Fischbeck, David, Hermann Müller. With the Majority Socialist, David, I had a long and interesting talk in the summer of 1917. Although our views, naturally, were anything but identical, we found many points of agreement. On my inquiring as to the next demands to figure on his party programme, he stressed the necessity for an Act to aid the unemployed. In reply to my objection that it would be very difficult to determine, in every case, whether the unemployment were really undeserved, he assured me that a very rigorous check would be exercised so as to exclude all possibility of abuse. When I read nowadays of the enormous sums expended by the realm and by the municipalities in assisting the unemployed, my mind occasionally reverts to that talk with " Comrade " David: have David and the other fathers of the Act really succeeded in carrying into practice their theory of a check to exclude all abuse ? I could wish it, but I am inclined to doubt it.

After David had left me, I received an account of a little incident that happened to him during his journey

PROGRESS OF THE WAR

through the war zone, an incident which reveals him as a very admirable man. In a small place were posted some *landwehr* men and some columns consisting mostly of elder men who had ceased to have much enthusiasm for the war. They recognized David and explained to him that they wanted to go home—wanted to fight no more. Thereupon the Social Democrat David made them a vigorous speech, in which he told them that every one had to do his duty, that striking in front of the enemy was quite out of the question. The speech did not miss its mark.

In July, 1918, I conversed with Herr von Heydebrand about our situation and our war aims; and I was touched by the optimism with which he regarded the future even at that time. He was quite dismayed when I disclosed to him the naked truth, when I told him that, for a long time, we had been conducting a war of desperation on the west front, conducting it with fatigued and exhausted troops against vastly superior forces. On my giving him accurate figures and other evidence in proof of my assertions and explaining to him our bitterly grievous position in regard to reserves, he appeared scarcely able to grasp the hard realities unfolded before his eyes. Afterwards my Chief of Staff confirmed for him what I had said and furnished him with further particulars. Herr von Heydebrand then told me that from what he had now learned he must recognize that, hitherto, he had cherished a totally false view of our situation; he and his party had been utterly misinformed in Berlin.

The over-rosy official view also explains the otherwise inexplicable and frequently exaggerated aims of the Pan-Germans, who have been so decried on account of their mistaken demands. Like many others, they really knew nothing of the actual situation. They wanted to point the people to some tangible war-aims. France was fighting for Alsace-Lorraine, England for the domination of the seas and for her trade monopoly, Russia for Constantinople and for ice-free access to the ocean, Italy for the "unredeemed provinces." What was Germany fighting for? To this the Pan-German party wished to give the answer; and the simple truth, "for her life, for her unscathed existence, for her unobstructed development," did not sound strong enough. And yet of all war-cries it was the only firm, strong and worthy one.

Out of a land of dreams millions of Germans were suddenly dragged into pitiless and harsh realities by the unfortunate events of the year 1918. It affords imperishable testimony to the fatal effects of artificially cultivating an ill-founded optimism, effects especially fatal when, in war-time, the judgment on the general situation is too favourable. Nay, I maintain that the collapse of Germany would never have developed into such a terrible catastrophe, if the severe reverses at the front, which they considered utterly impossible, had not torn the people out of all the illusions sedulously fostered by official personages. They had universally believed everything to be highly favourable and prosperous; and now, all of a sudden, they had to see that they had been duped by misleading propaganda. So effectually had this thoughtless, vague optimism been instilled into their minds that, even in times of the greatest excitement, tired people took refuge in it and very few had the energy or self-reliant courage to picture to themselves the results of a possible defeat. And, yet, it was just such as these few who drew from their inner conflicts with final bitter possibilities a stiffer power of resistance, since they learned thereby that supremest effort was essential for struggle and victory, that defeat meant destruction.

The lack of uprightness and truthfulness which

arose from loose thinking and which had become second nature to many gentlemen in responsible positions, has taken a bitter revenge. With the opiate of eternal reassurances that all is well you cannot stimulate either the individual or the community to the pinnacle of effort. A much greater effect is obtained by honestly pointing out that enormous tasks are to be accomplished in a life-and-death struggle, that this struggle is harder than any people has ever passed through, and that, unless *all is to be lost*, no nerve must weaken, no soul become lax, in the ups and downs of this vital conflict. Clear knowledge as to the results of a possible defeat ought not to have been withheld from the people at home, and the horror of the strife at the front ought never to have been disguised for them by a false mystification when failures occurred.

I am not here advocating any doleful damping of people's spirits ; all I say is that, from the outset, the German people ought to have been honoured by assuming it to be mature enough to face the whole hard truth and to steel its heart by gazing at it.

Hundreds and hundreds of times I said to my troops : " Comrades, things are going hard with us. They are bitterly difficult. It is a case of life and death for you and for all that we Germans have. Whether we shall pull through I do not know. But I have every faith in you that none will desert the other or the cause. There is no other way out of it ; and so, forward, for God and with God, for the Kaiser and the realm ! for all that you love and refuse to see crushed." Such things as these ought to have been told the people at home according as the situation called for it.

But the authorities preferred to ration the truth.

The result was that the nation, starving for news, snatched greedily at rumours and tittle-tattle as substitutes for what was kept from them, while distrust and disintegrating doubt grew apace. These false tactics began at the first Battle of the Marne; and we never got rid of them till the collapse came.

The German Press is not to be blamed for the mistaken views of its readers; the evil had its roots in the source from which the information was supplied to the Press. An honest desire for the truth was displayed throughout by the newspapers of all shades of opinion, though naturally party views and personal interests played their part. During the war, press representatives of the most diverse political opinions, and especially war correspondents who were my guests and whom I met over and over again with the fighting troops, complained to me that they were not permitted to write of the things as they saw them, that they might only give their readers an inkling of the truth, but not tell them the full seriousness of the situation. Very bad news it was thought preferable to suppress altogether. Especially when matters were critical at the front, the red pencil wallowed in the dispatches and reports; and what ultimately remained had often assumed quite a different air when denuded of its context.

The censor's office, by reason of its effect upon these reports of immediate eye-witnesses, was guilty of heinous sin against the country.

New Year's Eve, 1920.

Half an hour ago we rose from our modest celebration of New Year's Eve—Müldner, Zobeltitz and myself.

Thus quite a little party!

How delighted I was when, as soon as the ice permitted, Zobel came over.

But, after all, the evening has been a quiet and oppressive one. It was as though each of us hung secretly in the web of his own thoughts, and as if each, when he spoke, was anxiously choosing his words lest he might touch some old wound or sore.

It was fortunate that we had good old Zobel with us in his orange-coloured jersey. His melancholy humour is inexhaustible; and he has the knack of making the hardest things softer and more bearable by means of his dry, quiet, wise fooling.

What a lot passes through one's mind in such hours! Past, present, future—like the medley of a cinema picture, one's self being only a helpless spectator.

And my folk, wife, children, parents, brothers and sister—somewhere each of them on this last night of the old year has been thinking of me.

Dear comrades of the field—living and dead! Friends, even though the end was so different from what you sought, the sacrifices you made for our poor country, for our longings and for our hopes will not be lost. Your deeds remain a sacred example and the best seed for a new period in which the Germans shall again vigorously believe in themselves and their mission—for a period that will come, that must come.

And all the other faces out of pre-war years! But all that seems now to me to be much longer ago; it is as if a thin film of dust were settling upon it. There is so much that one cannot imagine again as it used to be. I fancy we have all learned a great deal by bitter experience. And yet it is only seven years ago.

How swiftly life rushes on!

And in another seven years?

God knows, the lot of us Germans is miserable

enough now, and I, personally, cannot exactly complain of any preferential treatment. But when I look forward into the future, I seem to feel that we must find the way up to the light again at no very distant date.

January, 1921.

It is still winter weather; but it is almost tolerable again; the unbearably depressing isolation caused by the floating ice has been broken; the post has arrived, and we are once again a part of the world. Spring tides and hurricanes are things which—considering the moods of the climate here—are best regarded as harmless excesses not to be noticed overmuch.

Almost as soon as we were " ice-free," Zobel left, disguised like an Arctic explorer.

I myself was over in Doorn again for a few days to make up for not being there at Christmas.

Now, those quiet hours with my mother and the long talks with my father belong to the past, and only the great winter silence lies before me.

Those talks with my father! There is hardly a problem of our past which did not crop up in the course of them. And, whenever I am with him and see how he worries himself to trace the road of our destiny, when I recognize that, with all our misfortunes, he sought always to do the best for the realm and the people entrusted to him, I feel the bitter injustice done him by a great section of our people in not allowing anything in his life's work to be of any value, in burying under the ruins of an unsuccessful peace policy all that was great and good and imperishable in the thirty years of my father's reign.

I believe myself to be fairly free from blindness to the mistakes of the throne in Germany during recent decades; and possibly these sheets bear testimony,

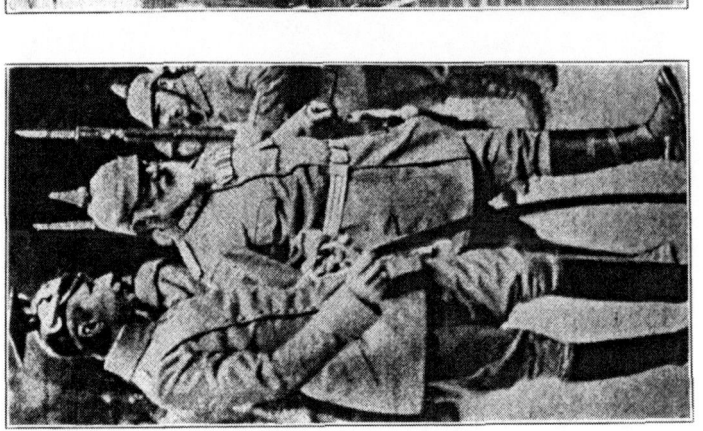

The King of Bavaria. The King of Wurtemburg. The King of Saxony.
THREE KINGS VISIT THE CROWN PRINCE AT HIS HEAD-QUARTERS IN FRANCE.

here and there, to my wish to see clearly and to speak frankly of what I see. That in my opinion much that, at the present time, is generally attributed to the Kaiser should rather be charged to the unhappy influence of unsuitable advisers has been stated already. With all that, however, these memoirs would give a one-sided idea of my views concerning the activities of my father, if they did not expressly record my full recognition of the great personal share taken by him in the prosperous development of the empire.

His services to the empire began when he was still a prince. In the years following the war of 1870–1, the army remained at a standstill for a long time. The officers were, in part, too old, but people did not care to pension off men who had done such excellent work in the war, and a very cautious attitude was adopted towards innovations as a whole. The well-tried principles on which the war with France had been won were to be kept, as far as possible, intact. It was, therefore, greatly to his credit that the young Prince William recognized the perils inherent in this stagnation. He used the whole force of his personality to effect an up-to-date reorganization of our army training, an effort which cost him many a severe conflict. I remember that my father, much to the astonishment of the great generals, caused the heavy artillery of the fortress of Spandau to take part in the manœuvres of the Potsdam garrison, a thing till then quite unknown. In further extension of this idea he subsequently, as Kaiser, took a large share in fostering the development of our heavy artillery. The development of our engineer troops is also largely due to his personal initiative. He also devoted himself energetically to the cultivation of a patriotic, self-sacrificing spirit in the army, and, wherever he could, he advocated the maintenance of traditions and the esprit de corps of the various troops.

The creation of our navy I regard as solely attributable to my father; in this he took the great step into the world which was essential for Germany if she were to become a World Power and not remain merely a Continental one. But we owe to him not only our navy; he likewise took an active share in the development of our mercantile fleet.

In the sphere of labour legislation he played a leading part; and there is a touch of the tragic in the fact that it was the Labour Party who finally brought about his fall, although for their sake he had gone through the first great conflicts of his reign and caused the Socialist Act to be quashed.

CHAPTER VI

THE GREAT COLLAPSE

FOR the great Rheims offensive in the month of July, 1918, the General Higher Command had brought together all our disposable forces, reserving only some fresh divisions and heavy artillery with the Prince Rupprecht Army Group for the Hagen attack. When this move upon Rheims failed, I no longer entertained any doubt that matters at the front as well as affairs at home were drifting towards the final catastrophe—a catastrophe which was inevitable unless, at this eleventh hour, great decisions were formed and energetically carried out. My Chief of Staff, Count von der Schulenburg, fully shared my views, and accordingly after the enemy's great offensive of Villers-Cotterets, we left no means untried to persuade the General Higher Command to adopt two measures above all; namely, the placing of affairs at the front and affairs at home on a sounder basis.

In consideration of our extremely difficult military situation, we regarded it as requisite that the entire front should be immediately withdrawn to the Antwerp-Meuse position. This would have brought with it a whole series of advantages. In the first place we should have moved far enough from the enemy to give our severely fatigued and morally depressed troops time to rest and recuperate. Moreover, the entire front would have been considerably shortened; and the naturally strong formation of the Meuse front in the Ardennes would have afforded us, even with relatively weak forces, a strong line of resistance. In this way a saving of reserves could be effected. The weak spots of the front naturally remained the right wing in Belgium and the left at Verdun.

Our views of the situation were laid before the Higher Command in a report in which we stated that everything now depended upon withstanding the attacks of the enemy until the wet weather set in, which would be about the end of November. If we had insufficient forces to hold the long front lines, we ought to make a timely withdrawal to a shorter one. It was immaterial where we halted; the important point was to keep our army unbeaten and in fighting condition. Our left wing between Sedan and the Vosges could not retire, and must therefore be strengthened with reserves.

The Higher Command replied that they could, at most, decide to withdraw to the starting-point of the spring advance of 1918. They adopted the view—in itself perfectly correct—that, in the first place, a further retirement would be an admission of our weakness, which would lead to the most undesirable political deductions on the part of the enemy; secondly, that our railways would not permit us to evacuate rapidly the extensive war zone beyond the Antwerp-Meuse position, so that immense quantities of munitions and stores would fall into the hands of the enemy; thirdly, that the Antwerp-Meuse line would form an unfavourable permanent position, since the railways, having no lateral communications, would render the transport of troops behind the front and from one wing to another cumbrous and slow.

We, however, were of opinion that a retirement was unavoidable and that it would be better to withdraw

THE GREAT COLLAPSE

while the troops were capable of fighting than to wait till they were utterly exhausted. Political considerations, we thought, ought to yield to the military necessity of retaining an army capable of showing fight. The loss of material and the unfavourable railway facilities could not be helped; we should have to fall back; and it would be better to do so in time.

At home we wanted energetic, inexorable and thorough leadership—dictatorship, suppression of all revolutionary attempts, exemplary punishment of deserters and shirkers, militarization of the munition works, etc., etc., expulsion of doubtful foreigners, and so on.

But our proposals and warnings had no effect; we knew, therefore, what was coming.

We soon saw ourselves in the midst of the *debâcle*; we had to watch with open eyes the inevitable catastrophe approaching nearer and nearer, day by day, ever faster and ever more insatiable.

When I look back and compare the past, that time is the saddest of my whole life—sadder even than the critical months at Verdun or the deeply painful days, weeks and months that followed the final catastrophe.

With an anxious heart I entered every morning the office of the Army Group; I was always prepared for bad news and received it only too often. The drives to the front, which had previously been a pleasure and recreation for me, were now filled with bitterness. The staff officers' brows were furrowed with care. The troops, though still almost everywhere perfect in discipline and demeanour—willing, friendly and cheerful in their salutes—were worn to death. My heart turned within me when I beheld their hollow cheeks, their lean and weary figures, their tattered and dirty uniforms; one would fain have said : " Go home, comrade, have a good long sleep, have a good hearty meal—you've done enough," when these brave fellows used to pull themselves together smartly on my addressing them or shaking hands with them. And the pity of it all was, I could not help them; these tired and worn-out men were the last remnants of our strength, they would have to be worked remorselessly if we were to avoid a catastrophe and obtain a peace at all bearable for Germany.

So, from day to day, I had to look on while the old fighting value of my bravest division dwindled away, while vigour and confidence were bled whiter and whiter in the incessant and arduous battles. As things stood, no rest could be allowed to the war-worn troops, or at most only a day now and then. Instead of a drastic shortening of the front, we had still the old extent to cover with our anæmic and decimated divisions. It soon became quite impossible to do so at all adequately. Clamours for relief and rest were made to me, which I found myself unable to grant. Reinforcements stopped almost completely; and the few grouplets that dribbled out to us were only of inferior value. They consisted mostly of old and worn-out soldiers sent back to the front again; often they were gleaned from the hospitals in a half-convalescent condition; often they were half-grown lads with no proper training and no sort of discipline. The majority of them were of a refractory and unruly disposition—an outcome of the agitators' work at home and of the feebleness of the Government, who did nothing to counteract these agitators and their revolutionary intrigues.

That the source of disintegration lay at home and that thence there flowed to the front an ever-renewed and poisonous stream of agitatory, mutinous and rebellious elements no unprejudiced observer could question. This conviction is not, by any means, based solely upon the views of military circles at the front;

during my journeys on furlough and otherwise, I saw for myself behind the lines and at home what was going on.

From these personal observations I became convinced that this movement had its source in the inadequate feeding and care given to the people at home; so that, especially in the last year and a half of the war, the revolutionary tendencies grew so rank that they smothered every sounder current of feeling. And I put the blame less upon the people, who hungered and pinched at home for their fatherland, than upon those who were called to provide for something better, to see that things were more equitably distributed and with an energy that showed no respect of persons. Finally, I blame those men at the head of affairs who, when they saw the failure of existing powers, omitted to create a post and appoint an official who, with unlimited powers and freed from all the hindrances and encumbrances of the old officialdom, should enforce the necessary measures with the authority of a dictator.

That, during the menacing years of crisis, we did nothing to make economic provision for the war, and that we were therefore quite unprepared in an economic sense, I have stated above in discussing the years preceding the catastrophe of 1914. The error of that period was immensely magnified during the war by lack of foresight and by clinging to a system which maintained itself by one makeshift after another. The decisions and schemes adopted were not precautionary; they came merely in reply to the incessant knocks of necessity. A characteristic example is the mania for commandeering that took possession of the State just when there was hardly anything left to seize, and which was doomed to failure also owing to a widespread corruption not infrequently winked at and encouraged.

All this does not, by any means, exonerate the Radicalism of the Left or its filibustering followers, whose policy was to draw party advantage and to profiteer by the war, from an inexpiable share of responsibility for our miserable collapse after four years' heroic fighting. It only postulates that minds cannot be enmeshed until circumstances have crippled their energy and rendered them open to the specious arguments of the agitator; it only postulates that those who ought to have nourished the people with spiritual and bodily food, who ought to have assured its will to victory and its patriotic spirit in a sound body—that these very men unfortunately helped to pave the way for its downfall.

Even as early as the beginning of the year 1917, I received, from conversations with many simple people in Berlin, the impression that weariness of the war was already very great. I also saw a great and a menacing change in the streets of Berlin. Their characteristic feature had gone: the contented face of the middle-class man had vanished; the honest, hard-working bourgeoisie, the clerk and his wife and children, slunk through the streets, hollow-eyed, lantern-jawed, pale-faced and clad in threadbare clothing that had become much too wide for their shrunken limbs. Side by side with them jostled the puffed-up profiteer and all the other rogues of like kidney.

It goes without saying that these contrasts aroused dissatisfaction and bitterness in the hearts of those who suffered, and whose faith in the justice and fairness of the authorities was severely shaken. Nevertheless, no steps were taken to do away with the evil; in the fullest sense of the saying, whoever wished to profiteer profiteered—profiteered in state contracts, in essential victuals, in raw materials, in party gains for the benefit of the " International."

THE CROWN PRINCE IN PRE-WAR DAYS.

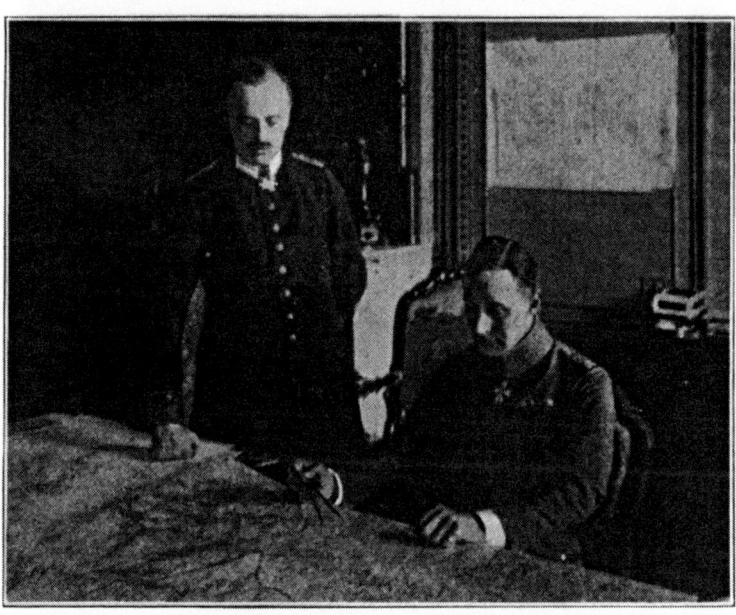
THE CROWN PRINCE AT HEAD-QUARTERS.
AT WORK WITH HIS CHIEF OF STAFF (COL. COUNT VON DER SCHULENBURG).

The effects of all this were severely felt, both behind the lines and at the front. Every bitter letter from home carried the bacillus; every soldier returning from furlough who had come into touch with these things and told his impressions to his over-taxed comrades, helped to spread the disease; and it was aggravated by every refractory young rascal who had grown up without a father's care and whom the home authorities shunted to the front because they could not manage him themselves.

The sources from which the losses of the troops were made good were the deputy general commands at home. Their enormous significance was not sufficiently recognized, nor their value properly appreciated in selecting the individuals who were to replace the commanding Generals and Chief of Staff. From the outset, old men were appointed—often worthy and deserving soldiers who enthusiastically placed their services at the disposal of their country, but who had no proper estimate of the energies and capacities left to them. People wished not to be ungrateful, wished to provide a sphere of activity for these willing patriots in which they could do no harm; it also gave an opportunity of liberating fresher forces for the front. All this may have been very well, so long as we could reckon with a short war and with the stability of home affairs as they stood in 1914; but it ought to have been drastically modified to fit in with new ideas, when the duration of the war could no longer be estimated even approximately, when it became necessary to consider carefully the possibility of new or recurrent movements that might exercise a destructive influence upon the unanimity that had originally been so reassuring. No such thorough adaptation to suit the altered circumstances ever took place. Whoever once occupied a deputy's post occupied it permanently; or if a post became vacant through death or because the substitute was really too utterly incapable, it was filled again from the ranks of those who had failed at the front or who, through illness or wounds, were now considered fit only for home service. A home post! What harm can the man do there? The man who was no longer a man, whose energies were used up, who knew nothing of the war, or who, if he had been to the front, had, in nearly every case, returned embittered to regard home service as a *buenretiro* after labours accomplished —this type of man caused us untold injury. Just in the last years of the war, all the human material that we called up and combed out ought to have passed through the strongest and firmest hands before being incorporated at the front. These men, who were for the most part worm-eaten by revolutionary ideas or tainted with pacifist notions, ought to have been trained by vigorous educative work into disciplined men worthy of their comrades at the front. With a few nice phrases such as were common at the meetings of " warriors' societies " or at memorial festivities, no such educative work could be performed. And what the homeland failed to do could never be done afterwards by instruction in patriotism, were it never so well meant. To my mind, the idea of instilling the patriotism they lacked into the men within hearing of the thunder of the guns was naïve in the extreme. We received as supplementary drafts men who had set out with the determination to hold up their hands at the very first opportunity. But it was the mistaken method of filling the responsible positions in the deputy commands that avenged itself most terribly. In the summer and early autumn of 1918, the spreading demoralization became more and more noticeable in the occupied territory. The order that originally existed behind the lines was visibly deteriorating. In the larger camps on the lines of communication, thousands of straggling shirkers and men on leave wandered about; some of them regarded every day that they could keep away from their units as a boon from heaven; some of them were totally unable to join their regiments on account of the overburdening of the railways. I remember at the time a journey to the front which took me through Hirson Junction. It was just dinner-time for men going on leave and stragglers, who stood around by the hundred. I mingled with the crowd and talked to many of the men. What I heard was saddening indeed. Most of them were sick and tired of the war and scarcely made an effort to hide their disinclination to rejoin their units. Nor were they all rascals; there was many a face there which showed that the nerves had given way, that energy was gone, that the primitive and unchecked impulse of self-preservation had got the mastery over all recognition of the necessity for holding out or resisting. Of course among the stragglers in Hirson there were also a number of fine fellows who maintained their courage and bearing. To meet this demoralization of forces which might have been concentrated into a valuable help for our daily increasing needs, nothing or next to nothing was attempted. New comprehensive and thorough measures were imperative here, and they should have been entrusted to the Higher Command to enforce. Within the sphere of our Army Group, we naturally did everything that lay in our power to introduce some sort of order into the chaos, but we received very scanty support in our efforts. The discipline behind the lines slackened ominously. This I could perceive in Charleville, the head-quarters of the Army Group. Men had constantly to be taken to task on account of their slack bearing and their failure to salute. Men returned from leave who had previously performed their duties in an exemplary manner were inclined to insubordination and mutiny. The younger supplementary drafts were, at best, utterly wanting in enthusiasm, and generally showed an absolutely frivolous conception of patriotism, duty and fidelity—things which, for a soldier, should be sacred matters. Unfortunately, the highest authorities resolved upon no energetic or exemplary measures in regard to these dangerous phenomena. The behaviour of the French population was, it is true, correct; but they did not disguise their delight at our obvious decline.

* * * * *

By the end of September, events came fast and furious. It was like a vast conflagration that had long smouldered in secret, and that, suddenly getting air, now burst into flame in innumerable places. Fire everywhere: here in the west and in the south-east and at home. The collapse of Bulgaria was the first visible sign. Bad tidings had arrived from the Balkan front on September 26. They reached us while our own Army Group was itself engaged in a severe defensive battle against heavy attacks to the west of the Aisne and on both sides of the Argonne from east of Rheims up to the Meuse, a battle which, despite all our heroic resistance, ended in our having to yield ground to the vastly superior masses of the enemy with their armoured tanks. The Bulgarians, under the heavy pressure of the united forces of the Entente on the Macedonian front, had retired on a wide line. They had lost a great number of prisoners and a large quantity of material; and, as we gathered from the brief telegrams and telephone messages, Malmoff, the

Bulgarian Prime Minister, believed that he could only meet these reverses by entering upon peace negotiations with the Commander-in-Chief of the Entente armies. The situation thus created spelled serious peril for us; the elimination of Bulgaria might mean the beginning of the end for the Central Powers; the Danube lay open to the Entente forces; the invasion of Roumania and Hungary had been brought within the bounds of more immediate possibility. The news caused the Kaiser and the General Higher Command at Avesnes the greatest consternation. For the time being, the gap was stopped; the influence of the King and of the Crown Prince Boris succeeded in stemming the rout; and the General Higher Command arranged for the immediate transport to the Balkans of some Austrian divisions and of several divisions from the east to buttress the severely shaken front.

Meantime the most vehement attacks upon the entire west front from Flanders to the east of the Argonne were continued by the Entente armies with a savage determination such as had never been displayed before. We received the impression of being at the climax of the concentric hostile offensive and—though the gigantic attack might compel us to yield ground—we felt that, by summoning up all our strength for the effort, we might after all maintain our position; only that, behind this desperate effort, still lurked the agonizing question: " How long yet ? "

On September 28, I visited my brother Fritz, who, with his First Guards division, was engaged in a severe struggle with the Americans at the eastern extremity of the Argonne. I know my brother to be a very brave, intrepid and cool-headed man, and one whose care for his troops was exemplary. He was accustomed to affliction and distress; the First Guards had all the time been posted where things had been about as hot as they could be, at Ypres, in Champagne, at the Somme, the Chemin des Dames, Gorlice, the Argonne. This time I found him changed; he was filled with unutterable bitterness; he saw the end approaching, and, together with his men, fought with the courage of despair. He gave me a description of the situation which filled me with dismay. His entire division consisted of 500 rifles in the fighting zone; the staff with their dispatch carriers were fighting in the front line, rifle in hand. The artillerymen were extremely fatigued, the guns were worn out, fresh ones were scarcely to be got from the works, the rations were insufficient and bad. What was to come of it all? The American attacks were in themselves badly planned; they showed ignorance of warfare; the men advanced in columns and were mowed down by our remaining machine-guns. No great danger lay there. But their tanks pierced our thin lines—one man to every twenty metres—and fired on us from behind. Not till then did the American infantry advance. Withal the Americans had at their disposal an incredible quantity of heavy and very heavy artillery. Their preliminary bombardment greatly exceeded in intensity and heaviness anything we had known at Verdun or on the Somme. In a report I made to His Majesty at Spa, I described to him in detail the desperate condition of the First Guards; the Kaiser talked about it to Ludendorff; but no decision to relieve them was arrived at; I may admit that perhaps it could not be done, for we now needed every available man for the last struggle.

At this time, all my attention and energy were devoted to the stormy events at the front and to the troops entrusted to me. Almost daily, I was in the fighting zone; and, till far into October, I was so occupied with my duties as leader of the Army Group

THE GREAT COLLAPSE

that I was unable to follow attentively the highly important political events which were taking place, although I recognized them to be of the most serious import. Hence, while in another place I can report from personal experience and from my own judgment as to the gigantic battle in which we were engaged, I can only briefly refer to those political happenings which may be regarded more or less as matters of common knowledge. On September 30 I received from His Excellency von Berg an unexpected telephone call to Spa, where, in the General Head-quarters, important decisions of a military character touching the question of peace and the situation at home had been made or were about to be made. Since I had hitherto been carefully confined to the scope of my military duties, this order suggested that something unusual was in the air. There was no reason to hope for anything good; and the information that met me at Spa was truly startling and dismaying even to one who, like myself, had come prepared to hear bad news. I will sketch in a few lines what I learned.

Field-Marshal General von Hindenburg and General Ludendorff had conferred with the Minister for Foreign Affairs and had been informed that, in pursuance of the negotiations of August 14, efforts had been made to approach the enemy States through the mediation of neutral Powers, but that these had failed to develop into peace negotiations, nor was there any hope of success in that direction. In reply to the Foreign Office's declaration of bankruptcy, the representatives of the General Higher Command had stated that, in view of their own breakdown in the field and at home and considering the enormous superiority of the enemy forces and the gigantic efforts they were making, they saw themselves faced with the impossibility of gaining a military victory. Even though this effort on the part of the enemy appeared to be the last possible spurt before the finish, success for us could no longer give us " victory," but as had been admitted in August, could only lie in our managing to outlast the enemy's will to continue the war—in a struggle as to whether one could hold out to the last quarter of an hour. In view of the utter failure of the home departments and the question of reserves, it had to be acknowledged that the only thing possible was to hold out through the late autumn and winter in better defensive positions of our own choosing. During that period, an armistice and peace negotiations should and must be begun. The Meuse position, which my chief of staff and myself had advocated immediately after the unsuccessful Rheims offensive in July and while we could with comparative ease have disengaged ourselves from the enemy, was now to be occupied for the winter defensive.

Still more threatening was what the Secretary of State had to report about the situation at home, where the people had glided faster and faster under the control and the influence of the majority parties. According to his statements, revolution, struggling to obtain control of the State, stood, as it were, knocking at the door. Induced by the conditions arising out of the unfavourable military situation, and quite regardless of the strength or weakness of the State, the majority parties—who desired the offensive for their own ends—had made a violent attack in the principal committee of the Reichstag, upon the Imperial Chancellor, Count von Hertling.

The main accusations brought against him were :— The supremacy of the deputy commanding generals at home, the Suffrage Act, and the influence without responsibility exercised upon home politics by the Higher Command. The demands put forward were aimed frankly at parliamentary control of the Government and the shelving of the military régime. The two ways of overcoming the crisis would have been, on the one hand, for the Government to assert its authority in unequivocal fashion by acting, in the one case, with all the powers of a dictator, in the other, to submit and grant the demands of the majority parties. The Secretary of State believed it possible to disarm the revolutionary movement by granting parliamentary government on a broad national basis; hence he advocated this policy, notwithstanding the fact that circumstances at home and our position with regard to the enemy were highly unpropitious for such a re-organization of the constitution. Thus, the revolution threatening from below was to be smothered with the mantle of a revolution from above; and a fresh welding together of the disintegrating national forces was to be effected under the cry of a "Government of National Defence." I will gladly assume it to be indisputable that these responsible statesmen who advocated this policy believed in the possibility of obtaining practicable conditions by these means, and that they hoped for a certain return from the new government firm, at any rate in the domain of foreign affairs, i.e., with a view to the peace negotiations. But I must confess that I could not resist the impression that it was all a matter of fine words, that the whole thing was only a form (evil in itself and made to look attractive by auto-suggestion) under which its advocates abandoned the power in the State to their opponents of the majority parties.

His Majesty agreed to the proposals of these gentlemen. The manifold difficultues now encroaching everywhere had already reached the steps of the throne, and the Kaiser, under the pressure of these problems, seemed to be suffering from a lack of psychical stamina; he appeared unable to assume a strong and self-reliant position of authority. Consequently, in the various proposals of his military and political counsellors, he saw succour and support, at which he eagerly grasped in order to feel that the dangers were surmounted, for a moment at least.

The position of the Imperial Chancellor, Count von Hertling, whose age and infirmities rendered him physically unfit for his office, appeared so severely shaken that the Kaiser, since the Count declined to take part in the change of constitution, declared himself willing to accept the resignation that had been tendered. As successors were mentioned, first of all Prince Max of Baden and the Secretary to the Imperial Exchequer, Count Rödern ; the selection of the latter appearing the more probable.

On account of the menacing and uncertain general situation at the front and at home, the gentlemen from Berlin, as well as those of His Majesty's suite and of the General Head-quarters, were in a very serious mood. In regard to the military difficulties, it was hoped, however, that the great battle on the west front might be fought out without any severe defeat. Moreover, a hope of keeping those allies who had become unreliable was also cherished. People likewise believed themselves able, by carrying out the intended constitutional change, to effect such an alteration of the mental trend at home that, on the whole, a firm front could be shown at home and abroad.

Personally, I could not share the optimism displayed in this view of home affairs. Both by nature and by lessons learnt from history and experience, I always possessed a leaning towards the British constitutional system, and I have thought much about the possibility of its being adapted to our form of State. As I have pointed out before, I was not spared a good many rebuffs and criticisms whenever, in pre-war years, I expounded and defended my opinions on this subject. What was now to take place appeared to fall into line with my notions. Appeared to do so, though in reality it had nothing in common with them.

Only what is given willingly meets with appreciation; what is ultimately extorted and claimed as a right, after it has been withheld time and again, has no value as a gift. To give up a thing voluntarily at the right moment and with discernment is manly and, if the word may be allowed, regal; but it is just as manly and regal to refuse what is sought to be levied as blackmail, as the question of a trial of strength in the hour of a country's bitterest need when it is struggling for existence. A liberal, voluntary and timely reconstruction of our constitution would have revealed the strength of the Crown; it would have disarmed the opposition and brought it back to a sense of duty. But for the Crown to yield to violent claims, backed by threats of revolution, was to display signs of helplessness and feebleness which could only increase the cupidity of the covetous within the country and without. At the moment when the flood was at hand, a dyke was razed, because it was believed possible to assuage and calm the approaching billows by removing the obstruction. Madness! One merely gave up everything that lay behind the dyke; the Spa decisions unconditionally abandoned the powers of the State to the parties of the extreme left who were "going the whole hog," aiming at revolution. Before the storm, one should have been strong and shown one's strength. But the rigid home programme of August 14, the programme of thoroughness, order, strictness, energy, the programme of no longer closing one's eyes, the programme which, in the days of the first sinister omens, had been demanded by Ludendorff as a *conditio sine qua non* and which had been promised by the Chancellor—that programme had never been carried out. Nothing had been done since then. Now, when the storm was howling, it was too late to strengthen the rotten bulwarks, to repair the neglected dykes. No dyke captain or dictator, were he ever so talented, were he the immortal dyke captain von Schönhausen himself, could undo or retrieve in a few hours the sins and the negligences of many years. That there was no longer a firm hand in the country, that the Government had for years not led, but suffered things to go as they pleased, brought about consequences that decided the question of supremacy. And on that day, men whose final wisdom it was to lay upon other shoulders the responsibility for the results of their own incapacity, abandoned monarchy, bowing to the democratic demands of our enemies and to threatening internationalism of every shade. As I have already said, His Excellency von Hintze, the Secretary of State for Foreign Affairs, took upon himself to report upon the situation in the interior as well, and to recommend as the best solution the "revolution from above," which, as things stood, was nothing but "surrender at discretion." Strange that this man, whose praiseworthy past entitled him to be held worthy and to be trusted, and who, as Kühlmann's successor, might have accomplished so much—strange that this man should have chosen this course.

In truth and honour, it must be said that what I have just written is, in part, the outcome of subsequent consideration and discernment. During the short hours of that conference such a pressure of exciting news was thrust upon me, and I was so anxious to get back to the troops and the battle from which I had been called, that I only grasped the general outline of affairs. Nor, indeed, was I asked for my opinion on all those seething problems, or on all that, in the main, was already unalterably fixed by determinations arising out of the agony of the moment. It was almost a wonder that people had remembered that the Commander-in-Chief of the army was also the Crown Prince of Germany and of Prussia. Without responsibility, without rights, but nevertheless. . . . And so I was summoned, and while a thousand voices called me away to the post of my soldier's duties, I had to look on at events irresistibly marching on to produce the great débâcle.

Immediately upon the conclusion of the conference, the Kaiser left for home; and the Field-Marshal General followed him on October 1, as he himself said, to be near His Majesty in those days of gravest decision, to give information to the Government now forming and to strengthen its confidence.

On October 2, indications accumulated that, in spite of the original doubts, Prince Max of Baden would be selected as Imperial Chancellor, his origin and personality affording a guarantee, as it was then thought, that the interests of the Crown would be safeguarded in the reorganization of home politics which appeared to have become necessary. In the preliminary negotiations, the Prince seemed to have adopted unreservedly the official programme of the majority parties.

February, 1921.

My Army Group was still struggling in the severest of defensive actions, when I learned of the actual appointment of Prince Max of Baden on October 1. A new Government had been formed, containing several social-democratic members. This innovation signified, in the eyes of the world, a reversal of the home policy of the empire, a change of system tending towards democracy and parliamentary government. Whether that which, to some extent, had been produced under the pressure of a very serious foreign situation would really prove capable of welding the nation together remained to be seen.

On October 4, my Army Group was again engaged in a very severe defensive action, the enemy having commenced a general attack along the entire western front. The battle raged bitterly on the ridge and the slopes of the Chemin des Dames between the Ailette and the Aisne, in Champagne, on both sides of the road leading northwards from Somme-Py, between the Argonne and the Meuse, to the east of the Aisne and on both sides of the Montfaucon-Bauthéville road. Since September 26, we had located no fewer than thirty-seven attacking divisions. And they had artillery, tanks and airmen in apparently inexhaustible numbers. On the whole, our older troops behaved magnificently and fought with undiminished tenacity. And yet we now suffered losses in men and material such as we had formerly never known. Oftener and oftener did individual divisions now fail us—partly from exhaustion, but also (and that was the most serious point) on account of the troops being contaminated by international and pacifist ideas. Troops that advanced courageously were howled at as " war-prolongers " and " blacklegs." Distrust of their comrades' reliability caused demoralization in the resisting powers of the whole body; failure on the part of certain contaminated troops led to our flank being turned and to the capture of groups that were fighting honestly; frequently, therefore, such unreliable troops had to be eliminated and the gaps filled with trustworthy but overfatigued divisions. And so I had to use up my best capital, although I fully realized what it meant. And yet, even now, I could weep when I think of the unbroken spirit of self-sacrifice shown by the trusty, brave and well-tried troops who faithfully performed to the last their severe duty. They upheld, through all that misery, our best traditions.

On that 4th of October, I drove over to Avesnes for a conference with Lieutenant-General von Boehn and his General Staff; from there I went on to Mons and discussed the military situation at length with the Crown Prince of Bavaria and his Chief of General Staff, His Excellency von Kuhl. We were unanimously of opinion that, in the present conditions, we could not continue to maintain the contested positions on our war-worn front in the face of continuous attacks by an enemy with superior forces at his command. We lacked the troops requisite for counter-attacking and for providing our soldiers with the necessary repose. Consequently, it appeared to us essential to relinquish further territory and, while covering our withdrawal, to take up positions farther back, and thus, by shortening our front, to obtain the reserves essential for a continuation of the battle, whose duration it was not possible to determine.

In the following night—while my brave divisions, ragged and tattered as they were, were retiring step by step and defending themselves as they went—Berlin dispatched to the President of the North American Republic, via Switzerland, the offer which suggested a "just peace," based in essence upon the basic principles put forward by Wilson—an offer which was coupled with a disastrous request for the granting of an armistice.

The struggle continued, and there was no end to the battle visible. Our troops were now opposed to enormously superior odds, both in men and material. They withstood them; they foiled attacks, and evacuated ground; they closed up to form a new front and offered fresh resistance. Almost daily I was at the front and saw and spoke to the men. They behaved heroically in the unequal combat, and faithfully fulfilled their duty to the death. He lies who asserts that the fighting spirit of the front was broken. It was stronger than the shattered and exhausted bodies of the men. The men grumbled whenever they had a moment's time to grumble, just as every genuine German grumbles; but, when it came to the point, they were ever ready again.

And these incessant battles had a curious result. They effected a kind of self-purification of the troops. Whatever was foul and corrupt filtered through into captivity with the enemy; what remained to us was the healthy kernel. All that these German warriors, emaciated and miserably cared for, over-fatigued and pursued by death in a thousand forms, could possibly give, that they gave. Gratefully my thoughts fly back to them—to those whose bodies lie where we left them, and to those living ones now scattered in German cities and German villages, who follow the plough, who stand at the anvil, who sit at their desks, to all who are peacefully labouring again in the homeland.

Still the enemy drove forward; every day brought a big attack; the air trembled with bombardments, and with unceasing concussions, roarings, long bursts of rolling thunder, the rattling peals never paused again.

On the night of the 5th, the left wing of the First Army had retired behind Suippes; in order to get into touch again with the retreating Seventh Army, it had to leave the salient of the Rheims front and to withdraw its right wing as far as Condé. On October 10, the Eighteenth Army, which at that time had also been ranged under the Army Group, retired, fighting hard, to the Hermann line, as yet little more than marked out.

And while all my thoughts were concentrated upon

the battle and upon the German soldiers entrusted to me, there reached me from home news that sounded distant and strange: the wording of our Peace Note to President Wilson; the brusque refusal voiced by the Paris press; the reply that evaded replying and demanded our consent to evacuate all occupied territory as a condition of an armistice. There was talk of consultations among the leading statesmen, of the formation by the Higher Command of an armistice commission under the expert, General von Guendell. The War Minister, von Stein, resigned his office and was replaced by General Scheüch.

We fought. The battle began to die down slowly at the end of the second week during which it had raged. Both sides were completely exhausted. We had yielded ground under the enormous pressure, but we were still standing; and nowhere had the enemy broken through. On the 10th, the Third Army stood in the new Brunhilde position from St. Germainmont on the north bank of the Aisne, passing through Bethel to the east of Vouziers and west of Grandpré. Gallwitz was fighting the Americans in the area between Sivry and the Forest of Haumont. By the 12th, the First Army had occupied, according to plan, the Gudrun-Brunhilde position, and the Seventh Army had retired to the Hunding position behind the Oise-Serre sector. A review of the military situation showed that the threatened collapse of the west front had been prevented by the transfer of the lines of resistance to stronger and narrower sectors. Despite the seriousness of the situation, we stood for the moment fairly secure; and, while the enemy was preparing for fresh concentration and new offensives, we could ourselves be recuperating and getting ready for defence—and such a breathing-space was more than necessary to the over-fatigued and over-taxed troops. There remained, therefore, in my opinion, the faint hope that the peace efforts now being undertaken might lead, before the winter began, to a conclusion of the war that would be honourable for Germany by reason of its being a righteous peace of reconciliation. Failing this, we could—again, according to my personal views—reckon with a possibility of holding out till the spring of 1919 at the furthest.

* * * * *

On October 12, in reply to the inquiry of President Wilson, Berlin gave a binding acceptance of the conditions drawn up by him and also signified that we were prepared to evacuate the occupied areas on certain conditions.

In all the news from the other side I seemed dimly to discover, as through a veil, two minds struggling for mastery. There was Wilson, who wanted to establish his Fourteen Points; there was Foch, who knew only one aim—our annihilation. Which would win? The pair were unequally matched—the sprinter Wilson and Foch the stayer. If things were quickly settled, Wilson's chances were good; if the negotiations were protracted, time was in Foch's favour. Every day's delay in arriving at an understanding was a gain to him; it allowed the dry-rot in the homeland to spread; it enfeebled and wasted the front, which was mainly buttressed upon auxiliary and defensive positions.

The 13th brought me news that caused me great uneasiness on my father's account. Developments in home politics had led to the resignation of His Excellency von Berg, the excellent and well-tried *Chef du Cabinet Militaire.* His departure removed from the permanent inner circle of the Kaiser a man who, by virtue of his old youthful friendship and his disregard of mere courtly conventions, was able, in loyal candour and simplicity, to show the Kaiser things as they really were.

On the 15th, formidable attacks were launched afresh against the Army Group of Crown Prince Rupprecht, against me and against Gallwitz. The enemy had pushed up to our new front and made a terrific onslaught. Loss of ground here and there. The troops were nearly played out. Next day, Lille fell. Things were worst with the Crown Prince of Bavaria. Losses were sustained wherever the enemy attacked. Now that they had heard something of a possible armistice and approaching negotiations, it was as though our people could no longer find their full inner strength to fight. Also as though, here and there, they no longer wanted to. But where was the dividing line between could and would with these men, who had a thousand times bravely risked their lives for their country, and whose heads were befogged by hunger, pain and privation? Does that one last failure make a coward of the man who has a hundred times shown himself a hero? No! Only it deprives him of one thing—the prize for which he has risked his life a hundred times.

Once more—while the new Government is making a quick change towards democracy and turning the Imperial constitution topsy-turvy—a note from President Wilson. It is in a new tone—implacable and arrogant, it imposes conditions which constitute an interference in Germany's internal affairs. It voices clearly the spirit of Foch, which threatens to overpower Wilson—the spirit of Foch, who brags of the military results of the last few days, who desires postponement and delay in order that the disaster that has swooped upon the German people and the German army may rage more madly than ever. I cannot refrain from quoting at this point a page from my diary that describes the position as I saw it at the time :—

"There is at the moment a marked contrast between Wilson and Foch. Wilson desires a peace by justice, reconciliation and understanding. Foch wants the complete humiliation of Germany and the gratification of French vanity.

"Every manifestation of firmness on the German front and in the German diplomatic attitude strengthens Wilson's position; every sign of military or political weakness strengthens Foch.

"Wilson demands surrender on two points only :—
1. Submarine warfare : no more passenger ships to be sunk.
2. The democratization of Germany. (No deposition of the Kaiser; only constitutional monarchy; position of the Crown as in England.)

"A military humiliation of Germany is not aimed at by Wilson. Foch, on the other hand, wants, with every means in his power, to bring about a complete military capitulation and humiliation (gratification of French revenge). Which of the two will get the upper hand depends solely and simply upon Germany. If the front holds out and we preserve a dignified diplomatic attitude, Wilson will win. Yielding to Foch means the destruction of Germany and the miscarriage of every prospect of an endurable peace.

"England's position is an intermediate one. The main difficulty in the peace movement is France.

"Attainment of a peace by understanding is rendered much more difficult for Wilson by the fact that our democratization and the peace steps have come at the same moment. This is regarded as a sign of weakness, and it strengthens Foch's position. If we want a peace of justice, we must put the brake on everywhere—especially in our hankering for peace and an armistice. Moreover, we must do everything possible to hold the front and to direct the further democratization along calmer, or shall we say more reasonably convincing, lines."

What was written above about Wilson was, at the moment for which it was intended, perhaps quite correct; but it was speedily no longer so. Still, I could believe even now that this self-complaisant theorist wanted, at first, to settle matters justly and conscientiously—till a stronger and more cunning man caught him and, with ironic superiority, harnessed him to his own chariot.

On October 17, Ostend, Bruges and Tournay were given up by the Army Group of my brave cousin, Rupprecht; on the nineteenth, the enemy settled down on both sides of Vouziers on the east bank of the Aisne and began preparations for further attacks.

From home there arrives news of feverish excitement among the people. Some are depressed and despairing; others are filled with the hope of a reasonable settlement. And then rumours of an approaching abdication of the Kaiser, of an election of the House of Wittelsbach in place of the Hohenzollerns, of a regency of Prince Max of Baden.

Fighting continues; we hold out fairly well. Any one who can keep on his legs is put in the ranks; for it is a question of the possibility of an armistice, of peace. The General Higher Command emphatically warns the leaders that, considering the diplomatic negotiations in progress, a further retreat might have the most serious influence upon events.

We must, therefore, hold tight to the Hermann and the Gudrun positions! Good God! What have these positions to offer? They are incomplete and, in many places, only marked out!

And yet the men who for four years have given their best, prove themselves now, in these days of blackest distress, to be the finest, the trustiest soldiers in the world! They hold this front!

On the 21st, we learn the terms of the Government's reply to Wilson. Everything has been done to meet his wishes. Surely, on this basis, he can find ways and means to conclude an armistice and to set peace negotiations on foot. Will he indeed do so? Will he still do so? More days pass during which thousands of Germans and men of all nations are mowed down, during which the gentlemen at the green-baize table take their time, during which our position at the front does not improve. The voice of Wilson's note of the 24th, that arrogant and haughty voice, was the voice of Marshal Foch—or the voice of a Wilson who had sunk to be the puppet of the French wirepuller and now equalled his master in hawking and spitting.

Once more, in those gruesome, gloomy days, in which I saw my poor battered divisions sacrificing all that was left of them, my heart was to be cheered by my brave fellows. It was on October 25 I motored to the front to convince myself of the condition of some of my divisions in the severe fighting. After visiting the Divisional Staffs of the 50th Infantry and the 4th Guards, I proceeded to a height from which I hoped to get a sight of the fighting lines.

In a green valley in front of the village of Seraincourt, I met the sectional reserves that were about to march into the fight. They consisted of the regiments of the First Infantry Division, and included my Crown Prince Regiment. When the troops caught sight of my car, I was at once surrounded by a throng of waving and cheering men. All of them betrayed only too clearly the effects of the heavy fighting of the last few months. Their uniforms were tattered, and their stripes and badges scarcely visible; their faces were often shockingly haggard; and yet their eyes flashed and their bearing was proud and confident. They knew that I trusted them and that they had never disappointed me. Pride in the deeds of their division inspired them. I spoke with a good many, pressed their hands; men who had distinguished themselves in the recent battles I decorated with the cross. Then I distributed among them my small store of chocolate and cigarettes. And so, in all the bitterness of those days, a delightful and never-to-be-forgotten hour was spent in the circle of my veteran front troops.

Meantime, the French had got the village that lay before us under heavy fire, and their artillery now began to sweep the meadows. I ordered the battalions to take open order; and, as I drove away, loud hurrahs were hurled after me from the throats of my beloved " field-greys "; on all sides there was waving of caps and rifles. Without shame, I confess that the cheers, the shouts, the waving brought tears into my eyes; for I knew how hard and how desperate was the entire situation.

My Grenadiers at Seraincourt! They were the last troops I saw march to battle with flashing eyes and volleying hurrahs. Dear, dear, trusty lads, each one of whom my memory gratefully salutes from this island of mine. A few hours later on arriving at the Army Group quarters, I stood again in that other world of anguish and anxiety; fresh tidings of a grave and doubtful character awaited me from home.

Next day, October 26, I received by telephone news of Ludendorff's resignation. In connection with the well-known incident of the Higher Command's telegram to the troops on October 24, he had fallen a victim to Prince Max of Baden's Cabinet question. I knew at once that this meant the end of things. I was informed that it was intended to appoint General Gröner as his successor. I rang up the Field-Marshal General. With a clear understanding of all it meant, I urgently implored him to reconsider his purpose and begged him not to choose this man in whom there was no trace of the spirit that was now our only hope of salvation. The Field-Marshal General, who doubtless felt constrained to comply with the views of the Imperial Government, was of a different opinion, and next day General Gröner was appointed First Quartermaster-General.

* * * * *

On October 28, my adjutant, Müller, returned from an official journey to the homeland. He brought the first evil news of mutiny in the navy. From his report, it appeared evident that the revolution was already menacingly at hand in Germany; but that apparently nothing was being done at the moment to suppress the rising movement. With a clear appreciation of the position, Müller proposed the posting of some reliable divisions behind the Army Group as soon as possible so that these troops might be ready at hand if necessity arose for their employment. This suggestion was unfortunately not considered further; our attention was all too deeply engaged at the front and riveted, as in duty bound, on the troops under our care.

From November 4 onwards, my four armies along their entire front, retreated towards the Antwerp-Meuse position, fighting hard as they retired and carrying out everything in perfect order and absolutely according to plan.

At this time, General Gröner, the new First Quarter-

IN THE TRENCHES AT LA FÈRE: A REPORT FROM GEN. VON GONTAR, 25/3/18.

THE CROWN PRINCE IN THE MIDST OF A CONVOY OF WOUNDED, ST. QUENTIN, 1918.

THE GREAT COLLAPSE

master General, paid us a visit. The chiefs of my four armies reported upon the situation of their various fronts. All of them laid stress on the overstrained condition of their troops and the entire lack of fresh reserves. But they were quite confident that the retreat to the Antwerp-Meuse position would be accomplished successfully and that the position would be held.

Afterwards my own chief of staff made a final report, two points of which I recall. They were definite demands couched in the plainest terms. The one was that the discussion of the Kaiser's position at home and in the press must cease, since the troops were quite incapable of bearing this burden as well as everything else. The other demand was that the General Higher Command must not issue orders which they themselves did not believe could be carried out; if, for instance, the retention of a position was ordered, the troops must be put in condition to hold it; confidence in the leadership was shaken by commands which the front was unable to obey because, in the existing circumstances, it was impossible to carry them into effect.

On November 5, the Higher Command of the Army Group shifted its quarters from Charleville to Waulsort, about 50 kilometres further north. This little place lies half-way between Givet and Dinant in a ragged rock-girt valley, which, at the time of our arrival, was filled with a thick clammy fog—sombre and depressing. I lodged with a Belgian, Count de Jonghe, a nobleman of the most agreeable tactfulness. In a long talk during the course of the evening, he summed up his views on the causes of our breakdown, which was now patent to the inhabitants. Germany, he said, had committed two grievious mistakes: she ought to have made peace in the autumn of 1914; if she then failed to obtain it, she ought to have appointed a civil dictator with unrestricted powers, which would have ensured the preservation of order at home.

On the same evening, Major von Bock, the first general staff officer of the Army Group, told me that he had been insulted in the open streets by a Landsturm soldier from the lines of communication. Two days later I made my first personal acquaintance with the revolution. I was driving with my orderly officer, Zobeltitz, along the Meuse road from Waulsort to Givet to visit once again the troops who were to hold the Meuse line. A few kilometres from Waulsort, just as we reached a spot where the railway runs close beside the high-road, we saw a leave-train which had halted and was flying the red flag. Immediately afterwards, from the open or broken windows my ears were greeted with the stupid cries of " Lights out! Knives out! " which formed a sort of catchword and cry for all the hooligans and malcontents of that period.

I stopped my car and, accompanied by Zobeltitz, walked up to the train. I ordered the men to alight, which they did at once. There may have been five or six hundred of them—a rather villainous-looking crowd, mostly Bavarians from Flanders. In front of me stood a very lamp-post of a Bavarian sergeant. With his hands thrust deep into his trousers pockets and displaying altogether a most provocative air, he was the very picture of insubordination. I rated him and told him to assume at once a more becoming deportment, such as was proper to a German soldier. The effect was instantaneous. The men began to press towards us, and I addressed them in urgent tones, endeavouring to touch their sense of honour.

Even while I was speaking, I could see that I had won the contest. In the end, a mere lad of perhaps seventeen, a Saxon, with a frank boyish face and decorated with the iron cross, stepped forward and said: "Herr Kronprinz, don't take it ill; they are only silly phrases; we mean nothing by them; we all like you and we know that you always look after your soldiers well. You see, we have been travelling now for three days and have had no food nor attention the whole time. No one troubles about us, and there are no officers at all with us. Don't be angry with us." A general murmur of applause followed. I gave the lad my hand, and then followed a comic close to the affair. The lad said: "We know you always carry cigarettes with you for good soldiers; we've nothing left to smoke." I gave the men what cigarettes I had, although these " good soldiers " really did not deserve them; I did it simply because I appreciated their condition, which certainly was in part responsible for their nonsense; I felt clearly that, if everything behind the lines and at home were not out of joint, these men would have followed the right path.

I narrate this episode of November 7 merely to show on what a weak footing the movement stood to a great extent; it was fanned into flame by violent agitation; and, as the above incident proves, a calm and resolute attitude did not fail of its end with the men who were, on the whole, not fundamentally bad. Unfortunately, there was a complete lack of determined action on the part of the home authorities, both civil and military. By the orders against shooting the road was paved for the revolution.

Concerning the behaviour of the troops in those days, it should be said that, despite the months of struggle that they had gone through, they carried out their retreat in perfect order and, in the main, without any important interference from the enemy, who followed hesitatingly. The prospect of the new

Meuse position, with its natural strength artificially increased, seemed to give the troops great encouragement as to the future.

One episode remains to be recorded. On the 6th, the negotiators despatched by the German Government crossed the road between La Capelle and Guise within the area of the Eighteenth Army.

CHAPTER VII

SCENES AT SPA

End of April, 1921.

IT is almost two months since I wrote the last of the above lines. As often as I have prepared myself to record those last and bitterest experiences, which have occupied my thoughts a thousand times, there has come over me a revulsion from the torture of recalling these still poignant sorrows. Moreover, other cares and other griefs have kept me away from these pages.

At the end of February I was at Doorn; on the 27th my parents celebrated the fortieth anniversary of their wedding-day. Celebrated? No, it was not a celebration. Everything in the beautiful and well-kept house was sad and depressed. My mother was confined to her couch; and her weakness permitted her only occasional hours of waking. She was so feeble that she could scarcely speak; and yet the slightest attention was received with "Thank you, my dear boy"; and then she gently stroked my hand. It made one lock one's lips hard together. The foreboding that on that day I held her in my arms for the last time never after left me.

All subsequent reports damped every hope of recovery. One could only pray: "Lord, let it not last long!" In six weeks' time the last sad news reached me in the island.

We went to Doorn; and during all the long hours of the journey, I was unable to grasp the idea that she would never speak to me again, that her kind eyes would never more be turned upon me. She was the magnet that drew us children, wherever we might be, towards the parental home. She knew all our wishes, our hopes, our cares. Now she had been taken from us for ever.

Changed, empty, strange appeared to me park and house and everything.

My poor father! Whatever his outward demeanour, I knew that his inmost heart was shaken. His old pride, his determination not to allow others to see his emotion, his resolve to bear himself like a king, supported him so long as we and other people were present. But the loneliness!

That night I was alone with my beloved mother for the last time. Through the hours of darkness, I kept a long quiet vigil beside her coffin. In that solemn, still chamber, with its heavy odours of wreaths and flowers and soft shine of the burning tapers, there floated before my memory an endless procession of pictures out of the past.

Her delight when I reported to her as a ten-year-old lieutenant, and that the parade went off all right in spite of the shortness of my legs and the difficulty they had in keeping step with the long-limbed grenadiers!

Her beaming face when she held my bride in her arms for the first time and said: " My dear boy, you have made a good choice "; from that day onwards till the end, a great love knit the two women together.

I saw her sitting at the bedside of my brothers Fritz and Joachim during a severe illness, night after night, untiringly—a devoted nurse, a mother who would have immolated her own self.

I saw her at court festivities, in all the splendour of

the crown—a tall and noble figure with a wealth of prematurely grey hair above the fresh, kind face; while every word showed a simple, cordial, generous nature, with the power of attaching and understanding others.

Then, ever and again, in her writing-room at the New Palace. It is in the interval between my morning and afternoon duties. I have ridden over to the palace, and now, while she listens and replies, I walk up and down before her. She is my confessor who always finds the right advice and the best solution in all my little difficulties; and in the heart of that woman, seemingly so unversed in politics, there was ample room for serious thought for the Fatherland in all its extent and all its greatness. Her clear recognition of many an error caused her to suffer—in a quiet hidden way—far more anxiety than the outside world ever imagined.

Then the war-time—care upon care, care upon care. And then all that followed.

I see her there in the garden of Doorn House. She is seated in a little pony-carriage; and I hold her hand and walk beside her. "My boy," she says, "yes, it is beautiful here, but oh! it is not my Potsdam, the New Palace, my little rose-garden, our home. If you only knew how homesickness often gnaws at me within. Oh, I shall never see my home again."

Now she lies at rest in the homeland earth to which her last longings went forth.

For a part of the way (as far as Maarn Station) I accompanied her on her homeward journey; then I turned back to my island here.

Days of sadness followed; not an hour went by in which my thoughts were not with her; but what was told me in a thousand letters of how unforgotten she was in the homeland, of the love that had sprung up from the seed she had sown, that, at least was a great comfort to me. Then, too, my brother-in-law, the Duke of Brunswick, was with me for a few days. Sissy is to remain for the present at Doorn, so as to lighten my father's sorrow in the first great loneliness and to bring a woman's voice into that beautiful and yet so friendless house.

But I must now proceed to set down what I have to say concerning that last and bitterest experience of our breakdown. God knows it is more difficult for me than all that I have recorded hitherto.

On the evening of November 8, 1918, I received at Waulsort an unexpected command from His Majesty to report myself to him next morning at Spa. Not a word as to what it concerned or what he wanted of me. I had only the knowledge that this summons could not portend anything good, and a foreboding of fresh agonizing conflicts.

In cold, gloomy weather, I motored through a heavy fog that seemed to smother the whole countryside. Everything apathetic, comfortless, dreary and devastated; the half-demolished houses, their plaster crumbling from their damaged walls; the interminable roads, ground by the violent jerkings of a hundred thousand wheels and pounded by the iron-shod hoofs of a hundred thousand horses. And those wan, haggard faces, so full of bitterness and sorrow and misery, as though their owners would never again be able to win through to fresh faith in life.

The car jolted through fields of mud, splashing the brown mire about it in huge fountains; it rushed heedlessly past columns of weary soldiers and troops and groups of men who had once been soldiers and who, now disbanded, trudged their way laden with a medley of odds and ends; it left behind it curses and cries and fists raised in the grey mist.

On and on.

Soon after midday we arrived at Spa, stiff and frozen to the marrow.

The Kaiser was lodged in! Villa Fraineuse, just outside the town.

General von Gontard, the Court Marshal, received me in the hall. His face wore a serious and very anxious look. In reply to my questions, all he did was to raise his hands helplessly; but the gesture said more than any words could have done.

My Chief of Staff, Count Schulenburg, was also there. He had been in Spa since the early morning, and, until my arrival, had been advocating our views with the Kaiser. Pale and manifestly profoundly moved, this strong man, full of a keen sense of responsibility and fine fidelity to his sovereign, proceeded, rapidly and in brief soldierly words, to give me an outline of the incidents into whose development we were now being dragged, and urgently begged me to do everything possible to persuade His Majesty against over-hasty and irretrievable decisions.

According to Schulenburg's report, the course of events so far had been as follows :—

In the early morning, my father had thoroughly discussed the situation with Major Niemann, of his General Staff, and had resolved boldly to face the threatening revolution. With this firm resolve, the Kaiser had taken part in a discussion at which the Field-Marshal General, with General Gröner, Plessen, Marschall, von Hintze, Herr von Grünau, and Major Niemann were present. The Field-Marshal General had opened the deliberations with a few words that revealed clearly that he was on the point of giving up everything : he must first ask His Majesty to permit him to resign, since what he had to say could not, he

felt, be said by a Prussian officer to his King and lord.
Only the Kaiser's head twitched. First let us hear what it is.

Then General Gröner had spoken. As Schulenburg sketched things, I could see and hear Gröner—Gröner the new man who had been only a fortnight in the place vacated by Ludendorff, and was hampered by no such considerations as those which choked the words in the throat of the old Field-Marshal General. A new tone, which brusquely and aggressively broke away from all tradition, which endeavoured, by despising the past, to gain inward strength for the coming death-blow.

General Gröner's words, as reported to me by Schulenburg, had they been the final truth, would indeed have signified the end: the military position of the armies desperate; the troops wavering and unreliable, with rations for a few days only, with hunger, dissolution and pillage threatening to follow after; the homeland blazing up in unquenchable revolution; the available reserves to be called up refractory, demoralized and rushing to join the red flag; the whole hinterland, railways, telegraphs, Rhine bridges, depots and junctions in the hands of the revolutionaries; Berlin at the highest pitch of tension which, at any moment, might snap and bathe the city in blood; to throw the army against the civil war at home with the enemy in the rear would be quite impossible. These views of his and the Field-Marshal General's had been endorsed by the divisional chiefs and by most of the representatives of the General Higher Command. Although not expressly, this report contained implicitly a demand for my father's abdication.

Speechless and deeply moved, my father had listened to these deplorably gloomy statements. A benumbing silence followed. Then, seeing from a movement on the part of my Chief of Staff, that he wished to be heard, the Kaiser sprang up and said :— " Speak, Count !—Your opinion ? "

Count Schulenburg then replied as follows :—

That he could not regard the remarks of the Quartermaster-General as a true description of the state of affairs. For example, the Army Group of the Crown Prince, despite great difficulties and hardships, had fought brilliantly through the long autumn campaign and was still firm and unbroken in the hands of its leaders. After its tremendous efforts, it was now exhausted, overtaxed, and filled with imperative longing for rest. If a definite armistice should come about, if the troops were granted a few days' repose, the refreshment of sleep and tolerably good rations, if the leaders were given a chance to come once more into closer touch with the men, and of exercising an influence over them, then the general frame of mind would improve. It would, indeed, be quite impossible to wheel round the troops of the whole west front to face civil war in Germany ; but this was not within the bounds of necessity. What was needed was resolute and manly resistance to activities which had unfortunately been allowed free play much too long, the immediate and energetic suppression of the insurgents at the centres of the movement, the rigorous re-establishment of order and authority !—The question of rationing had been depicted by General Gröner in much too sombre tints ; the effects of energetic proceedings against the Bolshevists in the rear of the army would be a fresh rally of the loyal elements in the country and the smothering of the revolutionary movement. Hence there should be no yielding to the threats of criminal violence, no abdication, but no civil war either—only the armed restoration of order at the spots indicated. For this purpose the mass of the troops would, without question, stand loyally by their Kaiser.

The Kaiser had accepted this view. Consequently, opposition had arisen between my Chief of Staff and General Gröner, who, in the course of this discussion, had persisted in his assertions that matters had gone too far for the measures proposed by Schulenburg to stand any chance of success. According to his version, the ramifications of the insurgent movement covered the entire homeland, the revolutionaries would cut off all supplies intended for any army operating against them, and, moreover, the army was no longer reliable, nor did it any longer support the Kaiser.

The views put forward by General Gröner found a certain confirmation in the many telephone messages which arrived from the Imperial Chancellory during the discussion; these reported sanguinary street fighting and the defection of the home troops to the ranks of the revolutionaries, and repeatedly demanded abdication. They evidently proceeded from a state of panic; and, on account of their urgent character, made a deep impression; but to what extent they were founded upon fact could not be tested.

In spite of all this, the Kaiser had stood resolutely by his original decision. But, in face of the irreconcilable opposition between the two views of the situation and the logical conclusions involved, he had ultimately turned to General Gröner and declared with great firmness that, in this exceedingly grave matter, he could not acquiesce in the opinion expressed by the General but must insist upon a written statement signed by Field-Marshal General von Hindenburg and by General Gröner—a statement based upon opinions to be obtained from all the army leaders of the west front. He would never for a moment entertain the thought of waging a civil war; but he held firmly to his desire to lead the army back home in good order after the conclusion of the armistice.

General Gröner had then adopted an attitude which seemed to indicate that he regarded all further discussion as a useless loss of time in face of a definitely fixed programme; he had brusquely and slightingly confined himself to remarking: " The army will march back home in good order under its leaders and commanding generals, but not under the leadership of Your Majesty."

In reply to the agitated question of my father: " How do you come to make such a report ? Count Schulenburg reports the reverse!" Gröner said: " I have different information."*

In response to a further protest by my Chief of Staff, the Field-Marshal General had finally relinquished his attitude of reserve. With every respect for the spirit of loyalty displayed in Schulenburg's views, he had come to the practical conclusion of General Gröner, namely, that, on the basis of information received by the Higher Command from home and from the armies, it must be assumed that the revolution could no

* It must be recorded here that General Gröner made this report to my father long before the vote had been placed before the commanders at the front. What " other information," then, did the First Quartermaster-General possess, and from which leader of the west front did it proceed? These questions still remain unanswered. From none of the four armies placed in my charge did I ever receive any report which could justify General Gröner's conclusion in regard to the front or even concerning the rear of my armies. The information referred to by General Gröner he must have received on the 7th or 8th of November, for at Charleville he was still in good spirits, on the 5th he had ardently taken the part of the Kaiser, and on the 6th the General Higher Command wrote to the armies on the west front that, for the armies, there was no Kaiser question and that, true to their oath, they stood immutably loyal to their Chief War Lord.

longer be suppressed. Like Gröner, he, too, was unable to take upon himself responsibility for the trustworthiness of the troops.

Finally, the Kaiser had closed the discussion with a repetition of his desire that the commanders-in-chief should be asked for their views. " If you report to me," he said, " that the army is no longer loyal to me, I shall be prepared to go—but not till then ! "

From these discussions and decisions it was clear that the Kaiser was willing to sacrifice his person to the interests of the German people and to the maintenance of internal and external possibilities of peace. At the conclusion of the parley, Count Schulenburg had called particular attention to the fact that, in any decisions of the Kaiser's, questions concerning the Imperial Crown must be carefully distinguished from those of the Prussian royal throne. At the very most, only an abdication of the Kaiser could be involved ; there was no need, even if the worst came to the worst, of any talk of a renunciation of the throne of Prussia. For this standpoint he had propounded weighty reasons ; and he had also expressed the opinion that the alarming telephone messages from Berlin needed careful investigation before they could be made the basis of any resolve.

My father had assured him that, in any circumstances, he would remain King of Prussia and that, as such, he would not desert the army. Furthermore, he had at once ordered an immediate inquiry to be made by telephone of the Governor of Berlin concerning the situation there ; he had then walked into the garden accompanied by some of the gentlemen of his suite ; while the Field-Marshal General, General Gröner and Count von Schulenburg had remained behind in the Council Chamber. In the ensuing discussion on the last statements of Schulenburg, the

Field-Marshal General also expressed the opinion that the Kaiser must, in all circumstances, maintain himself as King of Prussia, whereas General Gröner remained sceptical of this, and was indeed completely opposed to such a claim. He stated that a free decision to this effect, if taken by the Kaiser some weeks earlier, might perhaps have effected a change in the situation; but that, in his opinion, it now came too late to be of any value in combating the revolt now blazing in Germany and spreading rapidly every moment.

What had followed next, blow after blow, had seemingly been calculated to justify this view of General Gröner's—if it could be accepted as the actual truth with regard to conditions and feelings at home. The answer of the Chief of the General Staff with the Berlin Government, Colonel von Berge, had arrived and had brought a confirmation (though a qualified one) of the reports furnished by the Imperial Chancellory—bloody street-fighting, desertion of the troops to the revolutionaries, no means whatever in the hands of the Government for combating the movement; furthermore, an appeal by Prince Max of Baden stating that civil war was inevitable unless His Majesty announced his abdication within the next few minutes.

With these messages, the Field-Marshal General, General Gröner and His Excellency von Hintze had hurried into the garden and were now reporting the matter to the Kaiser, while Count von Schulenburg was explaining the situation to me.

I now went with my Chief of Staff to join the Kaiser.

He stood in the garden surrounded by a group of gentlemen.

Never shall I forget the picture of that half-score of

men in their grey uniforms, thrown into relief by the withered and faded flower-beds of ending autumn, and framed by the surrounding mist-mantled hills with their glorious foliages of vanishing green and every shade of brown, of yellow, and of red.

The Kaiser stood there as though he had suddenly halted with them in the midst of a nervous pacing up and down. He was passionately excited, and addressing himself to those near him with violently expressive gestures. His eyes were upon General Gröner and His Excellency von Hintze; but a glance was cast now and then at the Field-Marshal General, who, with his gaze fixed in the distance, nodded silently; and an occasional look was also turned towards the white-haired General von Plessen. Somewhat aloof from the group stood General von Marschall, the Legation Councillor von Grünau, and Major von Hirschfeld.

With their bowed attitudes, most of the men seemed oppressed by the thought that there was no egress from their entanglement—seemed, while the Kaiser alone spoke, to have been paralysed into muteness.

Catching sight of me, my father beckoned me to approach and, himself, came forward a few paces.

And now, as I stood opposite him, I saw clearly how distraught were his features—how his emaciated and sallow face twitched and trembled.

He left me scarcely time to greet the Field-Marshal General and the rest; hastily he addressed himself to me, and, while the others retired a little and General Gröner returned to the house, he burst upon me with all he had to say. He poured out to me the facts without the slightest reserve, reiterated much of what Schulenburg had reported just before, supplemented the particulars, and gave me a deeper insight into the character of the catastrophe which was threatening to spring from instability and demoralization of will and energy. As I had only just arrived from my Army Group and the seclusion of the front, I was still endeavouring to grasp and master all that Schulenburg had told me, but I now learned that yesterday evening, before he summoned me to Spa, a thorough discussion had taken place concerning the situation, in which General Gröner had urgently dissuaded the Kaiser from returning home—from attempting " to penetrate into the interior." Insurrectionary masses were on their way to Verviers and Spa, and there were no longer any trustworthy troops whatever! Nor, said he, durst my father proceed to the front with any such intention as to die fighting ; in view of the approaching armistice, such a step might give rise to false deductions on the part of the Entente, and thus cause even greater mischief and still further bloodshed. My father also informed me that, according to the statements of these gentlemen, the cities of Cologne, Hanover, Brunswick and Munich were in the hands of the Workmen's and Soldiers' Councils, while in Kiel and Wilhelmshafen the revolution had broken out, and that, in view of the apparent necessity for his abdication as Kaiser, he was going to transfer to the Field-Marshal General the chief command of the German Army.

Notwithstanding my great perturbation, I at once tried to intervene and to check wherever, in my opinion, it appeared possible ; despite the hitherto precipitate course of events, to call a halt, and wherever a halt was essential, unless everything were to be lost. Even if the abdication of the Kaiser as such could really no longer be avoided, he must, at any rate, unflinchingly remain King of Prussia.

" Of course ! " The words were uttered in such a matter-of-fact way and his eyes were so firmly fixed on mine that much appeared to me to have been gained already.

I also emphasized the necessity for his remaining with the army in all circumstances, and I suggested his coming with me and marching back at the head of my troops.

General Gröner now joined the other group again, accompanied by Colonel Heye, who, as I learned, had come from a conference of front officers convoked as a sort of council by the Higher Command without consulting the chief commanders of the army or the army groups, the vote of this council being taken by Gröner to be decisive.

In reply to the Kaiser's command, Colonel Heye reported to the following effect :—The question had been put to the commanders whether, in the event of a civil war at home, the troops could be relied upon : the answer was in the negative ; the trustworthiness of the troops had not been unconditionally guaranteed by certain of these commanders.

Count von der Schulenburg intervened. He adduced what we, who were familiar with our men, knew from personal experience ; above all this one thing, that the great majority of the army, if faced with the question whether they would break their oaths and desert their sovereign and chief war lord in the time of need, would certainly prove true to their Kaiser.

At this, General Gröner merely shrugged his shoulders and sneered superciliously: " Military oaths ! War lords ! Those are, after all, only words—those are, when all is said, mere ideas."

Here were two systems which no bridge could join, two conceptions which no mutual comprehension could reconcile. The one was the Prussian officer, loyal in his duty and devotion to Kaiser and to King, ready to live and die in the fulfilment of the oath which he had taken as a young man; the other, the man who doubtless never had taken things so earnestly or with such a sense of sacred obligation, who had regarded them rather as symbol and "idea," who was always desirous of being "modern" and whose more supple mentality now freed itself without any difficulty from engagements that threatened to become awkward.

Once more Schulenburg replied, telling the general that such statements as his only showed that he did not know the heart and mind of the men at the front, that the army was true to its oath and that, at the end of those four years of war, it would not abandon its Kaiser.

He was still speaking, when he was interrupted by His Excellency von Hintze, who had meantime received further reports from Berlin and wished to lay the evil tidings before the Kaiser. The Imperial Chancellor, Prince Max, he said, tendered his resignation and reported that the situation had become so extremely menacing in Berlin that the monarchy could no longer be saved unless the Kaiser resolved upon immediate abdication.

The Kaiser received the news with grave silence. His firmly compressed lips were colourless; his face was livid and had aged by years. Only those who knew him as I did could tell what he was suffering at this impatiently urged demand of the Chancellor, despite the well maintained mask of calmness and self-control.

When Hintze had finished, he gave a brief nod; and his eyes sought those of the Field-Marshal General as though searching them for strength and succour in his anguish. But he found nothing. Motionless, shaken to the depths of his being, silenced by despair, the great old man stood mute, while his King and lord, whom he had served so long and so faithfully as a soldier, moved on to the fulfilment of his destiny.

The Kaiser was alone. Not one of all the men of the General Higher Command, not one of the men whom Ludendorff had once welded into a strong entity, hastened to his assistance. Here, as at home, disruption and demoralization. Here, where an iron will should have been busily at work enforcing itself in every position of authority and gathering all the reliable troops at the front for heroic deeds, there was only one vast void. The spirit of General Gröner was now dominant, and that spirit left the Kaiser to his fate.

Hoarse, strange and unreal was my father's voice as he instructed Hintze, who was still waiting, to telephone the Imperial Chancellor that he was prepared to renounce the Imperial Crown, if only in this way general civil war in Germany could be avoided, but that he remained King of Prussia and would not leave his army.

The gentlemen were silent. The State Secretary was about to depart, when Schulenburg pointed out that it was, in any case, essential first to make a written record of this highly momentous decision of His Majesty. Not until such a document had been ratified and signed could it be communicated to the Imperial Chancellor.

The Kaiser expressed his thanks. Yes, he said, that was true; and he instructed Lieutenant-General von Plessen, General von Marschall, His Excellency von Hintze and Count von der Schulenburg to draw up the declaration and submit it to him for signature.

Accordingly, we went indoors again.

While the gentlemen were still at work on the document, there came another telephone call from Berlin. The *chef* of the Imperial Chancellory, His

Excellency von Wahnschaffe, asked urgently for the declaration of abdication; he was informed by Count von der Schulenburg that the decision already come to by His Majesty was being formulated and would be forthwith despatched to the Imperial Government.

The document *did not* contain *the abdication of the Kaiser*, but expressed his willingness to abdicate if thereby alone further bloodshed and, above all, civil war, would be avoided. It also stressed the fact that he remained King of Prussia and would lead the troops back home in perfect order.

According to this resolve there lay upon the Chancellor the duty of reporting afresh concerning the development of the situation at home. Then, and not before, the final Imperial decision would have followed.

His Excellency von Hintze undertook to telephone the wording of the document to the Imperial Chancellory.

It was now one o'clock, and we proceeded to lunch. That silent meal, in a bright, white room whose table was decked with flowers but surrounded only by bitter anguish and despairing grief, is among the most horrible of my recollections. Not one of us but masked his face, not one who did not make fitful attempts, for that half-hour, to hide his uneasiness and not to talk of the phantom which lurked behind him and could not for a single moment be forgotten. Every mouthful seemed to swell and threaten to choke the eater. The whole meal resembled some dismal funeral repast.

After this unbearably painful lunch, His Majesty remained in conversation with me and Schulenburg. A few minutes after two o'clock, he was called away by General von Plessen, as State Secretary von Hintze, while telephoning to Berlin, had been surprised by a fresh communication.

We others remained behind in anxious suspense,

fearing that some unforeseen incident had occurred which would still further complicate the already bewildered and confused situation. Those few minutes seemed like an age to me.

Presently Schulenburg and I were ordered to the Kaiser.

Notwithstanding the apparent self-control and dignity he had forced himself to assume, he was excessively agitated in mind. As though still in doubt whether what he had just passed through could be reality and truth, he told us that he had just received information from the Imperial Chancellory to the effect that a message announcing his abdication as Kaiser and as King of Prussia and, at the same time, declaring my renunciation in a similar sense, had been issued by Prince Max of Baden and disseminated by Wolff's Bureau without the Kaiser's declaration having been awaited and without my being consulted in the matter ; further, that the Prince had resigned his post of Imperial Chancellor and had been appointed Imperial Regent, while the social-democratic Reichstag deputy, Ebert, was now Imperial Chancellor.

We were all so dazed and paralysed by this startling news that for the moment, we could hardly speak. Then we immediately endeavoured to ascertain and establish the sequence of these unexampled proceedings.

His Excellency von Hintze had just begun to telephone the declaration drawn up by His Majesty, when he was interrupted. This declaration, he was told, was quite futile ; it would have to be the complete abdication, as Kaiser and as King of Prussia also, and Herr von Hintze must listen to what was about to be 'phoned him ! The State Secretary had protested against this interruption and had declared that the decision of His Majesty must now be heard before anything else. This he proceeded to read; but he had no sooner finished than Berlin informed him that a declaration had already been published by Wolff's Bureau and immediately afterwards communicated to the various troops by wireless telegrams; this declaration stated:—" The Kaiser and King has resolved to abdicate the throne. The Imperial Chancellor remains in office till the questions connected with the abdication of the Kaiser, the renunciation of the throne by the Crown Prince of the German Empire and of Prussia, and the appointment to the regency are settled. . . ." The State Secretary, von Hintze, had forthwith entered a categorical protest against this proclamation, which had been issued without the Kaiser's authorization and did not represent in the least His Majesty's decisions. Von Hintze had repeatedly demanded the presence of the Imperial Chancellor himself at the telephone; and Prince Max of Baden had then, in reply to Hintze's inquiry, personally acknowledged his authorship of the published proclamation and declared himself prepared to accept the responsibility for doing so.

Thus, he did not for one moment deny that he was the originator of this incomprehensible step, namely, publishing, without His Majesty's authorization, decisions ostensibly his which he had never agreed to in such a form and forestalling in a way that to say the least of it was casual, my own decisions in a matter that had not yet been even broached by a single word.

In the excited and credulous mood of the people at home and of the troops, it was clear to us that by the Prince's extraordinary behaviour the appearance of an accomplished fact had been created which was to cut the ground we stood upon from under our feet.

With a clearer judgment as to what had happened

to His Majesty and to me, and clearer views concerning what now needed to be done, we crossed over into the room where the other gentlemen were assembled.

Great consternation at the monstrous proceedings seized them also. Cries of indignation mingled with suggestions as to how this crafty *coup* was to be met.

Schulenburg and I importuned His Majesty never, under any circumstances, to submit to this *coup d'état*, but to oppose the machinations of the Prince by every possible means and to abide unalterably by his previously formed resolution. The Count also emphasized the fact that this incident rendered it all the more essential for the Kaiser, as chief war lord, to remain with the army.

For this advice we found some support from General von Marschall and specially also from the old Colonel-General von Plessen, whose faithful and chivalrous nature and strong soldierly instinct burst through the courtier-like formalities usually carefully observed by him and flared up indignantly at the disgraceful blow aimed at his Kaiser and the entire dynasty. It was of great importance that, by personal inquiry, he was able to prove the untenability of Gröner's assertion that the troops at head-quarters had become unreliable and no longer afforded the Kaiser sufficient protection.

Count von der Schulenburg and I offered to undertake the suppression of the revolutionary elements at home, proposing first to restore order in Cologne. But this suggestion the Kaiser declined to entertain, as he would have no war of Germans against Germans.

Finally, he declared repeatedly and with great emphasis that he abode by his decision to abdicate if necessary as Kaiser, but that he remained King of Prussia, and as such would not leave the troops. He instructed General von Plessen, General von Marschall and His Excellency von Hintze to report at once to the Field-Marshal General concerning what had happened in Berlin and his own attitude.

Somewhat encouraged by this firm mood of my father's, who now seemed to see his way clearly through all the entanglements and difficulties, I took leave of him, my duties as Commander-in-Chief requiring my presence in the head-quarters of the Army Group at Vielsalm.

As I held his hand in mine, I never imagined that I should not see him again for a year, and that it would then be in Holland.

Count von der Schulenburg remained in Spa.

It was from him, and not from personal experience, that I gathered my information concerning the further events of that fatal 9th of November in Spa.

Schulenburg, who, together with me, had taken leave of the Kaiser, had been called back by him once more. My father had repeated: "I remain King of Prussia and, as such, I do not abdicate; and I also remain with the troops!" Then, as it was impossible to recognize the revolutionary Government in Berlin, the question of the armistice was discussed. Who was to conclude it? His Majesty decided that Field-Marshal von Hindenburg should take over the supreme command and be responsible for conducting the negotiations. At the close of the conversation, the Kaiser held out his hand to Count Schulenburg and repeated: "I remain with the army. Tell the troops so!"

On leaving His Majesty, Schulenburg proceeded to the quarters of the Field-Marshal General, where, together with General Gröner, General von Marschall, State Secretary von Hintze and the Legation Councillor von Grünau, a conference was commenced at half-past three concerning the situation created by Berlin.

General Gröner declared that there were no military means of counteracting the abdication proclaimed in Berlin. At the suggestion of His Excellency von Hintze, it was decided to draw up a written protest against the declaration of abdication, which had been proclaimed without the consent or approval of the Kaiser, and to have this document signed by the Kaiser and deposited in a secure place. In discussing the personal safety of the Kaiser, for which General Gröner declined all responsibility, the question was raised as to what domicile the Kaiser could select if any development of affairs should force him to go abroad, and Holland was mentioned. Count Schulenburg stood alone in his opinion that it would be a grave mistake if His Majesty left the army. He urged that His Majesty should join the Army Group, the way being open.

Fully confident in the Kaiser's firm resolve, Count von Schulenburg, accompanied by the other members of the Army Group Staff, had then driven back to Vielsalm, where his presence was urgently required on account of the tense situation at the front.

As I stated in describing the events at Spa on November 9, the views obtained from a conference of officers from the front by Colonel Heye submitting to them certain questions were adduced as evidence in support of the Chief Quartermaster-General's opinion on the prevailing mood of the troops at the front. At my instance, an officer of the Army Group General Staff, who had accompanied Count Schulenburg to Spa, made a record of the character and the procedure of this council convoked direct by the General Higher Command. I append this document here as a key to the temper and the mental condition prevalent at Spa, and because it is necessary to a right understanding of what took place. On account of the relations of the officer to the service, his name is suppressed.

........, *November* 14, '19.
My Experiences at General Head-quarters on November 9, 1918.

(Written from memory.*)

In the night of the 8th–9th November, General Count von der Schulenburg received a telephone call from Major von Stülpnagel ordering him to come to Spa on November 9. Major von Bock took the message. No information was given as to why Count Schulenburg should come or who wished to see him.— Count Schulenburg was rather astonished when Bock brought him the message, but he at once gave orders for his departure on the 9th. He appointed Captain X of the General Staff, Orderly Officer Lieutenant Y, and myself to accompany him. The same morning, instructions had been given to transfer the quarters of the Upper Command of the Army Group from Waulsort to Vielsalm.

At 8.30 a.m. on November 9, we reached the Hotel Britannique in Spa. On our arrival, we were struck by the fact that in the hall of the hotel there was assembled a large body of officers not belonging to the Higher Command and that others were continually arriving. They were exclusively officers from the front; no commander-in-chief, commanding generals, *chefs* or other general staff officers were present.

Count Schulenburg at once proceeded to the Operations Department on the first floor in order to inquire the reasons for his being summoned. On the way upstairs he met Colonel Heye. This officer was

---

* Use has also been made of certain notes written by Captain X and myself on December 2, 1918, and now in the possession of Count Schulenburg.

manifestly surprised to see Count Schulenburg. After a short conversation, which I could not hear, Schulenburg returned to me saying: " We are evidently not wanted here at all. We have rushed into an affair which does not concern us, but we will see what is really going on ! "

From the numerous officers standing around, we learned that they had all been ordered to attend a meeting at 9 a.m. Apparently, from each of the divisions of the army groups Rupprecht, Kronprinz and Gallwitz, a selected officer, divisional commander and infantry brigade or infantry regiment commander had been summoned and had been rapidly brought along by motor-car. No information concerning these orders had reached the Upper Command of the Army Group. The reason for the conference could only be guessed. The first idea was that it concerned the expected armistice. But rumours were circulating about measures to oppose the spread of the revolutionary movement in Germany ; there was unverifiable news of civil war at home, of the westward advance of mutinous sailors through Aix-la-Chapelle, Bonn and Coblenz, of the blocking of the railways along the Rhine and the consequent entire stoppage of the commissariat. From the few members of the General Higher Command whom I managed to see, no further information was to be obtained in the hurry of the moment. Those whom I saw appeared dejected and rather desponding. It must be added here that, for nearly a fortnight, the Upper Command of the Army Group had received through the post neither newspapers nor letters, and that we were, therefore, inadequately informed as to the situation at home, while the front had been living for weeks on nothing but rumours. Hence I observed that the officers arriving from the front accepted without any criticism even very unfavourable reports circulating in the conference. A suitable soil for pessimism was, moreover, prepared in them by the fact that almost all had been fetched, just as they were, from the retreating battles in which they had been fighting for weeks and which were excessively exhausting and in every way depressing. Most of them, too, had travelled in many cases hundreds of kilometres, in open cars and clad in thin coats; and they were cold, unwashed and unfed.

Soon after the conversation with Colonel Heye, Count Schulenburg, together with Captain X and myself, went to the hotel dining-room, where the officers from the front were assembling. In talking to various acquaintances, my impression was strengthened that, for the reasons already adduced, these officers were in a very depressed mood. Meantime, Colonel-General von Plessen and General von Marschall had entered the room. Their dejected spirits were noticeable. When they caught sight of Count Schulenburg, who stood near me, they at once came up and began talking to him. I could only hear fragments of the conversation and guess its general tenor. But almost at the outset, Count Schulenburg said to the two of them very sharply: " Have you all gone mad here ? " Later he said, among other things: " The army stands firmly by the Kaiser." I noticed that Colonel-General von Plessen and General Marschall drew fresh confidence from the conversation with Count Schulenburg; and I heard the words " Schulenburg must go with us at once to the Kaiser." The meeting had not yet been opened, and Colonel-General von Plessen and General von Marschall very soon took Count Schulenburg out of the room and drove with him to His Majesty. Captain X, Lieutenant Y and I stayed behind. Captain X and I decided to remain at the meeting, although we both felt that we were anything but welcome there.

About nine o'clock, Field-Marshal General von Hindenburg, accompanied by Colonel Heye and a few other members of the Higher Command, entered the room. The Field-Marshal, having welcomed the officers assembled by his orders, thanked them warmly for all that they had hitherto done; he then characterized the situation as serious but not desperate, and proceeded to explain the object of the meeting. In Germany, he said, revolution had broken out, and, in some places, blood had already flowed. The resignation of the Kaiser was being demanded. The Higher Command hoped to be able to oppose this demand, if the requisite assurances were given them by the army at the front. On these questions which Colonel Heye would presently lay before them, the gentlemen were to express their views. In further delineation of the position of affairs, the Field-Marshal stated roughly that it was a question for His Majesty whether he could march to Berlin at the head of the entire army in order to recover there the Imperial and Royal crown. For this purpose, however—no armistice having as yet been concluded and the railways not being available—the whole army, with the enemy of course following rapidly in its rear, would have to wheel round and march for two or three weeks, fighting all the way, in the endeavour to reach Berlin. Special emphasis was laid by the Field-Marshal upon the difficulties of getting supplies of all kinds, since everything was in the hands of the insurgents, and he laid stress on the fatigues and privations to which the troops would be unceasingly subjected.

After this description of the situation—all of whose points were given by the Field-Marshal, not by Colonel Heye—the former left the meeting. I remember that my first impression, as I uttered it to Captain X, was something like this: It is regrettable that the generally revered Field-Marshal, whom many of those present had certainly just seen for the first time, should have been obliged to address them on such a sad matter and that he had given them a sketch of the military situation which many critical minds could only regard with considerable scepticism. For me there could be no doubt that, after such a representation of affairs, only negative answers could be expected.

Meanwhile, the attendance at the meeting was continually being increased by new arrivals, though many did not get in till after midday, when the answer to the questions had been long since reported to His Majesty. These questions—two or three in number—were put to the meeting by Colonel Heye. Their wording has escaped my memory; but roughly it was asked whether, under the watchword "For the Kaiser," the Higher Command could, with any prospect of success, call upon the troops at the front to march to Berlin and thus unloose a civil war, or whether the army could no longer be had for this purpose. Colonel Heye requested the gentlemen to consider this important matter each for himself and uninfluenced by one another. After the lapse of a certain time, he would invite the gentlemen to come to him and state their views, as far as possible, general command by general command, beginning with the right wing.

What replies Colonel Heye received is unknown to me; but, as already indicated, I do not doubt, from what had passed, that the vast majority of them were in the negative. As I learned afterwards, all the front officers who took part in the conference were pledged to secrecy by Colonel Heye and gave their hand on it. No such request was put to Captain X or myself.

My judgment upon the conference and the interrogation of the front commanders may be formulated as follows :—

Considering the importance of the verdict to be given by each individual officer ordered to Spa, it was bad management to interrogate these men, who in many cases were physically and psychically reduced, without giving them an opportunity of recuperation or giving them time mentally to digest the news placed before them in reference to the state of affairs at home. It was noticeable in the afternoon how changed these same officers were in appearance after they had rested a bit, had washed and dressed, had lunched and lighted a cigar.

It was an incomprehensible omission to leave unsummoned the commanders-in-chief, the commanding generals and the chiefs of staffs, to hear as it were the officers from the front behind their backs. Did the General Higher Command fear their judgment ? For that there was no occasion. From the Higher Command of the Crown Prince Army Group, at any rate, they had all along, and especially during the last few weeks and months, heard nothing but the most candid pronouncements as to the fighting capacity of the troops. Unfortunately, their statements had not always met with the proper consideration.

The picture of the situation from which the commanders were to form their judgment was so sombre that an answer in favour of His Majesty was scarcely to be expected. On such a hypothesis, the army was not to be won over for the Kaiser. Moreover, a large proportion of the front officers doubtless lacked the analytic capacity and tactical judgment requisite for getting to the very heart of this momentous situation.

If, as it would now appear, the significance of the

interrogation was whether the Kaiser could remain with his army or not, it was a culpable omission not to have pointed out more explicitly the consequences which might ensue from their replies and that no detailed representation was given of what the position would be if His Majesty failed to remain Chief War Lord. So far as I am aware, the question whether His Majesty would be safe with the troops was never put.

Not until 4.30 p.m. did Count Schulenburg return to the hotel. Captain X, Lieutenant Y and I had spent most of the time waiting in the hotel, without being able to ascertain anything of any significance from anyone. Count Schulenburg was greatly agitated. Briefly and with intense indignation he described what had happened. As the most essential points of what he told us, I recall especially the following : " We have no longer any Kaiser. A consultation has just been held at the Field-Marshal's villa as to whether His Majesty shall be sent off to-night to Holland. Gröner says he can no longer guarantee his safety for another night. Bolshevists are, he asserts, marching on Spa from Verviers. The verdict of the front officers brought by Heye has turned out to be in the negative. My objections that the army is loyal and abides by its oath were shelved by Gröner with the words : ' Loyalty to king and military oaths are, after all, mere ideas ! ' I could not carry my demand that the commanders-in-chief and the commanding generals should have a hearing. On my departure, His Majesty promised me he would remain King of Prussia and stay with the army." Concerning everything else that occurred in His Majesty's villa and the Field-Marshal's and what Count Schulenburg told us further, exact information is to be found in the record of the events at Spa on November 9, as since published in the Press. I would emphasize the fact that the particulars contained therein coincide perfectly with what Count Schulenburg told us at the Hotel Britannique and during the return journey to Vielsalm, i.e. while still under the first impressions of what he had just experienced.

Signed..................

pro tem., ... in the General Staff of the Higher Command of the Crown Prince Army Group.

On the top of all the exciting events of that day the night brought me a letter from my father which was irreconcilable with the last impressions I and the Chief of my General Staff had carried away with us from Spa, and destroyed all the hope and confidence we had cherished concerning a restoration of the old order of things. The letter confronted me with unalterable facts that could not but change the course of my destiny and turn me aside from the path which I had hitherto regarded as the only proper one and which, relying upon my rights and obligations, I had intended unswervingly to follow.

My father's letter ran :—

" MY DEAR BOY,—

" As the Field-Marshal cannot guarantee my safety here and will not pledge himself for the reliability of the troops, I have decided, after a severe inward struggle, to leave the disorganized army. Berlin is totally lost ; it is in the hands of the Socialists, and two governments have been formed there—one with Ebert as Chancellor and one by the Independents. Till the troops start their march home, I recommend your continuing at your post and keeping the troops together ! God willing, I trust we shall meet again. General von Marschall will give you further information.

" Your sorely-stricken father,

(*Signed*) " WILHELM."

I had no particulars concerning the circumstances which had been urgent enough to force the Kaiser, in a few hours, to give up everything and to desist from his determination to maintain his throne. For the present, we could only assume that the Kaiser had been rendered pliable by the influence of those men whose views Count Schulenburg and I had combated with all our might and who had thus been rendered powerless so long as we were in Spa.

Details of what took place on that fatal afternoon only came to my knowledge very much later. I gathered them from conversations with His Majesty and the gentlemen of his suite and from the written records of various persons who were present.

From these it appeared that, after the departure of Count Schulenburg, a report was made to His Majesty, the Field-Marshal, Generals Gröner and von Marschall, His Excellency von Hintze and Herr von Grünau. Later on Admiral Scheer also joined the party. The Kaiser was most urgently pressed to issue his abdication and to start for Holland. Emphasis was laid on the fact that fifty officers from all parts of the army had expressed the opinion that the troops at the front were no longer to be trusted. It was declared that, in these circumstances, the Kaiser must leave the collapsing army and go to Holland. Gröner declared that the General Staff was of the same conviction. For His Majesty, the attitude adopted by the Field-Marshal General was decisive. No final decision seems to have been formed. His Majesty only agreed to preparatory steps being taken for his journey to Holland.

After the conference had been closed, the Kaiser said to Count Dohna, who reported himself back from leave : " I have answered Gröner categorically that I have now done with him ; despite all suggestions, I remain in Spa." To his two aides-de-camp he remarked : " I am staying the night in the villa ; provide yourselves with arms and ammunition. The Field-Marshal tells me that we may have to reckon with Bolshevist attacks."

It was not until after a further discussion with Colonel-General von Plessen and Herr von Grünau, that the Kaiser decided not to pass the night in Villa Fraineuse but in the train at Spa, for which he gave the necessary orders. Further representations—made at the instance of the Field-Marshal General after supper and based upon the great danger of Bolshevist attacks from Aix-la-Chapelle and Verviers—were needed to induce the Kaiser to set off upon his journey. Major Niemann, the General Staff officer of the Higher Command attached to the Kaiser, has furnished a description of what occurred. According to this account, the resolve of His Majesty developed in the course of the afternoon and evening of November 9 as follows :—

" Between 4 and 5 o'clock in the afternoon, Field-Marshal von Hindenburg and State Secretary von Hintze reported to His Majesty that the situation was continually growing worse, and requested him to consider crossing the frontier into neutral territory as the last resort. The Field-Marshal made use of the words : ' I cannot assume the responsibility for the Kaiser's being dragged to Berlin by mutinous troops and there handed over as a prisoner to the Revolutionary Government.' His Majesty declared his assent to *preparatory* steps being taken by His Excellency von Hintze for the possible reception of His Majesty in Holland. After this conversation, His Majesty again gave personal instructions for measures of security to be adopted during his stay in Spa.

" Towards 7 p.m., His Excellency von Hintze and

SCENES AT SPA

Colonel-General von Plessen again came to request His Majesty, in their own names and in the name of the Field-Marshal, to leave for Holland that night. The situation at home and in the army, said the State Secretary, made a speedy decision by His Majesty essential. The possibility of His Majesty's being seized by his *own* troops, as already stated by the Field-Marshal, was getting nearer and nearer. At first, His Majesty yielded to this pressure. Subsequently, however, on calm reflection, His Majesty came to the decision not to leave, but to remain with the army and to fight to the last. On the way to the royal train, in which the greater part of the suite lived and in which all meals were taken, His Majesty, about 7.45 p.m., communicated this decision to his aides-de-camp, von Hirschfeld and von Ilsemann. On reaching the royal train, he went to General von Gontard and told him explicitly that he would not follow the advice given him by the Higher Command to leave the army and the country; on the contrary, he would stay with his army to the end and risk his life. The demand that he should leave the army was, he said, preposterous.

" His Majesty expressed himself in the same sense to Colonel-General von Plessen and to General Baron Marschall.

" By supper-time (8.30 p.m.) the idea of departure appeared to be finally given up.

" After supper, i.e., about 10 o'clock, Herr von Grünau appeared under instructions from His Excellency von Hintze, and reported to His Majesty that both Field-Marshal von Hindenburg, and State Secretary von Hintze had come to the conclusion that His Majesty *must* start for Holland without delay. The situation had become untenable, as the insurrectionary movement threatened to travel from Aix-la-Chapelle and Eupen to Spa, and insurgent troops were already marching on the town; while the route to the front was blocked by mutinous troops on the lines of communication.

"His Majesty, yielding to these renewed urgent demands of the leading responsible military leaders and competent political advisers, gave orders for the journey to the Dutch frontier to start at 5 a.m. on November 10."

All these facts seem to me to prove that His Majesty did not resolve, of his own accord, to go to Holland. On the contrary, he protested against the idea to the very last. But all his advisers, with the Higher Command at their head, employed the most forcible means to wrest this decision from him. The leading persons of his suite seem also to have gone over to the other side in the course of the afternoon and to have exerted themselves to obtain the early departure of His Majesty.

Only in this way can it be explained that, in Vielsalm, a bare hour by motor-car from Spa, we did not get news of this decision in time for us to intervene and to induce the Kaiser to join our Army Group. True, the situation at the front was very critical, and our presence in the Vielsalm Head-quarters extremely necessary. Nevertheless, it was a mistake for Schulenburg and me not to have remained in Spa or to have taken the Kaiser along with us when we left. We relied upon the promise of the Kaiser and upon those around him, who knew our views and attitude, to give us a call immediately any change occurred in the Kaiser's resolve.

Looking back upon the abdication of the Kaiser, it seems to me that there was only one suitable moment for such an act. That moment was at the end of September, when Kaiser and people were startled by the military collapse and by the demand of the Higher Command for an immediate armistice proposal. The revelation of the bald truth was so crushing that the people would have understood the Kaiser's taking upon himself the responsibility and sacrificing himself. *Such* an abdication would have been voluntary and would not have weakened the monarchy. In October, one privilege after another was wrested from the crown. Even the Higher Command, in the middle of October, agreed to the supreme command in war time being torn from the Kaiser—from the Chief War Lord. Ultimately came the demand for abdication, and it grew louder and louder as the hostile propagandists acted more and more in concert. If it had been accorded in response to this pressure, the Crown would have been surrendered to the absolute control of parliament and of the mob—the end would have been just the same.

Or does anyone still believe that the dynasties would not have been overturned, if the Kaiser had abdicated in the days of November or in the forenoon of November 9. The revolution was not directed against the person of the Kaiser but against monarchy.

For months, the ground had been undermined, and the favourable moment was being awaited. This moment had arrived when the people's confidence in Hindenburg and Ludendorff received such a severe blow by the recognition that the war was lost. The people were worn out; the masses were worn out and ready for the revolution; the middle classes were worn out and apathetically let things slide. The will to fight and to resist was paralysed; and people yielded to the delusion that they would obtain a better peace by removing the Kaiser.

The revolution had an astoundingly easy game to play. A few hours sufficed to sweep away the hereditary princes and their governments. Without fighting and without bloodshed, the revolution was accomplished—a proof of how thoroughly it was prepared, partly by the moving and swaying forces of our unfortunate destiny and partly by the systematic work and influence of the revolutionaries.

The Kaiser recognized that the abdication demanded from him would be the commencement of chaos. He recognized that, in the difficult times ahead of us, one thing above all was essential: and the one thing needful was the maintenance of authority and of the fighting powers of the army so that it might resist any attempt to dictate peace. Was he not right? The German people had received the most extensive democratic rights. The old authority could not be dispensed with in the hour of greatest peril. The Higher Command were forced to sign the ignominious armistice, not because we were defenceless, but because the field army could not continue the campaign with the revolution in its rear.

The entire blame for their misfortune our people have heaped upon their old Kaiser. As his son, but also as one who never was his blind admirer, I must demand justice in any verdict pronounced upon my father. For three years he has been overwhelmed with abuse by the parties of the present Government, who still impute every failure to the old régime and specially to the Kaiser, by the heroes of the extreme left as well as those of the right. Like everybody else, my father was, after all, only human, and he too was worn out. Did not stronger men also experience their hours of weakness in the war?

To what trials was not this sensitive and most pacific of princes exposed in the war? The last year of the war brought disappointment after disappointment. In its last wretched months, adverse intelligence was followed by evil tidings and evil tidings by bad news; and in the closing days and hours everything collapsed. He had resolved to tread the path of duty, and in that path to fall fighting. He relied upon the Higher Command, who till the 6th of November took his part with the whole weight of their authority. In the decisive hour, when the nation, the home army and the navy deserted him, that man also failed him who for him and for the nation was the greatest authority, and to whom he, the Emperor, had made himself a subordinate.

Is it any wonder that my father trusted this man, this responsible adviser, more than he did me or my Chief of Staff? Is it any wonder that, in the enormous excitement and tension which had seized him, he, after prolonged opposition, eventually yielded because his great Field-Marshal strove for it with all the means at his disposal? Is it not natural that he should have shunned a bloody struggle against two fronts, a struggle withal which, in the judgment of the Field-Marshal General, the German army was no longer morally capable of conducting. What enormous difficulties lay in the fact that the enemy alliance was prepared to negotiate only with a so-called popular government! Without a doubt, our enemies, in the event of a conflict, would have made the surrender of the Kaiser a preliminary condition for the continuance of the armistice and peace negotiations. Was my father to place army and country in such a terrible dilemma? And so he acquiesced in his fate, rather than involve his people and army, who were enduring many ills, in civil war on his account. It was but logical that he should go abroad after he had given up the struggle with the revolution.

I ask, on the Kaiser's account, that people should exercise humanity in deliberation and righteousness in judgment; and yet I fear I shall not convince his adversaries—those adversaries who cast stones at him because he went to Holland and who would have stoned him just the same if, after abdicating, he had marched back home. But I hope to meet with understanding for my father among those nationally disposed Germans who have the honest courage to look back and to beat their own breasts: " He that is without sin . . . ! "

CHAPTER VIII

EXILED TO HOLLAND

May, 1921.

IN the early morning of November 10, I deliberated with my Chief of Staff, Count Schulenburg, about the situation created by the departure of the Kaiser and the possibilities left open to me. My own inclination was still towards resistance.

Combat the revolution then? But only Hindenburg, the man into whose hands the Kaiser committed the supreme command over the troops at the front and the troops at home, and to whom I, myself, am subordinate as soldier and as leader of my Army Group, only this one man has the right to summon us to such a combat.

And while we are still talking of him and of the decisions which he may perhaps be making, there comes the report from Spa that he has placed himself at the disposal of the new Government!

Therewith, every thought of fighting is blasted in its roots—any enterprise against the new rulers is doomed to futility. With Hindenburg and the watchword of order and peace, much might have been saved; in opposing him there was only more to be lost, namely, German blood, and the prospect of an armistice and of peace.

Hence, every temptation to regain my hereditary power by force of arms must be repudiated; and all that can persist is my desire in any case to do my duty as a soldier who has sworn fealty to his Kaiser and owes obedience to the representative appointed by that Kaiser. Accordingly, I will retain the command in my hands and will safely lead back home, in order and discipline, the troops entrusted to me. Count von der Schulenburg endorses this resolve with his advice; and like views are expressed by my army leaders von Einem, von Hutier, von Eberhardt and von Boehn, some of whom present themselves among the Staff of the Army Group in the course of the morning while the others are communicated with by telephone. Not one of them but is deeply affected by these unhappy decrees; not one of them who does not regard the events of Berlin and Spa with bewilderment. The same question again and again : " And Hindenburg ? " And again and again the one answer: " General Gröner——"

After a long discussion of the pros and cons, I left Vielsalm in the afternoon. Schulenburg advises me urgently to proceed nearer to the troops at the front during the negotiations with Berlin, and to await the decisions of the Government in a spot more remote from the demoralization that was likely to find more ready expression behind the lines. On the other hand, it is necessary to select a place accessible by telephone. Therefore, in the end, it is agreed that I shall, for the present, proceed to the head-quarters of the Third Army.

That drive I shall never forget. My orderly officer, Zobeltitz, and the courier officer of the Army Group, Captain Anker, accompany me; while my two adjutants, Müldner and Müller, remain behind to conduct the further negotiations with the Government.

In one place we passed through, my car was surrounded by hundreds of young soldiers, who greeted me with shouts and questions. It is a depot of recruits of the Guards; none of the lads will believe in the reports of the revolution, and they beg me to march home with them. They are prepared to batter everything to pieces! When they hear that Hindenburg also has placed himself at the disposal of the new Government, they become quite silent. That seemed beyond their comprehension. I press many hands; I hear behind me the shouts of the young voices: " Auf Wiedersehen!"—Dear, trusty German lads— now doubtless German men!

We toil along incredible country roads and forest tracks; and, about nine o'clock, we reach our goal. But no Staff is to be seen anywhere! Accidentally, a veterinary surgeon turns up in the dark and informs us that no Staff has ever been located here. The name of the head-quarters of the Third Army occurring twice, it has been incorrectly indicated on my map. But he will show us the way to the next place, where von Schmettow's Staff was located yesterday.

Our route traverses a vast and pitch-dark forest. In an hour's time we arrive at a house where every one has already retired to rest. After much shouting and sounding of our motor horn, an officer appears at length and explains that this is a school for ensigns; von Schmettow's Group has already left. The young man is exceedingly kind, as though he must apologize for Schmettow's having gone. He begs me to stay the night; he does not know where the Third Army Staff is located, but presumes Einem to have taken up his quarters in the neighbourhood of the little town of Laroche.

We proceed therefore on our night journey. Eventually we find Laroche. It is a railway junction. It is a terrible chaos through which we drive: bawling, undisciplined men going on leave, shouts and screams;

and storming of the trains. At the commandant's, we learn that the Third Army Staff is lodged in a house quite close by.

We start off again!—On a deeply rutted road we have to pass under a narrow railway arch. Here an Austrian motor howitzer battery has jammed itself into some German munition vans in a hopeless entanglement. It is pitch dark to boot. The small lights flicker: the men shout and curse. Our car sinks deeper and deeper into the mud; and a fine, cold drizzle pours down. And thus we sit there and wait in that chaos for two whole hours. The yelling and bawling at the railway station reverberates over our heads; groups of muddy shirkers and soldiers from the lines of communication drift mistrustfully past, casting greedy sidelong looks at us as they go by. Two such hours, after that flood of terrible events and with one's heart full of pain and bitterness. It is like a picture of the ghastly end of our four and a half years of heroic struggle: confusion, insanity, crime.

I would not wish my worst enemy the burning torture of those hours.

It was past midnight when we eventually reached the Army head-quarters, where we were welcomed with cordial friendship by His Excellency von Einem and his Chief of Staff Lieutenant-Colonel von Klewitz. They had been expecting us since late in the afternoon, and had begun to fear some misfortune might have overtaken us and they would not see us again.

We soon retire to bed; but again I find it scarcely possible to sleep.

The eleventh is a cold, sombre day. At the Third Army head-quarters, not a trace of the revolution is observable. From the chief down to the lowest orderly, everything is irreproachable; and it is a pleasure to see the smartness and alacrity of the men.

Were it not that all the unspeakably bitter experiences of the last few days are burnt indelibly into my brain, I could, at the sight of this perfect order, imagine myself awaking from a horrible dream. Klewitz told me, by the way, that a soldiers' council had been formed among his telephone staff; but he had soon put an end to it, and the men came to him afterwards to apologize.

In the course of the forenoon, the leader of the First Guards, General Eduard von Jena, and his general staff officer, Captain von Steuben, reported to me. They are both fine well-tried men. We were much affected, and when they took leave of me, tears were in their eyes.

In the afternoon I telephone to my adjutants at Vielsalm. They report that, in regard to the negotiations with the Government, they are again communicating with Berlin, but no decisions have been come to yet. One thing I request, namely, that no sort of conclusive settlement shall be made, that the final decision be left to me.

Hence, wait on! Wait? Wait for what miracle? Is not, in all that I already know, all that is barely concealed under the form of discussions and negotiations, the " No " of the gentlemen in Berlin clearly audible? And indeed, if they are to retain the power they have usurped, can they act otherwise? And if I wish our poor and oft-tried country to have peace, can I repudiate their " No "?

One unforgettable impression of that day I must set down here. It is evening. Sunk in agonizing thought, I am walking alone in the park of the château. I have taken refuge in this solitude and seclusion in order to look in the face the finalities which are about to be consummated.

And I reason thus. When that " No," which is

surely coming, has robbed you of your place beside your comrades, and has reft from you your responsibilities and duties as an active soldier—what then? Are you then to take one of the trains at Liège or Herbesthal and travel to Berlin in order not to become the nucleus of disturbances by remaining with the troops? Will you live there as an idle gentleman passively watching them—in the wild frenzy and raving delirium of their jaded, goaded and misguided brains—violate all that tradition had made so sacred to you and to them? Or would you like to be there as the person on whom all their quarrels turned?

"No!" But a way opens out at the moment when you are forced by their "No" to give up your desire to return home with the troops, at the moment when you are deposed by the new rulers and discharged from the service. That way is the way across the frontier.

Over there, away from all fermenting conflicts, you might wait a few weeks till the worst tempest is over and reason and discernment have helped to restore order. Then, at the latest on the conclusion of peace, you could return to your wife and children and to the fresh labours which await you and every other German.

I think of my father, whom, in this way, I should see again—

And the whole bitterness of this separation and this exile comes over me.

Early dusk veils the autumn trees; sleet is falling, and a penetrating chill arises from the wet, mouldering leaves and the soddened earth.

Suddenly, along the road outside, a company marches by. The men are singing our fine old soldiers' song: "Nach der Heimat möcht' ich wieder—"

Singing! Marching!—" Good God," I think to myself. I struggle with my feelings as best I can;

THE CROWN PRINCESS VISITS THE CROWN PRINCE AT WIERINGEN.

but they are too strong for me, I cannot resist them. Still they sing—softer now and more distant—
I kept up until then. But that—in the darkness and solitude in which no one could see—that overcame me.

Late in the evening arrived the declaration of the Government that, having heard the advice of the War Minister, General Scheüch, they must refuse to allow me to remain any longer in the Higher Command of the Army Group. The new Commander-in-Chief had no further use for me. And so nothing was left but to write my farewell letter. It ran as follows:—

Head-quarters of the Crown Prince Army Group,
November 11, 1918.

DEAR FIELD-MARSHAL GENERAL,—

In these days—the most grievous of my father's life and of mine—I must beg to take leave of your Excellency in this way. With deep emotion, I have been forced to the decision to avail myself of the sanction accorded by your Excellency to my relinquishing my post of commander-in-chief, and shall, for the present, take up residence abroad. It is only after a severe inward struggle that I have been able to reconcile myself to this step; for it tears every fibre of my heart not to be able to lead back home my Army Group and my brave troops to whom the Fatherland owes such an infinite debt.

I consider it important, however, once again to give your Excellency, at this hour, a brief sketch of my attitude; and I beg your Excellency to make whatever use of my words may seem at all fitting to you.

Contrary to many unjust opinions which have endeavoured to represent me as having always been a war-inciter and reactionary, I have, from the outset, advocated the view that this war was, for us, a war of defence; and, in the years 1916, 1917, and 1918, I often emphasized, both by word of mouth and in writing, the opinion that Germany ought to seek to end the war and that she should be glad if she could maintain her *status quo* against the entire world. So far as home politics are concerned, I have been the last to oppose a liberal development of our constitution. This conception I communicated in writing to the Imperial Chancellor, Prince Max of Baden, only a few days ago. Nevertheless, when the violence of events swept my father from the throne, I was not merely not heard, but, as Crown Prince and heir-apparent, simply ignored.

I therefore request your Excellency to take notice that I enter a formal protest against this violation of my person, my rights, and my claims.

In spite of these facts, I held to my view that, considering the severe shocks which the army was bound to sustain through the loss of its Kaiser and Chief War Lord as well as through the ignominious terms of the armistice, I ought to remain at my post in order to spare it the fresh disappointment of seeing the Crown Prince also discharged from his position as military commander-in-chief. In this, too, I was led by the idea that, even though my own person might be exposed to the most painful consequences and conflicts, the holding together of my Army Group would avert further disaster from our Fatherland, whom we all serve. These consequences to myself I should have endured in the conviction that I was doing my country a service. But the attitude of the present Government had also necessarily to be taken into account in deciding whether I was to continue in my military command. From that Government I have received notice that no further military activity on my part is looked for, although I should have been prepared to accept any employment. I believe, therefore, that I have remained at my post as long as my honour as an officer and a soldier required of me.

Your Excellency will, at the same time, take notice that copies of this letter have been despatched to the Minister of the Royal Household, the Prussian State Ministry, the Vice-President of the House of Deputies, the President of the Upper House, the *Chef du Cabinet militaire*, the *Chef du Cabinet civil*, and a few of the military leaders with whom I am more intimately acquainted.

I bid your Excellency farewell with the ardent wish that our beloved Fatherland may find the way out of these severe storms to internal recovery and to a new and better future. In conclusion, I am, yours,
(Signed) WILHELM,
Crown Prince of the German Empire and of Prussia.

To His Excellency Field-Marshal General von Hindenburg, Chief of the General Staff of the Field Army. General Head-quarters.

Soon after these incidents, I felt the desire to have a short account prepared of all that had taken place, including more especially the progress of the negotiations between my Army Group in Vielsalm and the Government in Berlin during my stay at Third Army head-quarters. As a supplement to the description given by me, I insert here the account drawn up and signed by my chief-of-staff, Major-General Count von der Schulenburg and my two acting adjutants Müller and Müldner :—

Account of the Events of the 10th and 11th of November, 1918.

On November 10, 1918, the Chief of the General Staff of the Army Group, under the German Crown

Prince, Major-General Count Schulenburg, urgently advised His Imperial Highness the Crown Prince to remain at the head of the Army Group. The Commanders-in-Chief von Einem, von Boehn, von Eberhardt and von Hutier, some of whom appeared personally at the head-quarters of the Army Group, endorsed this view, each expressing his opinions independently to the Crown Prince. On November 10, the Crown Prince betook himself to the front, viz., to Third Army head-quarters, in order not to come prematurely into contact with various signs of demoralization.

In Vielsalm, the head-quarters of the Army Group, a conference was held on November 11 with His Excellency von Hintze, in which Count Schulenburg and the two personal adjutants, Major von Müller and Major von Müldner, took part. Count Schulenburg advocated the Crown Prince's remaining at the head of his Army Group. He pointed out that the Field-Marshal and Gröner were also of this opinion. In general, the two personal adjutants agreed with this view, but they called attention to the fact that, before his departure for Holland, the Kaiser had declared that under no circumstances must civil war be inflamed in Germany. Willingly or unwillingly, however, now that the Kaiser had crossed into Dutch territory, the Crown Prince, as things stood, would, in all probability, become the cause of such civil war.

Even if this factor were excluded, it might be assumed with certainty that the new Government would bring about, with all convenient speed, the termination of so commanding a military post as that held by the Crown Prince. At the latest, this would have to take place at the Rhine; and then there would no longer be left to the Crown Prince any decision as to his further actions. He would presumably be forced to accept

THE CROWN PRINCE WITH A WIERINGEN NATIVE.

EXILED TO HOLLAND

any conditions imposed upon him, and would not even have any choice as to his future domicile. If he chose it in Germany he would always remain the nucleus of movements that might lead to incalculable consequences. His Excellency von Hintze declared that the question whether the Prince was to remain or to depart was one to be decided by the responsible military authorities. It was agreed to inquire of the Government, and His Excellency von Hintze offered to transmit the question. He requested the Imperial Chancellor to come to the telephone. The Chancellor was at a sitting and could not be spoken to. His place was taken by Herr von Prittwitz and Herr Baacke. While His Excellency von Hintze was talking with these gentlemen, Count Schulenburg dictated to Major von Müldner the inquiry put to the Government by the Crown Prince :—" The Crown Prince has a fervent desire to remain at the head of his Army Group and, in these serious times, to do his duty like every other soldier. He will lead his troops back home in strict order and discipline, and he engages to undertake nothing against the Government in these times. What is the attitude of the Government in this matter ? " His Excellency von Hintze telephoned this inquiry to Herr Baacke, who wrote it down and verified it. During these negotiations, the Crown Prince called for Count Schulenburg and His Excellency von Hintze, and demanded that no final arrangements should be made and that, in any case, he reserved to himself the decision.

Late in the evening, Major von Müldner received a telephone message to the effect that, after having consulted the War Minister, Scheüch, the Government must answer the inquiry of the Crown Prince in the negative, and that they had no intention of leaving the Crown Prince in command.

Thereupon, and with the consent of Field-Marshal von Hindenburg, the Crown Prince laid down the command and, after a severe internal struggle, resolved in favour of the journey to Holland, saying to himself that, after the decisions already formed, his remaining would not bring about any change in the situation, but would only aggravate and confuse it, so that he was convinced he ought to make this sacrifice for the Fatherland.

The departure took place in the forenoon of November 12.

Berlin, April 4, 1919.

   (*Signed*) VON MÜLLER,
       Major.

     MÜLDNER VON MÜLNHEIM,
       Major.

     COUNT VON DER SCHULENBURG,
       Major-General.

The next night is sleepless, restless. It is one long horror to a tortured heart which must now tear itself away by the roots from its affections, horror against the brain which vainly racks itself for a better solution of the problems.

In the end, only one thing stands clear, namely, that not through me or on my account must further bloodshed come about at home, that I dare not be a hindrance to any possible restoration of tranquillity at home, or to the finding of a peace which the Fatherland can bear.

We intend to travel in the early morning—to travel across the frontier into Holland. Two cars with only the most absolutely indispensable luggage. We have talked about it for days; and I have thought of scarcely

EXILED TO HOLLAND

anything else at night; yet now that it faces me in all its reality, I can hardly realize it.

I should like to leave the Third Army head-quarters quite quietly and with but few words. What can be said, has been said. And every military duty has been fulfilled up to the last moment. The command of the Army Group hitherto entrusted to me passed to Lieutenant-General von Einem with the advent of the armistice. Departure—stern compulsion ordains it. Why make the heart still heavier?

But, when I enter the hall, the whole head-quarters staff is there in full regimentals and with their helmets on—all of them, even the clerks and orderlies. In front of them, leaning upon his sword, stands the fine old Colonel-General, von Einem; next to him is his Chief-of-Staff, my good Klewitz—that admirable soldier, never daunted though things were often so black! Only that, in his sturdy features, there is something I have never seen there before.

Einem speaks—encouraging, deeply-felt words, belief in a new future!—Three cheers for the Commander-in-Chief of the Army Group fill the hall and re-echo over my head.

Commander-in-Chief of the Army Group? Am I that still? Perhaps at this moment the Field-Marshal General holds my letter of resignation in his hands.

I cannot speak, cannot answer. I press the hands of the old and well-tried officers; and I see tears on the cheeks of the men.

We must be off.

On the way, we have to halt with the Staff of the First Army, which has its quarters in the picturesque Rochefort Château in the Ardennes, not far from Namur. There, at General von Eberhardt's—the general was for a long time a trusty leader in my Army

Group—I have to meet my chief-of-staff. Thus, I have another bitter farewell to take from him also, from the man who, during the hardest period of the war, stood nearest to me as my military assistant and adviser, and to whom, for all that he gave me as a soldier and a man, I am so deeply indebted.

We are all deeply moved as I now sign the last army order to my troops.

"To my Armies!

"His Majesty the Kaiser having laid down the supreme command and the armistice being concluded, I am compelled by circumstances to retire from the leadership of my army group. As ever heretofore, so also to-day I can only thank my brave armies and each man in them from the bottom of my heart for the heroic courage, self-sacrifice and resignation with which, in prosperity and in adversity, they have faced every danger and endured every privation for the Fatherland.

"The army group has not been defeated by force of arms! Hunger and bitter distress have conquered us! Proudly and with heads erect, my army group can leave the soil of France which the best German blood had won. Their shield is unblemished, their honour untainted. Let every one see to it that they remain so, both now and later in the homeland.

"Four long years I was permitted to be with my armies in victory and in distress; four long years my whole heart was given up to my troops. Deeply moved, I part from them to-day, and I bow my head before the splendour of their mighty deeds which history will some day write in words of flame for later generations.

"Be true to your leaders as you have been heretofore, till the command comes which shall set you free for

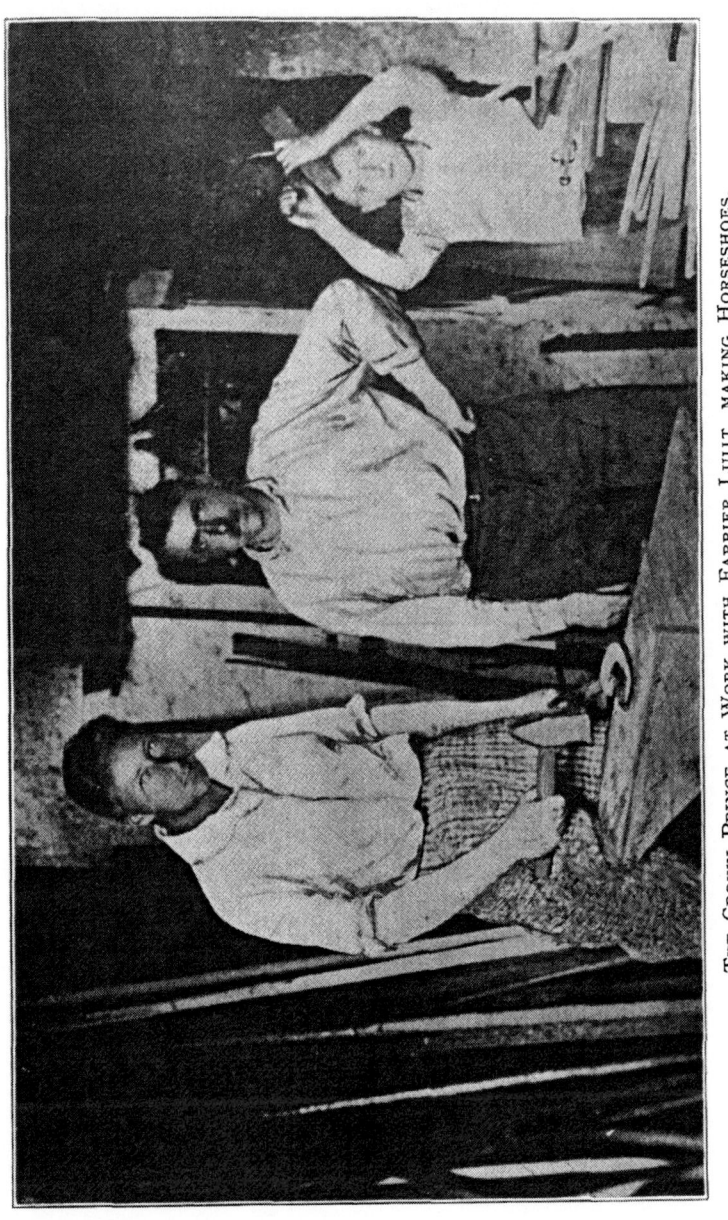

THE CROWN PRINCE AT WORK WITH FARRIER LUIJT, MAKING HORSESHOES.

wife and child, for hearth and for home. God be with you and with our German Fatherland!
"WILHELM,
"Commander-in-Chief,
"Crown Prince of the German Empire and of Prussia."

And now the moment of separation has come here too. I can scarcely tear myself away.

But it must be—my people urge me. Müldner has been holding a cap ready for me for some time—a grey infantry cap; he thinks, I suppose, that I shall not notice what it is in this torment and distraction; he wishes to disguise me with it, in his affectionate care imagining that I shall be safer and less easily recognized in that unaccustomed colour.

"No, I want my Hussar cap for this last journey, too! No one will do me any harm!"

And now they pretend to be unable to find it. But I wait; and, at last, the black one with the death's head turns up, and I don it once again.

I look into their faithful eyes; we can only nod; words stick in the throat. Schulenburg jerks out: "If you see my lord and Kaiser over there in Holland ——"; then he falters, too.

The motor whirrs; and we start.

We drive through the back areas of two disintegrating armies, districts which are disengaging themselves in mad haste from the firmly established order of a four years' campaign.

Our cars are grey; they carry my three trusty companions and myself to the bitter end. In the front car are Müller and Müldner, myself following them in the other car with the sick Zobeltitz.

There are soldiers everywhere, saluting and shouting. No, I was right; no one will interfere with me.

I return their salutes; and I can't help thinking, again and again: "If you lads only knew how I feel just now."

Our route goes via Andenne to Tongern. Belgian soil; everywhere the Belgian flags are flying in the towns and the population makes jubilee.

Moreover, the look of our own people changes as we get further and further from the front. Crowds of men who once were soldiers now drift along without discipline. Shouts that are no longer friendly greet our ears. There is the incessant repetition of the silly catchwords of those days; swaggering and bragging, each boaster tries to outdo the other in his display of rebelliousness and insubordination, shouting: "Knives out!" "Go for 'im!" "Blood up!"

But we are stopped nowhere.

At one spot we pass a cattle transport driven by Landsturm men. One old chap, passing close to the car and waving a red flag above his oxen, curses me roundly; the officers, he says, are to blame for it all; they've kept heyday—he is half famished!—That is really too much for me, and I give the miserable man such a dressing down that, trembling and white as a sheet, he makes salute after salute. Wretched rabble that have never faced the enemy and are now playing at revolution!

Just before Vroenhoven, we see the last German troops; Landsturm they are, making off towards home.

Near Vroenhoven we halt in the Dutch barbed wire.

My heart thumps loudly as I jump out of the car. I am thoroughly conscious that the few paces before me are decisive. As though all crowded together in one moment, the pitiless and tormenting scenes of the last few days pass through my mind once more: Spa; the Kaiser; the Field-Marshal; Gröner's face; my

Schulenburg, adjuring and undauntedly opposing the others; my father's letter; and the decision from Berlin which gives me my discharge and cuts the ground from under my feet.

No, it must be; it must be; there is no other way.

Suddenly there came into my mind the words that General von Falkenhayn used to call out to me when, as a boy, I had to take some difficult obstacle with my horse :—" Fling your heart across first; the rest will follow."

Then I take the few steps in front of me.

Veiled, blurred and uncertain is my impression of what followed next. People surround me, comrades (Müller, deadly earnest; and Müldner, self-possessed, soldierly, practical and clear as ever) and strangers.

There is a young perfectly correct Dutch officer, who at first is so surprised that he cannot grasp the situation and does not know what to do with us. But he sees that we cannot remain here; consequently we are taken past a presenting guard into a small inn, where amiable and silent attendants serve us with hot coffee.

Meantime Maastricht is rung up. The young officer returns. He is, himself, oppressed by the duty incumbent upon him: he must request the surrender of our weapons——. Then follows a moment of intense bitterness, which is rendered endurable only by the tact of the petitioner.

Baron von Hünefeld and Baron Grote come over from Maastricht. Soon Colonel Schröder of the military police arrives with his adjutant. Our further destiny lies in his hands. He acts energetically. Telephones ring and telegrams are despatched. Reports, inquiries, regulations to be observed. Thus our destiny begins to shape itself.

In any case, we are first to proceed to the prefecture

in Maastricht and to await the Government's decision at the residence of the Governor of the Province of Limburg.

Again we drive off. Everything is warlike here also. The streets of the town are blocked with guards, wires and chevaux-de-frise. The news of our arrival, too, has spread with incredible celerity; and the people regard us with sinister looks. "The Boches are here! The Crown Prince!"

It is nearly one o'clock when we enter the prefecture.

On the square below is a raging, yelling crowd, consisting mostly of Belgians.

Baron van Hoevel tot Westerflier receives us with a thoroughly humane and magnanimous comprehension of our position, and endeavours in every way to alleviate our melancholy situation. He, too, declares that our arrival has come as a complete surprise to the Dutch Government, and that further decisions must be awaited. He then leaves us alone in the cold splendour of the large hall of the prefecture.

However tactfully it may be done, however skilfully the veil may be drawn over the reality, one feels oneself to be, after all, a prisoner, to be no longer a free man, master of one's own decisions, to be a person who may be compelled to stay or forced to go. To all the other torments is now added the feeling that one wears invisible shackles.

We sit doing nothing round the table on highly ceremonious chairs; or we range restless round the room, or stare dumbly out of the tall window.

What is going to happen now?

The hands of the timepiece seem scarcely to move; sometimes I think they have stopped altogether.

And, to make things worse, good Zobeltitz, poor fellow, lies doubled up with pain on the plush-covered bench.

EXILED TO HOLLAND

Occasionally one of us talks—rather to himself than to the rest. It is always the same thing, one of those thoughts that go buzzing through our heads and which we cannot properly grasp; and no one makes any answer.

Now and then there is a knock at the door. Everyone is filled with expectation. But it is nothing; only the Governor sending to inquire after our wishes, or the Commandant of Police informing us that he is still waiting for instructions.

And again we are alone, our thoughts busy with the past from which we are physically separated, or turned towards the future into which we cannot see. Broodingly we ask ourselves: "What is happening behind us while we wait here like caged animals? What in the field, among the men who have been our comrades for four and a half years? What in the homeland? What at home among our wives and children?"

Zobel has got up with difficulty and is creeping about the room. Now and again his honest dark eyes catch mine. In spite of all the tortures of his stomach, which ought to have been under the surgeon's knife long ago, he looks at me as though he would fain do something for me. Then he stops in a corner before the white bust of William of Orange, who gazes down comfortably and in dignity from his pedestal. Zobeltitz nods to him and says philosophically: "Aye, aye, my dear Van Houten, you never dreamed it would come to this, did you?"

How much bitterness may not be mitigated by such a sudden sally of humour in the midst of despair! The martyrdom of waiting is almost rendered easier.

The Baron has dinner served for us. Notwithstanding all our protestations, a real dinner. It is all so well meant; but, in the mood which now holds us in its clutches, we can scarcely swallow a mouthful.

At last, by midnight, things are settled. We are, for the present, to find shelter in Hillenraadt Castle, belonging to Count Metternich.

Again we are in open cars, with the police officer beside us. The streets through which we pass are cordoned off by patrols of *marées chaussées*, in accordance with the wise and proper orders of Colonel Schröder.

A bitterly cold fog lies over the landscape and makes the night still more impenetrable. Only the search lights bore white funnels in the dark into which we hasten. It is as though, at one moment, they threaten to swallow us up and the next have hurried phantom-like away.

Two hours pass thus.

Then we stop before the Count's castle near Roermond.

We remove our coats in the great hall which is faintly lighted by candles. Stiff with cold we are, wretched at heart and rootless on foreign soil.

Suddenly, the lady of the house descends the stairs —young, blonde, dressed all in black, a chain of pearls round her slender neck. All feeling of strangerhood vanishes before those warm and sympathetic eyes.

From that moment onwards throughout the unspeakably difficult ten days which we spend in Hillenraadt Castle, this kind woman looks after us with the most delicate tact, and becomes to me a good friend with whom I can talk over many a torturing question. The Countess is a believing Catholic and suffers severely under the misfortune which has come upon our country ; moreover, she is deeply anxious about her husband, who, during these days of revolution, is in Berlin.

Thus ten days pass, during which, while bad news follows bad news from the field and from home, negotiations are carried on with the Dutch Government concerning our future. In the course of these proceedings, it appears that outward circumstances compel Holland to couple the question of my internment with my arrival and my wish to sojourn temporarily on neutral soil. Only under guarantees to the outside world is it possible for the neutral State to afford me hospitality or to endeavour to oppose the demands already being made for my "extradition." Thus I have suddenly found myself in a position of constraint. In view of the conclusion of the armistice on November 11, the possibility of such a situation arising never occurred to anyone in considering the pros and cons of my journey—neither to me, nor my Chief of Staff, nor the gentlemen about me, nor the State Secretary of the Foreign Office, nor His Excellency von Hintze, nor the General Higher Command. We all cherished the assured conviction that I could claim exactly the same rights as all the gentlemen of the Imperial suite, none of whom had been interned or were to be interned, and whose movements were left to their own discretion. Despite the difficulties and torments involved, these discussions and negotiations are conducted by the representatives of the Dutch Government in a spirit of genuine humaneness. In full accord with the character of the Dutch people, every one of the men with whom we came into contact over the matter proved to be just, impartial and ready to stand up for his own personal convictions.

At length, we receive some sort of indication as to my future. Colonel Schröder brings me news that the Dutch Government have appointed the Isle of Wieringen for my residence.

Wieringen? The Isle of Wieringen?

No one in the house knows where the island may lie!

Wieringen?

I hear the name for the first time in my life; I can form no notion of it, attach no idea to it.

And now, as I write these reminiscences, I have been living for nearly three years on this small spot of sea-girt earth.

Even this last phase of the journey into exile is full of little hindrances, vexations and annoyances.

Early in the morning we bid farewell to our kind Countess, for the train leaves Roermond station at seven o'clock. A Dutch captain is appointed as our companion.

Towards one o'clock we are in Amsterdam—many inquisitive people throng the station, and there is a cordon of soldiers—and by three o'clock we reach Enkhuizen, an out-of-the-way place on the shores of the Zuyder Zee. As we had learned on the way, a steam-yacht of the *Waterstaats* Department is to meet us here and take us across to the Isle of Wieringen.

But, in the fog, the yacht has run herself fast on to a sandbank off Enkhuizen and begs to be excused. During my consequent enforced stay at Enkhuizen, the population gives utterance to its feelings in cries, yells, hoots and curses. By an unmistakable gesture towards the neck followed by an upward movement of the hand, the crowd, with a remarkable expenditure of mimicry, makes it clear to me how thoroughly the caricature of my person produced and disseminated by Entente propaganda has fixed itself in their minds. In any case, all this does not exactly tend to enliven one's feelings.

After a long palaver, it is eventually decided to go on board a little steam-tug and to search for our yacht.

So off we go. The fog on the Zuyder Zee is so thick

THE CROWN PRINCE, CROWN PRINCESS AND FAMILY, WITH THE MAYOR AND MAYORESS OF WIERINGEN.

that we can scarcely see twenty yards ahead, and an icy wind is blowing from the open sea. We stand on the deck of the little pitching and rolling steamer and stare into the fog for hours together. It is a cheerless business.

At last we find the yacht. But there is not much comfort to be gained from her. Her screw is broken. First, we have to tug her off. Then she is lashed alongside the tug; and we are then, it would seem, in a position to steer for Wieringen.

Aye, if we only knew where Wieringen lay. In the fog and the deepening darkness and the heavy storm and the turbulent sea, our magnificent navigators spend hours in searching for the island. But the island cannot be found; it has vanished, as though devoured by the sea and the fog. In the end, somewhere about ten o'clock at night, they give up the search and decide to drop anchor till the morning. But this again proves to be fool's wisdom, for the sea is so rough that the two ships are bumped against one another all the time. A number of rivets have already been loosened, and, if things go on like this, there is every prospect of our being drowned—man and mouse. And so up comes the anchor again!

Next we try to reach the harbour of Medemblik on the mainland, and—bold seafarers being often blessed with good luck rather than with brains—we at last manage to get there towards midnight.

Wieringen? Just a foretaste which prevented our expectations from running too high; that was all that this day brought us.

But next day the effort succeeded. The sea having quieted down, we go aboard in the morning and make the island about noon in calm, clear winter weather.

Uneffaceable is the impression of that moment in

which I first set foot upon the firm ground of this little corner of earth.

The harbour is again crowded with people. There are the quiet and distrustful natives of the place staring at this curious billeting; and there are reporters from all parts of the world and deft-handed photographers.

It makes you feel like some rare animal that has at last been successfully caught. I should like to say to each of these busybodies: "Ask nothing, and get out of the way with your quizzing camera. I want quiet; I want to collect my thoughts and to arrange my ideas after all this disaster—and nothing more!"

In a primeval vehicle—assuredly the best the island boasts—we proceed to the village of Oosterland. The venerable jolting-car smells of oil and mustiness and old leather. Even still, if I close my eyes and recall that hour, I can smell that ineradicable odour.

We are set down at the little parsonage, which is very much out of repair. Everything is bare and desolate.

A few rickety old pieces of furniture—absolute cripples! Chillness and solitude ensconced like phantoms between them.

The decrepit chariot outside turns groaning and moaning on its axles and jogs off homewards through the fog.

Home! The thought of it almost chokes me.

Days and weeks ensue that are so cheerless and leaden as to be almost unbearable.

Like a prisoner, like an outlaw, I move among this small group of people, who turn away their lowering, shy visages as they pass or, at most, look askance at me with inquisitive half-closed eyes. I am the bloodthirsty baby-killer; people are embittered against the Government for having imposed such a burden upon this honest island and for letting me roam about it untrammelled.

The burgomaster, Peereboom, has his work cut out for him; it is a difficult task to calm these agitated souls.

And absolutely heartrending news dribbles in from home concerning the course of events! We have no German newspapers. Only from Dutch journals—which are out-of-date by the time they reach us—can we spell out the tenor of the London, Paris and Amsterdam telegrams; and their tenor is "blood and tumult," the palace shelled and pillaged, domination by the sailors, Spartacist battles, a threat of invasion by the Entente.

One would like to cry out for a little hope, for a little light to be granted to the land to which every fibre of one's heart is attached and for whose peace and security one would willingly make every sacrifice!

Sacrifice? Yes, they ask one from me, of which I will speak here.

On December 1, von Pannwitz, Secretary to the German Legation at The Hague, arrives with a fresh demand sent by the new German Government. The secretary is an old member of my corps in my student days at Bonn. God knows, the task can scarcely have been an easy one for him, and he doubtless undertook it only because what he had to tell me was less painful to listen to from the lips of a friend than from those of a stranger.

He is to obtain from me a formal renunciation of my personal claims.

A renunciation! Why? What for? The gentlemen in Berlin who hold the power in their hands and who, according to their own assertions, represent the will of the majority of the German people, have not hitherto been so pedantic and punctilious in their dealings with the rights of the Hohenzollerns. Did they not, on November 9, announce the abdication of His Majesty and my own renunciation, without waiting for the Kaiser's decision or even advising me? And did not the same lips which, a few weeks before, had sworn fealty to His Majesty, proclaim the German republic without a scruple? What can my renunciation signify to those gentlemen? It has not been their custom heretofore to trouble about such small matters!

But other considerations press for attention. What is the true foundation of the rights exercised by a ruler who regards himself as the chief servant of the State, or by the prospective heir to a throne who, according to traditional law, is some day to take over that service? Is it merely his ancestry and his inherited and guaranteed claims? Or is it not rather only by gaining the confidence of the nation, which entrusts itself voluntarily to the leadership of one who is carrying on the tradition, that he earns afresh the real substance of those actual rights? Is not the one without the other void and empty? And can I, without further consideration, believe that I have the confidence and attachment of the majority of Germans, after our collapse, in this hour of deepest distress and humiliation, when so many hundreds of thousands see before them a portrait of me which is nothing but a disfigurement, a vilification, a distortion of my true self? No, that is impossible!

Shall I present to my German fatherland the spectacle of one who persists in demanding his rights when they deny him the best element in those rights— their love and confidence? Shall I, by a rigid insistence " upon my bond," provide a war-cry for all those who stand for monarchy in the State, and that at a time when, according to my deepest convictions, the

Potsdam, 1914.   The New Palace, "Sanssouci."

Wieringen, 1922.   " The Parsonage."

fatherland—whether as republic or as monarchy—demands from all of us internal solidarity against the rapacious desires of the "victors" around us and work, work, work? Once more, No!

And if, under the stress of circumstances and for the benefit of the whole, the individual renounces a prescriptive right, does he thereby relinquish any particle of that sublimer free right of obeying a possible summons issued to him by the will of the majority? My renunciation, proceeding from my love of the fatherland, cannot be regarded as blameworthy; it is evidence of one thing only, that in the fateful hours, with the enemy at our gates and divided counsels at home, when the great need of the moment was to save the country from further dissensions, I obeyed the demands which were calculated to serve her interests.

And so, I yielded to the somewhat belated wishes of the new Government; but I repeat that it was not for their sakes and not because I recognized any of the traditional rights of my position as in any way affected by the violent doings of the revolution; no, it was because, so far as in me lies, I desire, as much as any one of my compatriots, honestly to help in preventing conflagration and in healing and strengthening by devotion and self-abnegation our so severely-tried fatherland, till the hour shall come in which I, too, may take active part with my fellows in productive labour in my home country.

September, 1921.

I have perused again the pages describing my journey to Holland and the almost unbearable first weeks of my sojourn on the island here. Vividly present is the recollection of that painful past. And yet it is so distant—almost three years! Those who then regarded me with deep-rooted distrust, with reserve and even with repulsion, have long since become friends who admit me to their joys and sorrows, small as well as great—friends whose simple and straightforward fairness lightens my solitude by many a token of genuine good-will.

It is true, too, that the tranquillity and seclusion of the island have doubtless tended to deepen and enrich my powers of discernment; and yet, all this and all that the Dutch people have given me in their hospitality could not make me forget my German homeland. My old love for her and my longing for the people who are my kindred are as strong in me as ever.

The hour of fulfilment has, alas, not yet struck, and I cannot yet actively co-operate in the work of restoration; all I can do is to await that hour in self-control and patience, enduring meanwhile the hardships of exile and solitude without complaint.

I have sketched in these pages the most important matters of my life up till now, and I have not wittingly suppressed any essentials.

I have finished.

But I would not say good-bye to those Germans who have followed my course in this narrative without expressing to them the wishes that fill my heart for them, for us all, for our sacred fatherland which gave us birth and which, whether it flourish or whether it fade, is the source from which our life's blood issues.

What in our great depression and misery we need most of all, in order to regain our old position, is internal solidarity founded upon self-sacrificing love of the fatherland, coupled with national consciousness and national dignity.

Away with the acrimonious cries that tend to

perpetuate internal strife and prevent the return of peace! It cannot be our aim continually to reproach one another with having broken the dish. In some way we were all of us sinners; and what we need is a new vessel instead of the shards of the old one.

Let every one who may be called to share in determining the destiny of the German people to-day feel the full weight of the responsibilities entrusted to him! May that much-abused and often misconstrued saying " Room for the competent!" at length be turned to deeds! Let us have only the best men at the helm! Let the most tested experts, the most capable, the stoutest come to the front! It is not a question of whether they come from the right or from the left, whether they have or have not a past, whether they are republicans or monarchists, employers or workmen, Christians or Jews; all that should be asked is whether they are honest men inspired with German feelings and prepared to work for the reconstruction of their country with all their might and all their combined vigour—united at home and strong towards the world without.

Fettered by the chains which the impossible and criminal Treaty of Versailles has forced upon our powerlessness, Germany has lain prostrate and helpless for three years. She is helpless because she squanders her strength in internal feuds, because a large proportion of her people continue to listen to the " Pied Piper " melodies of those rogues or madmen who sing them the alluring lay of universal brotherhood in the paradise of internationalism. How long is it to last, how long? Open your eyes and look around you; and you will see that this world by which you are encompassed is one homogeneous proof that nowhere is a hand held out to help you, and that only he who helps himself finds recognition. Above all, be Germans, and take your stand firmly on the ground of practical politics in this world that is so eminently practical, reserving your romanticism for better days in which it will be less fatal to the whole fabric.

Believe me, a German people which buries its party quarrels, which emancipates itself from the miserable materialism of these recent years and which, united in its love for our impoverished and yet so gloriously beautiful fatherland, struggles for freedom with an indomitable will—such a German people can shake off its shackles and burst its manacles.

But you must display sternness, and you must wrestle with that fervour which knows only the one ardent longing and cries: " I will not let thee go, except thou bless me."

I do not summon to revenge or to arms or to violence. I call upon the spirit of Germany; let that be strengthened; *for the spirit makes the deed and the destiny—and senseless is the tool without it.* Possibly this saying is the key to that destiny through which we have been passing for a generation, and also to that which lies ahead and into which we may enter as victors over all our opponents if we do but bind together all the best of our energies into a potent whole.

INDEX

Abdul Hamid 47-50
Alexandra, Empress, 62
Alexis, Tsarevitch, 65
Alsace-Lorraine, 96, 112–14, 184
American anti-German war propaganda, 127
American Army, 206
Anker, Capt., 268
Anschütz, 47
Armistice, 215
Austrian ultimatum, 119

Baacke, Herr, 277
Ballin, Herr, 135
Bassenheim, Count, 31
Beck, Major, 93
Behr, 52
Benedik, 165
Bentinck, Count, 128
Berg, von, 18, 127, 207, 218
Berge, Col. von, 239
Bethmann Hollweg, 71, 84, 95–101, 112, 120–4, 135–6, 138–41, 150, 185
Betzold, 47
Bismarck, Prince, 16, 33–5, 75, 106
Bock, Major von, 226, 251
Boehn, General von, 215, 268, 276
Boer War, 76
Boris, Crown Prince, 184
Brandis, Capt. von, 175
Brunswick, Duchess of, 182, 232
Buchholz, Gustav, 120
Bulgaria, 204
Bülow, General von, 165
Bülow, Prince, 28, 75, 76, 78–80, 85–6, 95

Carol, King, 100
Chamberlain, Joseph, 76
Clemen, 47

Clemenceau, 151
Court festivities, 53–6
Czernin, Count, 184–5

David, Hermann, 186–7
Deimling, General von, 113
Deutschland in Waffen, 112
Dohna, Count, 111, 259
Dommes, Col. von, 170
Douaumont, Fort, 175

Eberhardt, von, 268, 276, 279
Ebert, 246, 258
Edward, King, 67–8, 74, 80–4
Einem, von, 268–70, 276, 279
Eitel Friedrich, 16, 35, 153
Eitel Fritz, 47, 171
Enver Pasha, 184
Erzberger, 140
Eulenburg, Prince, 22

Falkenhayn, General von, 33, 173, 177
Fashoda, 77
Federal princes, 183
Finckenstein, Count, 40
Fisher, Lord, 70, 132–3
Foch, 218–22
Forstner, Lieutenant von, 114
Francis Ferdinand, Archduke, 84, 106–7, 119
Frederick Charles, Prince, 115
Fredericks, Baron, 63
Fritz, Prince, 16, 205
Frobenius, D. H., 120

Gallwitz, 217
George, David Lloyd, 98, 151
German censorship, 187–90
German Revolution, 208–13, 234–50

INDEX

Giesl, 107
Gontard, General von, 233, 261
Goschen, Sir Edward, 101, 123
Gothein, 47
Grey, Earl, 101, 105–6
Gröner, General, 87, 224, 233–44, 248–50, 257, 259, 268, 276
Grote, Baron, 283
Grünau, Herr von, 233, 240, 249–50, 260–1
Guendell, General von, 217

Haldane, Lord, 101–2
Hardinge, Lord, 103
Hedin, Sven, 184
Heine, Heinrich, 89
Henry, Prince, 121–2, 173
Hentsch, Col., 167–9
Hertling, Count von, 208, 210
Hewett, Sir John, 103
Heydebrand, Herr von, 187
Heye, Col., 242, 250–7
Hindenburg, Field-Marshal von, 154–8, 177, 207, 233–43, 249, 254–78
Hintze, von, 212, 233, 239–40, 243–50, 259–61, 276–7, 287
Hirschfeld, Major von, 240, 261
Hopfgarten, Count, 61
Huenefeld, Baron, 31
Hülsen, von, 60
Hünefeld, Baron von, 283
Hutier, von, 268, 276

Ilsemann, 93, 261
India, 103

Jagow, 99, 101
Jellicoe, Lord, 72
Jena, General von, 271
Jena, Herr, 173
Joachim, Prince, 153
Joffre, General, 176
Jonghe, Count de, 225
Jutland, Battle of, 69

Kan, Mr., 127
Kapp *Putsch*, 129, 131–2
Karl, Kaiser, 184
Keppel, Sir Roos, 103
Kiderlen-Wächter, 98–100
Klewitz, Col. von, 270–1, 279
Knobelsdorf, General von, 116, 176
Koenigsmarck, Graf, 21

Kolff, Mr., 163–4
König, Capt., 127
Kruger telegram, 76
Kuhl, General von, 167, 215
Kummer, 57
Kurt, Major, 128

Labour Party, 194
Leo XIII, 47
Lichnowsky, Prince, 102
Litzmann, 47
Lloyd George. *See* George
Louis of Battenberg, Prince, 45
Ludendorff, General, 133–4, 151, 154–62, 185–6, 207, 211, 223, 263
Luijt, 57
Lyncker, General von, 35, 109–10

Malimoff, 204
Maltzahn, 153
Mangin, General, 176
Maria, Dowager Empress, 62, 64
Marne, Battle, 169–72
Marschall, General von, 233, 240, 244, 248–9, 253, 258–9, 261
Max of Baden, Prince, 210, 213, 221, 224, 239, 243, 246–8, 274
Menzel, Adolf, 53–5
Michaelis, Herr, 139–40
Mitzlaff, von, 40–1
Moltke, General von, 118, 165–6, 169, 171–2
Morocco affair, 98
Müldner, 94, 127–8, 173, 182, 190, 268, 276–8, 281, 283
Müller, 71, 128, 224, 268, 276, 278, 283

Naumann, Dr. Victor, 141
Navy, British and German, 68–73, 101
Nicholai, Grand Duke, 62, 65, 107, 136
Nicholas, Tsar, 61–5, 107, 136
Niemann, Major, 233, 260

Oldenburg, von, 86
Oscar, Prince, 153

Pannwitz, von, 291
Panther, 98
Peace Note, 217
Peace Treaty, 90

INDEX

Peereboom, Burgomaster, 31, 109, 163, 291
Planitz, Captain von der, 61
Plessen, General von, 19, 233, 240, 244–5, 248, 253, 260–1
Plettenberg, Col. von, 39
Plüskow, Major von, 39
Pohl, Admiral, 71
Poland, 139
Prell, Herr, 127
Prittwitz, Herr von, 277

Rantzau, Count, 39
Reuter, Colonel von, 113
Rödern, Count, 210
Rostock, Mr., 127
Rupprecht, Prince, 221

Salisbury, Lord, 75
Scheer, Admiral, 259
Scheuch, General, 217, 273, 277
Schiller quoted, 114
Schlieffen, 134, 166, 169
Schmettow, von, 269
Schönhausen, Count, 212
Schröder, Col., 283, 286–7
Schulenburg, General Count von der, 153, 195, 233–53, 257–9, 267–8, 275–81
Schumacher, 47
Serbia, Ultimatum to, 107
Spender, Harold, 85
Stein, von, 217
Steuben, Capt. von, 271
Steurmer, 136–9
Stuart, Sir Harold, 103
Stülpnagel, Major von, 52, 251
Suffrage question, 152

Talleyrand, 25
Tappen, Col., 166, 169
Third Party System, 17–18
Tirpitz, Admiral von, 68–73, 79, 96, 101
Tisza, Count, 184

U-boat warfare, 142, 144

Valentini, 139, 153
Verdun, Battle of, 173–9

Victoria, Queen, 37, 44–5
Von der Tann, 104–5

Wahnschaffe, von, 245
Wartenburg, Count York von, 162
Wedel, von, 40, 54
Wergin, 51
Westerflier, Baron van, 284
Widemann, 50
William, Crown Prince, *passim.* At coronation of George V, 105; childhood, 14–37; exiled to Holland, 267–96; extract from Diary on Germany's military collapse, 220; " Laughing Murderer of Verdun," 178–9; learns a trade, 36; letters on leaving army, 273–5, 280–1; lover of sport, 20, 42; marriage, 58; matriculates at Bonn, 45–7; Memorial after Battle of Aisne, 141–6; opinion of British administration, 103, 117; relations with Kaiser, 15–29, etc.; relations with Kaiserin, 14–15, 44, 56, 87, 93, 109, 172, 183, 229–32; representative of Kaiser, 87–8; tour in the East, 102; Wieringen, 130, 287
William, German Emperor, *passim.* Abdication, 221, 238, 243–66; at Spa, 233; character, 91; letter to Crown Prince on abdication, 258; services to Germany, 192–4; the *Daily Telegraph* interview, 85–8, 98; various references on pages 107, 109, 114, 125, 128, 206, 209, 230, 233, etc.
Wilson, President, 217–22
Witte, Count, 63
Wolff's Bureau, 246
Wortley, General Stuart-, 85
Wrangel, Baron, 43

Zabern incident, 112
Zitelmann, 47
Zobeltitz, 190–1, 226, 268, 281, 284, 285
Zorn, 47

Printed in Great Britain by Butler & Tanner, *Frome and London*

LaVergne, TN USA
30 April 2010
181138LV00003B/35/A